TAX POLICY

AN INTRODUCTION AND SURVEY OF THE PRINCIPAL DEBATE

By

STEPHEN G. UTZ

University of Connecticut, School of Law

WEST PUBLISHING CO.
ST. PAUL, MINN., 1993

Library of Congress Cataloging-in-Publication Data
Utz, Stephen, 1947–
   Tax policy : an introduction and survey of the principal debates /
Stephen Utz.
     p.   cm.
  Includes index.
  ISBN 0–314–01930–8
   1. Taxation—Law and legislation—United States. 2. Taxation—Law
and legislation. I. Title.
KF6219.3.U89 1993
343.7304—dc20
[347.3034]

93–9795
CIP

ISBN 0–314–01930–8

Utz, Tax Policy

*In Memory of
My Father*

*

Foreword

This book offers law students a guide to contemporary tax policy analysis. The issues and arguments covered are multi-disciplinary and have not previously been assembled in a single work. Accordingly, a guide must both convey background information about the relevant disciplines—their methods, preoccupations, and strengths—and discuss the foreground tax policy debates to which they make contributions. That dictates the plan of these chapters.

There are of course classic lawyerly approaches to a number of broad problems about taxation, which deserve careful examination in the round. It is no surprise that the development of the tax law in a number of countries has stimulated legislatures, courts and the bar to bring forth durable insights into aspects of public finance, with only marginal assistance from nonlegal experts. To the extent that legal training enables us to grapple with unfamiliar information and relationships, we may be well placed to approach the peculiar task of designing and justifying a tax regime. Lack of specialization may be a practical advantage. It may also hinder the solution of complex problems. Legal methods of advocacy and adjudication are not always even superficially adequate to the task of formulating public policy.

Some specialized fields of study are obviously relevant. Taxes affect economic behavior. They can also reinforce or undermine a society's quality of life, self-image, aspirations, long-term political arrangements, and so forth. It follows that moral and political theory as much as positive and normative economics promise to enlighten tax choices. Historical and psychological studies tell us vital things about the workings of real tax systems that mainstream tax economics and political science might otherwise ignore. The horizon of tax policy continues to widen.

The following chapters are therefore organized with the goal of permitting easy access to these analytical tools of the trade. Part One (Chapters 1 through 5) provides a historical survey of what those who shaped income tax theory thought they were doing and of their styles in doing it. The Part also includes separate introductions to the elements of the tax policy as seen by economists, philosophers, political theorists, and other specialized inquirers. Part Two (Chapters 6 through 8) gives an overview of some classic debates that form the shared culture of countries in which income taxation is prominent. These debates are about what income is and why we might choose to tax it rather than some other base quantity. My summary of the high points naturally relies on what American legal authorities have made of these debates, but the goal is to reflect a wider set of concerns. Part Three (Chapters 9 and 10) includes short studies of the case for taxing expenditures rather than a combination of expenditures and retained income, and of the interaction of public debt and the taxing function. Part Four (Chapters 11 through 13) addresses the goals and shortcomings of the classic corporate tax (therein dealing somewhat more broadly with comprehensive business taxation), international taxation, and state and local taxation. Part Five (Chapter 14) describes sophisticated efforts to model the economic effects of taxation.

I have tried to bring together in one place the techniques and insights that many tax students know are out there but would have a hard time finding for themselves in the trackless recesses of tax scholarship. Tax specialists disagree about the relative importance of the parts of the field thus surveyed. Most, however, regularly draw on this material. Although my own views have inevitably shaped the course and depth of the mainstream as I portray it, my intention has been to give a balanced account of the best of many professional approaches. The book will, I hope, serve as a base for the detailed study of primary works by some of the authors discussed herein. Footnotes, which have otherwise been kept to a minimum, cite important books and articles.

* * *

I would like to thank the Southern New England Telephone Company for a grant that supported my writing in its crucial last stages. I would also like to thank Peter Bloom, Jonathan Hamilton, Frank Kirkpatrick, Tracey Lenox, Rolf Th. Lundberg, Sr., Susan Pennybacker, my wife and the participants in my Tax Policy Seminar in the Spring 1992 for reading and commenting on all or part of the manuscript.

STEPHEN G. UTZ

February, 1993

Summary of Contents

*

Table of Contents

*

TAX POLICY

AN INTRODUCTION AND SURVEY OF THE PRINCIPAL DEBATE

*

Chapter 1

HISTORICAL FOUNDATIONS
OF TAX POLICY

1.1 A SURVEY OF STYLES IN TAX ANALYSIS

The term "tax policy" covers a great deal. It applies to the persistent debate over whether the basic tax of a society should be levied on income or expenditures, and to the isolated lobbyist's ephemeral plan for a targeted tax credit. It describes the use of economic models to illustrate the distributive justice of various broad types of tax levy as well as the prevailing grass-roots preference for sales over income taxes. Important contributions to the subject are to be found in philosophical treatises and in newspaper opinion pieces. Tax policy might with some plausibility claim to include all public policy, since government programs almost always have tax implications, at least by creating or reducing the need for government revenues.

The extent and influence of taxation in our lives is so overwhelming that we do not expect every discussion of the subject to reflect all issues. No one is surprised that those concerned with minute changes in tax laws do not always think in the most basic terms, or that those whose perspective is more grand do not decorate their views with detailed statutory proposals. Some discussions, for example, try to be purely technical and free of controversial values while others are about values and nothing else.

It is worthwhile, however, to be aware of any continuity there is from the general to the more practical and definite parts of the subject. This is especially so in view of the patently different purposes for which economists, philosophers, politicians, lobbyists and others discuss taxation. Consider economics. As a field of study, public finance—the part of economics that encompasses tax theory—is driven by obsessive interest in hypothetical economic relationships that are not always, if ever, especially helpful in predicting the unfolding of real-world events.[1] Thus, tax policy through the lens of the economist may not be

---

1. George Stigler's observations about "progress" or what is better described more neutrally as shifts in perspective among professional economists apply with

1

particularly relevant to what ails or would prosper the world. She may, for example, have something to say about how taxes could most effectively be collected in a state that is not limited by respect for civil rights, even though there is no straightforward application of her generalizations to the liberal state that does recognize such rights.[2]

There are other sorts of theorist. Philosophers, for example, question the common assumptions of tax policy, more skeptically perhaps than any taxpayer would think relevant. (No one will probably thank the philosopher for this skepticism, even if it implies greater solicitude for the taxpayer's rights than is otherwise accorded them.) Among other things, philosophers are more concerned than the ordinary citizen with the puzzles of interpersonal comparisons of well being.[3] Since relatively naive approaches to welfare distribution are the starting point of most tax policy, a philosophical critique might show that tax theory and practice should proceed from a completely different kind of measure of human well-being, or that no objective measure of well-being is possible even in principle, so that rational tax policy must be based on something else.

No simple ordering of tax theoretical thought from applied to abstract seems possible. There are not only different levels of generality within tax policy but different standards of argument and perhaps incompatible goals. There are, however, common problems and related solutions, even among the products of very differently oriented tax analysts. Tracing the common elements is no easy task. The remainder of this chapter illustrates that point with important episodes in the history of income tax policy. (Although income taxes are not necessarily the best and highest kind, they dominate contemporary tax thinking for a variety of reasons, some of which become clear from the following historical sketch.)

1.2 THE COMPREHENSIVE STYLE

One might suppose that tax theory typically tries to tell us what moral or political goals a tax system should pursue, examines the economics of production and distribution in relevant respects, and then deduces a tax system fit for the real world. With some highly eccentric exceptions, contemporary tax analysis disappoints this expectation, concentrating instead on specially framed difficulties, from which intractable problems of value theory and economics are remarkably absent.[4] But a comprehensive style of tax policy analysis has at times been the norm.

special force to public finance specialists. See George Stigler, *The Nature and Role of Originality in Scientific Progress,* in his Essays in the History of Economics 1–15 (1965).

2. But see Patricia Apps, A Theory of Inequality and Taxation (1981).

3. See, e.g., Beyond Utilitarianism (ed. Amartya Sen & Bernard Williams 1983)

(essays by philosophers and economists debating the analysis of welfare).

4. Contemporary economists concerned with so-called "public" choice theory come closest to the nineteenth century standard in this regard, but even the most forthright of them present their views in terms of models that may at best illustrate but

Classical economists—Adam Smith, David Ricardo, John Ramsey McCulloch, Nassau Senior, and their contemporaries, with John Stuart Mill as a later but important standard-bearer—invented their subject largely in order to pinpoint the effects of different tax policies and evaluate them. For this naive generation, evaluation meant unabashed value judgment. Economic growth and the alleviation of poverty figured large in their openly avowed agenda. They also *dis*favored government intervention on moral and empirical grounds. From the outset, then, political economy was partly (for Ricardians, mostly) about tax reduction and social engineering through taxation. How often have these two goals of taxation been united in a single cranium?

The classical interest in taxation had an immediate and polemical basis in the broadly shared perception—at least among entrepreneurs and the influential press—that tariffs and impediments to free trade were costing the country more than they contributed to its economic health. The existing Corn Laws in England had imposed stringent tariffs on agricultural imports, ostensibly in order to shore up domestic food production pending the threat of a French military invasion. Similar tariff laws in other countries indicate that these restraints of trade could be popular for other reasons. Protectionist tax measures remained in force, however, long after Napoleon's British campaign had fizzled. A perceived crisis of agricultural protectionism spurred Ricardo to the holistic task of analyzing markets and government's role in them, with a view to putting tax policy on a firm footing. He devised a model of what could have been any economy in transition from the exclusively agricultural to predominantly industrial, and his efforts caught the imagination of both moralists and business folk.

A tripartite division of the social product into "rents" from land, profits from capital and wages for personal services provided the groundwork for the whole theory. Wages of course differ from profits in that labor is the only factor responsible for "producing" them. Capital is accumulated wealth that may be added to labor to augment the production of new wealth, and profits are the difference between the resulting product and the wages that must be paid to produce it. There might seem to be no room for a third factor of production. Ricardo's reason for distinguishing rents from profits turns on the peculiar role of land in the expansion of the labor supply (at least in an economy that depended on seemingly exhaustive exploitation of arable land to produce a minimal food supply). He postulated that the work force necessary for exploiting new capital could grow only if a society's agricultural product increased, and this in turn could happen only if lower quality land was put into production. Living as he did in a time of severe unemployment, it was natural for him to assume that wage earners were generally forced to work for the minimum that would

certainly do not purport to chart the actual functioning of any society's actual economy. See, e.g., James M. Buchanan, *From Private Preferences to Public Philosophy: the Development of Public Choice*, in his Constitutional Economics (1991).

sustain them and their families. He concluded that landowners would inevitably demand more for the use of lower quality land as capitalists found use for a larger work force. The additional return on inferior land was paradigmatic "rent," as Ricardo understood the term: it was the difference between the earlier (and perhaps normal) market value of the land's use and what could be had for it, given the higher agricultural use for which there was a demand. Higher rents would keep wages at a minimum and ultimately eliminate the possibility of further profit from the exploitation of capital, to the general injury of society as a whole.

From these elementary relationships, and building on earlier work by Adam Smith and Malthus, Ricardo developed a model in which rents, profits and wages interact. We will return to the details later. For the moment, it need only be noted that Ricardo's basic views were very widely thought for a decade or so to support tax measures that discouraged rent-taking and encouraged capital accumulation and the further expansion of the economy. British economists of Ricardo's generation exhaustively studied and defended these not-quite-laissez-faire principles.[5]

Although the Corn Laws stimulated Ricardo's thoughts on the British economy, the first decades of the nineteenth century saw a rapid shift of public concern from protectionism to the public debt. The staggering cost of the American colonial war and of military response to the scare of Napoleonic invasion lived on in undischarged and growing public deficits. Although temporary income taxes were adopted from time to time to restore national solvency, experiments with taxes directly levied on the wealth, income or head count of the populace, as opposed to taxes on things and activities, had not convinced the public or major political parties that a general tax could work. The perceived intransigence of the public debt, however, at last prompted formal bipartisan political debates during the 1840's, 50's and 60's concerning the introduction of a permanent British income tax.[6]

John Stuart Mill was one of several prominent economists who testified before parliamentary committees charged with considering the merits of a permanent direct tax, but many who testified represented pure economics and ethical theory in as full-blooded a sense as did Mill. Political economy as a field was still closely allied to moral philosophy. The combination of moral, political and economic concerns was characteristic of the "governing values" that defined Victorian debates about public morality.[7] Against that background, the younger Mill's *Principles of Political Economy*,[8] based in part on his public testimony, became enormously popular and apparently influential for the rest of

5. See Mark Blaug, Ricardian Economics (1973); Denis Patrick O'Brien, The Classical Economists (1975); Carl S. Shoup, Ricardo on Taxation (1960).

6. F. Shehab, Progressive Taxation, chapters 4–6 (1954).

7. Stefan Collini, Public Moralists 60–118 (1991).

8. John Stuart Mill, Principles of Political Economy [first published 1948] (ed. William Ashley 1909) [reprinted 1987].

the century. It is a grand restatement of Ricardian principles, in language far more comprehensible than Ricardo's or any other classical economist's, coupled with an elegant defense of the special sort of income tax that Great Britain finally adopted.

Mill rejected the taxation of income as such on the grounds that this meant the double taxation of retained capital. His argument is discussed in section 9.5 below. But income could properly be taxed, he thought, as a proxy for what a person consumed. Consumption deprives society of something of value, and the portion of a person's income that is likely to be consumed obviously depended on his or her circumstances. These could largely be inferred from the sources of the taxpayer's income—wages, profits from professional or business activities, rents from land.

At this juncture, Mill, whose father had been one of Ricardo's principal collaborators and admirers, pressed Ricardo's grand conclusion into service—the idea that economic growth depended on curbing rents. With some qualifications, Mill contended that, if there had to be income taxes as a surrogate for consumption taxes, they should fall most heavily on rents, less heavily on profits, and less heavily still on wages. Like the majority of his contemporaries, Mill assumed that what we call capital gains should not be taxed at all, on the grounds that these will typically be reinvested.

His ideas were eventually reflected in the first permanent British income tax laws, which taxed income from land ownership, from business enterprise, from professional services, and from wages at different tax rates. Since the tax statute specified these rates by reference to schedules of activity (with headings like those just broadly set forth), the resulting form of levy came to be known as a *schedular* income tax. Although the British income tax is now levied nominally at the same rates across the board, the schedules survive. Thus, in part through Mill's efforts, the Ricardian theory of economic growth and normative dispreference for rents was preserved and transformed to become the basis for modern direct taxation in a paradigmatic form.

What is most striking about this development—a practical political point of departure as well as a triumph of sorts for theorists—is how far ahead of self-conscious legislation in other fields it was. Long before Ricardo, Jeremy Bentham had pioneered the analysis of law and its processes in terms of utility rather than tradition. But the public debate about existing legal institutions lagged far behind, and only learned from the newer, less tradition-bound project of controlling the economy through rational taxation. Roughly a sixth of John Stuart Mill's *Principles* is devoted to an inventory of legal institutions and their assessment from the standpoint of the same social and political analysis that supported Mill's views on taxation. The popularity of Mill's book helped finally put legal reform on the general agenda.[9]

9. Collini, supra note 7, at 256–58 (on J.S. Mill and the slow progress of law re- form until the second half of the nineteenth century); Phyllis Deane, The State

Classical economics, especially in Mill's revision, offered a dynamic macroeconomic model of the economy. That is to say, it was intended to provide a measure of the aggregate and average value of goods and services and an explanation of how they came to be what they in fact are. The short-term movements of market prices were of secondary concern. What most mattered were long-term changes in the relative values of economic resources. The model purported to show how the accumulation of profits from capital, normally reinvested in productive enterprise, favors economic growth, and how improper levels of wages and rents (where rent is the difference between what a property user pays for its use and what would be paid for its next most profitable use) retard growth and can even stop it. Ricardians, in particular, took for granted that wage earners could not control wage levels and that other economic forces determined them. They also believed a priori that the gains from productive enterprise could be diverted from profits to rents by artificial price supports for food—price supports like the controversial Corn Laws. In brief, almost all of them concluded that market forces should be permitted to set food commodity prices in order to curb excessive rents. (Karl Marx was of course a Ricardian, in that he too believed that "classes" of participants in the economy could be distinguished by whether they earned wages, reaped profits or exacted rents; he went further and drew the conclusion that business cycles based on the unbalancing effect of rent-taking on capital accumulation would eventually destroy any economy based on capital accumulation.)

The classical macroeconomic model no doubt beguiled and provoked skepticism simultaneously. In retrospect, it seems as if the whole field of modern economics was called forth by the stimulus of its grand constructive simplicities, which foreshadowed the persistent habit of model-building. Mainstream classical economists, though obsessed with hypothetical gross economic quantities (value, cost, profit, rent) that interacted similarly at the national and more down-to-earth levels, were invariably tinkerers. Eventually their efforts demolished the mysterious parallelism.

1.3 TAX POLICY IN MICROECONOMIC MODELS

The Ricardian spell didn't last much beyond Mill's day. Flaws in Ricardo's arguments, apparent from the beginning, prompted economists to notice relationships that depend on the marginal unit of production or consumption and to recognize that some of the Ricardian generalizations misdescribe what happens at the margin of production. William Stanley Jevons in England and Carl Menger in Austria started a "marginalist revolution" in economic thought that was also eventually a revolution in tax policy.

and the Economic System 105–12 (1989); Joseph A. Schumpeter, History of Economic Analysis 544–50 (1954) (on J.S. Mill and the classical economists' interest in *Sozialpolitik*).

Classical economists had been concerned to find both a measure of the value of goods and services and an explanation of the causes of their value. They had all, in different ways, sought the ultimate cause in the labor impressed on natural resources and had all agreed that in later stages of society as well the cost of production determined the normal value or natural price of goods. This almost dogmatic concern with labor probably reflected both a commitment to justifying the valuation of economic resources and a concern with changes in the wealth of society through time. By the same token, the classical theory of economic distribution was mainly an attempt to explain the proportion of the total real income of society received by wage earners, capitalists and landlords, and the causes of changes in these proportions, again over time.

The marginalists, who were the avant-garde of what is now called neo-classical economics, insisted on a shift in the content and character of the field. Value and distribution remained major concerns of the new approach, but now no longer in subordination to the question of how social wealth increases. The new central question was how an economy with a certain population, with given tastes, and known resources and technology, will allocate its resources through the market system. The important elements of the answer necessarily were the individual actors, consumers and producers, who must react to the stimuli of prices and profits. What gave unity to the answer was the presumption that general features of consumer and producer motivation allow at least broad generalizations about how a hypothetical economy would stabilize in the short run—generalizations about the conditions for economic equilibrium.

These changes in the problem economists set themselves amounted to a shift of interest from macro-analysis, or the scrutiny of major aggregates (such as the share of labor in the national product) to micro-analysis, or the scrutiny of economic variables associated with individual people (such as the weekly wage of a plumber). From a different point of view, the shift was also from the broad dynamics of a complex growing economy to the precise statics of the allocation of given resources. A change of method made this shift possible and attractive. If individual consumers and producers are assumed to be motivated in broadly similar ways, especially, if rational behavior is assumed to consist in maximizing satisfaction or minimizing costs under suitable circumstances, many microeconomic problems have a simple and elegant mathematical solution: supply (a function of marginal productive cost) and demand (how many can be sold at what price) together determine the level of output.

The observation that slight increases or decreases in prices, wages, or rents could have unexpected and almost qualitative effects on other economic variables, which was central to marginal utility analysis, had also been important to classical economic thought. For example, Ricardo devoted considerable attention to unpacking the idea that the cultivation of inferior agricultural land would increase the price of all agricultural products, because product from better land would command the same price as that of the inferior land. His reasoning was that the old price of the product of better land would have been just sufficient to compensate the fewer laborers needed for its cultivation and pay normal rent and a normal return on the capital invested; since the inferior land would require more hands to produce a unit of the same agricultural commodity, the price of that commodity would have to be higher by the amount of the additional wages. (This assumes that the wages paid to the workers on the prime land are already rock-bottom, and that the same level of wages is now being paid to the workers on the inferior land.) The increase in the price of all units of the commodity would benefit the land owner and not the capitalist or the laborer, because the land owner would auction the use of the land to the highest bidder, who would inevitably be the capitalist willing to pay the highest possible price (assuming perfect competition of course), and this highest possible price would be the difference between the gross price of the unit and the cost of the unit attributable to a normal return on capital and a minimum wage for the labor involved.

This central argument, accepted by Mill with slight revision, depends on the observation that the marginal unit of a given product can command as high a price as the average unit, but that the land that produces the marginal product cannot command as high a rent (indeed it commands no rent at the margin) as other productive land. The difference between average and marginal quantities is basic to the theorem.

Setting out to understand the effects of economic growth, or deviations from economic equilibrium, on welfare distributions, Jevons and Menger were careful to distinguish between differences in the distribution of economic power and distributions of welfare. They independently applied a similar insight to the utility of fungible goods and commodities. It now seems elementary to observe that more of a good thing does not always proportionately increase one's well being. Two apples are not necessarily twice as valuable to a person as one apple would be. When this insight is applied scrupulously to the task of comparing the welfare of individuals who have different amounts and perhaps different kinds of money, goods, commodities, or other equivalents, the result is to undermine the simple picture of economic growth Ricardo and the classical economists presented.

In fact, Jevons and Menger found ingenious ways to insulate their hypotheses about tax effects from the simplistic assumption that objective economic power and welfare are the same thing.[10] They responded to the difficulty of comparing the utility individuals derive from the same goods or events offering satisfaction by relativizing their discussion to the effect of changes of economic state on relative satisfaction along a decreasing continuum. More specifically, they postulated that

---

10. Jevons may have made interpersonal comparisons of utility, despite his precautions not to do so. See George Stigler, *The Development of Utility Theory,* Journal of Political Economy 59 (August and October 1950): 307–27, 373–76.

marginal utility to the individual tends to decrease as units of the same good accrue to the individual's benefit, and this postulate of the decreasing marginal utility permits at least broad averaging among individuals.

Later marginalists bowdlerized the analysis. Soon Jevons's and Menger's more careful approach to marginal utility had been simplified by followers to the proposition that diminishing utility of wealth provides a normative argument for progressive taxation.[11] While it may be true that progressive tax rates result in a fairer distribution of the tax burden, at least under appropriate assumptions about the tax paying public and the uses to which government expenditures are put, nevertheless the hypothesis of diminishing marginal utility does not by itself yield that result.

The point of this brief sketch of the marginalist episode in public finance history is to stress the new limitations economic analysis indirectly imposed on tax policy. The marginalists knew perfectly well that their assumptions about the relative satisfaction or utility of economic goods were simplistic. They were content to limit the explanatory power of their arguments accordingly. But this is to say that their arguments were only true for models that starkly differ from the world as we know it, so starkly that no one knows what allowance to make in order to correct their implications about the real world.

Models, like other metaphors, by definition differ from what they represent. They are helpful because they simplify, and because they induce us to think about analogies rather than unique details. In some cases, the behavior of a model differs only slightly from the behavior of the object or system it represents. Economic models notoriously differ so drastically from the behavior of the closest analogue in the real world that even their advocates cannot tell precisely how to allow for the differences. At best they can only claim that the models suggest other models that will be susceptible of such evaluation. The marginalist revolution abandoned the description and prediction of concrete economic results in favor of greater precision and the elimination of earlier, classical errors.

It also happened to offer a framework for analyzing the equity of tax burdens within a hypothetically static economy. The postulate of the decreasing marginal utility of goods and services suggested a simple correlation between the monetary reckoning of tax burdens and individual welfare. If the motivational basis of neo-classical economics had any basis in reality, it surely condoned the working hypothesis that marginal income conferred decreasing benefits on the individual. Progressive income taxation therefore found prima facie support in prevailing economic theory.

11. The Dutch mathematical economists exposed this corruption of Jevons' and Menger's views in 1889, by demonstrating that if utility falls as rapidly as income advances, equal sacrifice is achieved by *proportional* and not by progressive taxation. *Bijdrage tot de theorie der progressieve inkomstenbelasting* (1889). A part of this work appears in translation in Richard A. Musgrave and Alan Peacock, *Classics in the Theory of Public Finance* 48–71 (1958).

But the mood in tax policy discussions had changed by this time (roughly the last decade of the nineteenth century). In England, where both the public and public figures had arrived at some clarity about the issues, the income tax, which had been till then a temporary measure, became permanent in 1906 amid a flurry of political compromises that deprived the resulting tax regime of any clear theoretical justification. It was a schedular tax, as Mill had proposed, but it no longer differentiated significantly among rent, profits and wages: although it set different nominal rates of tax for these categories of income, it permitted profits a wider range of deductions than it permitted rents, and wages were allowed no deductions at all.

1.4 THE MARRIAGE OF BROAD THEMES WITH FISCAL AND ECONOMIC PLANNING

The next worldwide fashion in tax policy accompanied the rapid adoption of complex income tax systems in most European countries, parts of the British Commonwealth, and the United States. It brought a new role for tax economists primarily as technical analysts and as advocates only by default. During the great British debate over the income tax, philosophers and economists (often indistinguishable from each other) had both analyzed and advocated approaches to taxation, but the chief issue for them, as for politicians and the public, had been social improvement, class-based fairness, and broad fiscal planning. By the beginning of the twentieth century, it was taken for granted by politicians and by parts of the public that some broad new kind of national taxation was inevitable; the fairness of income taxes, as compared with indirect taxes on property or commodities, ceased to be a big issue. Instead, the issue was what kind of broad levy could raise enough revenue and win popular acceptance. Direct taxation was virtually synonymous with income taxation, although the details had to be worked out. Indeed, what was "income" had to be worked out. The task of the economist—public moralists need not apply—was now to convince the rest of the communities to which they belonged that, for reasons both technical and moral, income had to be defined in a certain way.

Prominent economists in America were about to become prominent figures in the debates leading to the enactment of an income tax here, notably E.R.A. Seligman and Irving Fisher. Both were expert in the arcane subject of who bears the burden of the tax, or tax incidence. This set them at odds with the macroeconomic approach of their British forerunners, who had of course come before the marginalist revolution. Part of the baggage of classical economic views about taxes was some very amateurish guesswork about how tax burdens may shift from some taxpayers to others. Ricardo, for example, had reasoned that a tax on wages had to be shifted to employers (who were by definition capitalists), because wages were normally merely enough to sustain life and any reduction by government intervention would simply drive the wage earner out of the work-force—by death or if the effect took longer to be realized then by a reduction in the sizes of workers' families. (In fact, during the heyday of free trade, there were substantial local government subsidies in kind to many wage earners' incomes, and these subsidies sometimes offset the effects of taxes either on wages or on rental property. Ricardo was simply wrong to assume that the market for labor was perfectly competitive in this respect. He was probably also wrong to assume that wages were merely enough to sustain life even in those parts of Great Britain where wage earners received no government help.)

At any rate, Seligman, spurred perhaps by greater national experience of the income tax, began to speculate more shrewdly and even to collect a little empirical information about the actual incidence of income and other taxes. As is typical of intellectual debates, when the spotlight shifted to this relatively unexplored new topic, the importance of earlier topics seems to have been forgotten. Now, the grounding of tax policy in principles of distributive justice and overall utilitarian planning for society got short shrift.

Technical inquiry strongly influenced the prevailing climate in which the United States became interested in the idea of an income tax. Seligman wrote the best critical summary of what others in other countries had had to say about tax policy, but his own contribution emphasized the neutral virtues of income taxation in general.[12] Others agreed or dissented largely on grounds of practicality and administrability. Most importantly, politicians and the public said little about the justice of the income tax, and were content to wrangle over details like the size of the tax burden that should fall on capital income.

This may have been because projected income tax burdens were going to be small in comparison with the burden of existing taxes, especially pervasive and sizeable local property taxes. Local taxes had grown to become the main instrument of government finance, and were backed by an elaborate body of legal doctrine. The idea that taxes should correspond to benefits was strongly felt in the rhetoric of legislative tax policy. If a street was to be paved, those who lived on the street were the chief beneficiaries and they should pay for the work. If a dam was to control floods, the riparian land owners should pay for it. And so on. As you might expect, the rough-and-ready analysis of benefit was frequently open to question. As a matter of legal principle, it eventually broke down altogether, and courts simply refused to try to make sense of it any longer.[13] Other taxes also paid the way of government: these were primarily indirect taxes and direct taxes on imports, or for brevity, excise taxes and customs. Such taxes still account for a significant part of the fisc, both here and in other industrialized democracies.

12. Edwin R. A. Seligman, The Income Tax: A Study of the History, Theory and Practice of Income Taxation At Home and Abroad (1911).

13. Stephen Diamond, *The Death and Transfiguration of Benefit Taxation: Special Assessments in Nineteenth–Century America*, 12 J. Leg. Stud. 201 (1983).

Legal analysis of the new federal income tax centered on the problem of making a national direct tax pass muster under the Constitution. Article II denied the federal government the power to impose a direct tax without apportionment among the States (whatever that meant), and Congress adopted the prudent course of seeking ratification of a constitutional amendment to bless the individual income tax they had in mind. (The corporate tax was enacted before the amendment was ratified and survived Supreme Court review.) The constitutional problem may have eclipsed the question of the overall design of the shared federal and state tax scheme. Or perhaps no one noticed that there even was a shared federal and state tax scheme. Whatever the case, the conglomerate effect of federal and state taxes struck no one as a central problem, judging by the written record, and fragments of prior tax policy debates left irrelevant fingerprints on the design of the federal revenue acts. A likely explanation for the serendipity of legislative and public reactions to the momentous innovation of the income tax lies with the comparatively low rates, and high exemptions, from the initial corporate and personal income taxes.

The gist of the episode, however, was that tax policy took shape against the backdrop of Progressive Era commitment to government programs that required a broad federal tax, without much concern for the basic moral or political issues that had animated the comparable British debate. Perhaps not everyone saw that the income tax would last.

1.5 PRAGMATISM AND/OR ABILITY–TO–PAY AND ECONOMIC STIMULATION

The next big style in tax policy evolved during Franklin Delano Roosevelt's administration. One of the inevitable consequences of the prosperity that followed World War I was that the federal government must take bold steps to restrain economic perils—inflation, recession, etc. No one put it that way. Whatever the public mind was thinking, central figures in the academic discussion of tax matters, notably, the charismatic Henry C. Simons (1899–1946), began to speak again about the justice of alternatives in tax system design.[14] They did so, however, in peculiarly narrow terms.

Simons set the tone for this new approach by advocating utter clarity of tax structure (this meant a tax system limited to a federal income tax and practically no local taxes) and a strictly progressive, i.e., redistributive, tax structure. The element for which he was perhaps best known, and which he himself advertised quite effectively in his classic *Personal Income Taxation*, was strict accrual taxation. The effect of accrual taxation is to deny property holders the advantage they enjoy under the so-called realization principle: gains are not taxed until appreciated property is disposed of or the gain is somehow severed

14. Walter Hettich, *Henry Simons on Taxation and the Economic System*, 32   Nat'l Tax J. 1 (1979).

from it.[15] Interestingly, Simons proclaimed himself, and was received as, a political conservative.

The ambiguity of Simons's position in terms of partisan politics made his approach to tax policy all the more beguiling. He set a novel example for tax policy writers, since he was both powerfully technical (or was taken to be) and could yet be understood.

His work is still honored as the last word on the definition of income for all practical purposes. In effect, Simons championed an uncompromising definition of income, thereby advocating revision of the tax law to broaden the income tax base by repealing exceptions and deductions. But all this was based on arguments that merely emphasized obvious propositions concerning the duplication of tax incidence. In other words, he argued in the most general terms for a fairer income tax by reference to an intuitive sense of tax equity.

Simons was therefore the first of the op-ed tax economists. He had devised a new style: he brandished economic analysis but argued from noneconomic hunches. His *Personal Income Taxation* devotes considerable space to debates with earlier economists that must have been meaningless to most readers. He solemnly argued that income should be understood to include savings as well as consumption. But his arguments for these propositions are cursory. He says nothing about the effect of taxes on the distribution of value among the members of society. He in effect brushes aside the problem of distributive justice, treating tax law instead as government intervention in an unquestioned status quo. His advocacy of progressive taxation established a pattern that has been continued by economists close to legislative matters.

What of macroeconomic analysis and the demands of justice? Simons managed to make it seem natural to leave both to fields other than tax policy. He makes no arguments and declares no assumptions about the likely course of the economy under the direct tax system he advocates. By default he can therefore be taken to accept the free market as normative. The *status quo ante*, the actual welfare distribution to which taxes are applied, is treated as if it must have been morally and politically acceptable, or as if whatever faults it contained could not be worsened by taxes that alter market decisions as little as possible. How could either of these sweeping propositions be demon-

---

15. By taking this position Simons placed himself squarely in opposition to E.R.A Seligman, the earlier standard-bearer of income taxation as a politically attractive strategy. Seligman had pressed on his readers the accounting advantages and conformity with tradition of the realization principle, with little in the way of argument. He also wrote the amicus brief that guided the Supreme Court majority in Eisner v. Macomber, 252 U.S. 189, 40 S.Ct. 189, 64 L.Ed. 521 (1920), the case that read the realization requirement into the six-teenth amendment, thus making it a constitutional limit on our tax laws. Commentators immediately took issue with the economic wisdom of the holding. It is common today for legal scholars to speak as if *Macomber* has been implicitly overruled, for example, by implication in Taft v. Bowers, 278 U.S. 470, 49 S.Ct. 199, 73 L.Ed. 460 (1929), although the Supreme Court's statements on the topic are less than direct. See Marvin Chirelstein, Federal Income Taxation 71 (6th ed. 1991).

strated, either in the brief compass of a book like Simons's or in a life's work of detailed distributive analysis? What makes Simons's work a tour de force is that it purports to pre-empt such discussion, to show by implication if not explicitly that there is no point in examining these issues. Not only is it necessary to begin the discussion of tax policy *in medias res*, but it is also mete and just to do so.

Today, the distinguished Brookings Institution, the National Bureau of Economic Research, and a variety of partisan think-tanks play host to tax policy experts of a similar pragmatism, though agenda differ considerably. Typically, these experts have established their credentials as pure public finance economists; they have published detailed studies of abstract economic models that have only tenuous application to current problems of tax policy. Their advice to legislators and the executive branch consists largely in the advocacy of particular political choices; confusingly, these political choices are often "non-partisan," i.e., they are carefully framed not to reflect the perceived advantages of political interest groups, with the main political parties as prime examples.

Economic credentials are not essential for this line of work. Prominent tax lawyers are found in the ranks. A particularly distinguished example is that of Stanley Surrey, who left his mark both as a Harvard law professor and as Assistant Secretary of the Treasury for Tax Policy. His name is closely linked with the ideal of expanding the income tax base so as to eliminate deductions and exclusions that are prompted by policy considerations distinct from those of revenue maximization and tax fairness. He also popularized the concept of tax expenditures, i.e., implicit government expenditures in the form of tax relief for preferred taxpayers or transactions. Today, the Treasury Department regularly publishes a "tax expenditure budget" to accompany each tax act, as a kind of caution to legislators of their disguised largesse.

But there are now many variations of tax policy analysis as open advocacy. I have already mentioned the op-ed columns of the Wall Street Journal, in which eminent economists speak with authority on behalf of policies that could not conceivably find support in explicit economic theory. But not all such opinion amounts to disguised lobbying. Certainly, much of it is intended to be statesmanlike. It is important to recognize, however, that this strain of policy analysis does not always declare its foundations and that no single variety of foundations could be claimed for analysis of this sort. It belongs ultimately to the same continuum as the ordinary voter's observations about the wisdom of particular tax measures, which of course does not mean that the opinions expressed are without value or should have been hedged in with disclaimers and qualifications, but may mean that the mantle of the technocrat clothes only a Wizard of Oz.

1.6 THE PROBLEM OF PERSPECTIVE

This short survey of changing styles in tax policy is much less than a history of the field. Yet it suffices to show that theoretical approaches to tax questions can conceal powerful assumptions, and that these assumptions can function as biases with respect to fundamental issues. John Stuart Mill examined the design of income taxation from an openly utilitarian perspective. This enabled him to consider in the round governmental functions other than taxation and argue forcefully for a specific relationship between taxation and the general good. He presumed, however, that the natural unit for utilitarian analysis is the state. Later, less comprehensive tax theorists have effectively taken this bias further by focusing on the equilibrium of economic systems that are invariably national rather than local or international. Similarly, early and more recent economists assume without saying so that the effects of taxation on people are properly evaluated by reference to a welfare analysis inherited from utilitarian ethics. These perspectival biases are natural, given the implicit desire of theorists to have an impact, preferably on legislators at the national level. The arguments produced are not necessarily good or persuasive ones from the standpoint of the citizen or the legal professional who is as often concerned with the deficiencies of the state as with its interests.

The basics of traditional tax policy are surveyed in the following four chapters. The objective is to reveal in what respects they are analytically strong, theoretically controversial, partisan, or out-of-date. The concepts and arguments developed in these chapters serve as stepping stones in later chapters that examine more specific tax design issues.

Chapter 2

ECONOMIC CONCEPTS
AND TAX POLICY

2.1 BASIC ISSUES AND ASSUMPTIONS

To get an idea of the extent to which the design of a tax system requires scientific inquiry as well as value judgment, a survey of what economists regard as the basics of the subject will prove useful. Chapter 1 illustrates that, since the dawn of modern income taxation, economists have been in the vanguard of tax theory. Whatever the merits of their disciplinary biases, economists' assumptions and interests underlie many tax policy debates.

Modern economic writing, however, discloses its assumptions reluctantly. The naive reader may not readily detect that economists usually assume no ethical or political constraints on the taxing power of the state. It is as if a despotic government of complete benevolence and unrestricted power—the philosopher king, not the average citizen—were the intended recipient of the economist's advice. For economic theory as such, the question does not come up whether governments have the right to intervene as sweepingly in their subjects' lives as to implement the best economic advice.[1]

Moreover, as we will see in section 3.2 below, most economists' unswerving adoption of some philosophical tenets about human welfare (which happened to be derived from utilitarian moral theory) complicates this lofty attitude toward political justification. A principal attraction of utilitarianism has always been that it conveniently appears to justify governments in doing what is best for those governed.[2] Methodological paternalism, however, may be thought to obscure the real problem for the public policy maker, how to design social measures for a public that is not unanimous in their assessment of what is

---

1. The generalization that all work on tax economics takes an omnipotent state for granted now has exceptions—mostly in social and public choice theories—that will be discussed in Chapter 4.

2. See, e.g., John Austin, The Province of Jurisprudence Determined, Lecture 3 (1832) [H.L.A. Hart ed. 1954].

needed. The problem of political justification receives separate attention in the next chapter.

Finally, since the late 1900's tax economists have usually further limited their attention to what the benevolent despot should do, *given a perfectly competitive economy*. Fortunate progress in understanding economic equilibrium states has made perfect competition (or more rarely some other equilibrium state of the economy) the baseline by default for the discussion of governmental goals and the means of achieving them. Doing its best in those terms, i.e., in equilibrium, the free economy still may underprovide some goods for which there is a collective demand. It may also, though producing the greatest possible sum of wealth, distribute that wealth unfairly or unwisely. These two shortcomings of competitive equilibrium have been allowed further to define the task of tax economics.[3] Summarizing the limitations mentioned thus far, mainstream economic tradition assumes that government should step in and use the taxing power only to supplement the benefits to individuals of an ideally functioning but otherwise unconstrained economy.

Some potential hazards are evident in these assumptions about taxation. First, the common approach devotes primary attention to the broadest governmental intervention to provide the social and merit goods that would be chosen by a central and infallible expert. This prejudges the options for justifying tax policy in a less comprehensive fashion; it takes for granted that unless any tax measure that maximizes social welfare is rationally acceptable, no tax measure that improves social welfare can be. If it is wrong to levy taxes for certain purposes, e.g., to promote religion or secularism, we must learn that elsewhere than from economic theory. Economic theory thus effectively assumes that constraints other than those dictated by market necessities or market failure are forced on us only by the contingent facts of particular communities of people. Again, if it is wrong for a government to impose taxes that interfere with certain rights, e.g., with free speech or with some economic right like that of collective bargaining, this has nothing to do with what taxes are all about; such limitations must be based on judgments made elsewhere, perhaps at the ballot box, and not attainable by general reflection on the nature or purpose of taxation.

Second, although most economic analysis of taxation suppresses the broad problem of political justification, it does take up a sort of justification problem. As has been mentioned, economists identify the broad goals of taxation as those of maximizing the welfare of the members of society in general by causing goods to be produced and transfers to occur that the market is not likely to cause, despite a collective need for them. In other words, economists assume measures that achieve the provision of these socially desirable goods are justified

---

3. See, e.g., Charles M. Allan, The Theory of Taxation 13 (1971).

and others are not. In order to see what this amounts to, we must look more closely at the broad categories of goods in question.

Social goods are goods that will not be produced at all if people are not coerced to pay for them; the market usually does well to prevent the production of goods to the extent that people will not pay for them, but that is because most goods can be produced in different amounts or at different times, in accordance with demand; social goods, by definition, are goods that cannot be produced so flexibly. Some social goods are not goods in the sense we may be familiar with. They include the elimination of market imperfections, if any, that threaten an uncontrolled market—monopolies, wasteful competition, failures of locational planning, cyclical problems like recessions that *shouldn't* occur, and monetary instability among parts of the economy (such as the national components of an international economy).

Merit goods are goods an efficient market will not produce because consumers fail to make rational choices in favor of these goods and because externalities prevent the market from confining the cost and benefit of the production of these goods to those who produce or consume them. It is worthwhile to note that there are also demerit goods that the market may produce for the same reasons that it fails to produce merit goods. The problem of producing merit goods may be thought of as including the squelching of demerit good production.

These governmental goals do not point to taxation as the expedient means. A government might finance merit goods by piracy, for example, or more fashionably, by borrowing. Since Keynes, economists have acknowledged that government debt may not indicate that the economy is not in equilibrium, and this removes one reason for thinking that ever-increasing national debt cannot finance all government activities. David Ricardo is credited with the observation that taxing and borrowing are interchangeable means of public finance in a closed economy, which is another way of saying that what singles taxation out as an instrument of public finance (again, in a closed economy) is government's need to prevent the public from consuming that part of the national product that should go for public goods, and not the need to extract the wealth needed by coercion from those to whom the market would otherwise allocate it. A closed economy is one that cannot import or export goods or borrow or lend with outsiders. Hence, Ricardo's "theorem", as it is sometimes called, calls our attention to the ill effects of *too much* borrowing as the real justification for taxation. The relationship of public debt to the goals of taxation is discussed in chapter 10, below.

What ill effects? An illustration will suffice. In an open economy, a borrowing government would claim for itself, through market transactions, a large part of the public wealth, just as it would take that wealth directly if it used taxation as a means of public finance. But it must compete with other borrowers by paying higher interest rates (absent coercion of its lenders, which would be a kind of taxation if exercised against citizens of the country whose government is in question). Paying higher interest would not be a problem in a closed economy, because the government could by fiat increase the supply of money at its disposal for interest payments. In an open economy, however, such inflationary measures may cause a spiral of increased government borrowing. This is because higher domestic borrowing may be needed to reduce the inflation-prompted demand for imports and to reduce domestic demand for goods that can be exported. Higher borrowing would lead to the printing of more money, and so forth. Thus, inflation and balance-of-payments problems must be added to the account in order to explain why taxation rather than some other strategy is needed to finance government spending.

This bit of the typical economist's analysis of taxation has the corollary that whatever government debt there happens to be should be regarded as partly accomplishing the ends of taxation. The effects of government borrowing should be added to the effects of taxation in any evaluation of the latter for its justice, efficiency, neutrality in influencing business decisions, and any other relevant parameter. In fact, economic models have yet to be developed to permit such bifocal analysis of the borrowing and taxing functions of government.

Many tax policy analysts of the recent past would have added the general Keynesian program to the goals of taxation just described. They would, in other words, declare the principal objective of taxation to be the regulation of private expenditure on goods and services to a level that produces full but not over-full employment. Hence, employment, inflation and balance-of-payments would be among the inevitable topics for consideration in designing a national tax system.

What further standards should taxes be judged by? Adam Smith in *The Wealth of Nations* was the first to set forth as "canons" of taxation a list of criteria that include some still respected criteria of efficiency. Economists are frequently concerned to explain these criteria and to illustrate how they may be served by various tax strategies. The criteria include: equity (similar treatment of economically similar taxpayers); neutrality (or the nondistortion of market mechanisms); four kinds of certainty—certainty of incidence, certainty of liability, certainty of the evasion ratio, and the certainty with which the authorities can predict the revenue that will fall due within a given period; evidence to the taxpaying public; administrative efficiency; and net revenue restraining effect.

Much that has been written about these tax goals is based on partial equilibrium analysis—that is, the analysis does not take into account the reaction of a firm's suppliers to any tax on the firm's profits, and the effect of government expenditures of the tax revenue on the firm's business environment. Actually, partial equilibrium analysis is largely a form of microeconomic analysis (analysis of what happens to an individual firm engaged in isolated but typical transactions) and not a form of macroeconomic analysis (macroeconomic analysis is typically analysis of the economy as a whole in operation, though based on drastically simplifying assumptions as well). Several prominent tax policy analysts have questioned the value of partial equilibrium analysis for investigating criteria of tax efficiency.[4] In layman's terms this is merely one of many possible criticisms of economic analysis that assumes away the compounding of tax effects within the economy.

2.2 PROBLEMS OF TAX INCIDENCE

Public finance economists have always devoted much of their attention to the problem of determining whose income is ultimately affected by a tax. The underlying thought is the obvious one that the payor of a tax is not necessarily stuck with the loss it represents but may be able to pass that misfortune on to others—to suppliers or customers, to an employer, to parents or to heirs. A tax is said to fall *nominally* on the person who is required to pay it, usually the taxpayer in the eyes of the law. But the person or persons who are left with the economic pinch of the tax bear the *ultimate incidence* or, for short, the incidence of the tax.

Most analysis of tax incidence was a matter of armchair speculation until quite recently. Such a priori analysis of tax incidence was usually based on highly simplistic assumptions about the knowledge and rationality of taxpayers. Empirical research is difficult to justify, because of the practical impossibility of distinguishing tax effects from each other in a world of complex and changing tax levies (though in some respects the tax laws do not change often enough to permit empirical comparisons of their effects). Nevertheless, empirical research has often contradicted a priori predictions—perhaps for the obvious reason that real people don't know as much or act as exclusively from economic motives as is assumed by a priori models. Nevertheless, tax incidence remains of central importance, precisely because most criteria of efficiency are concerned with tax effects on those who bear the tax.

The questions about tax incidence raised by individuals and by enterprises are widely thought to be of different orders of difficulty, the firm having much more control over whether it pays a tax or shifts it to other taxpayers than the individual does. A manufacturer who is required to pay a tax on the sale of heavy trucks, for example, may hold prices at their pre-tax level or try to pass the tax on to consumers in the form of higher truck prices—this is called forward shifting of taxes. If the manufacturer is in a position to insist on lower prices for parts purchased from suppliers, in order to compensate for the tax, this is called backward shifting of taxes. Any combination of bearing the tax, shifting it forward or shifting it backward is conceivable, and some business firms have the opportunity to indulge in all the varieties.

4. Carl S. Shoup, Public Finance 41 (1969); John B. Shoven & John Whalley, Applying General Equilibrium 3, 153–93 (1992); Jeff Strnad, *Taxation of Income from Capital: A Theoretical Appraisal*, 37 Stan.L.Rev. 1023, 1024 (1985).

Hence, the effective taxpayer may be someone other than the nominal taxpayer.

A lump-sum tax on business in equilibrium in perfect competition would in the short run be borne by the business firm itself, at least if the main opportunity for shifting is towards the consumer. This is because the tax would raise the firm's average cost curve but would not affect the marginal cost and marginal revenue curves, the determinants of optimal pricing for such a firm.

In Figure 1, marginal cost (mc) is a rising function of output, and marginal revenue or demand is constant for all outputs, a symptom of perfect competition. Note that an increase in average cost does not change where mc and mr intersect. That is because marginal cost does not include any part of a one-time lump-sum tax; the tax increases average cost alone.

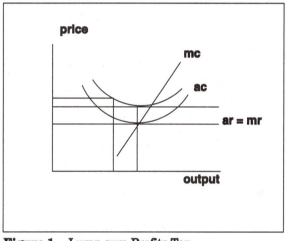

Figure 1 - Lump-sum Profits Tax

[310a]

In the long run, however, the perfectly competitive industry to which the firm belongs would produce less and charge higher prices; this is because the marginal revenue or demand for the industry as a whole must decline beyond some level of output, and because the price increase caused by the shifting forward of the tax would accordingly curtail demand to some extent. Some firms would be eliminated. This long-term effect probably accords with what anyone would expect.

If we discard the restrictive assumptions of perfect competition and equilibrium, the picture can change drastically, for example, when any of the following circumstances obtains:

(1) *Durable vs. perishable commodities and tax capitalization.* If the tax falls repeatedly on a durable, as opposed to a perishable, commodity, the original owner will usually bear the entire tax. Purchasers will discount the price to be paid for the commodity by the

amount of the tax. What this means for firms producing commodities is complicated by the fact that if the tax stays with the firm, its value is reduced at once (capitalized), and hence the normal return on its value just after the imposition of the tax is proportionately smaller. This will of course give the owners of the firm an incentive to advertise their ability to shift the tax to others. The credibility of this claimed shifting may vary from firm to firm.

(2) *Monopoly.* If the firm has a monopoly or shares a monopoly in the sale of its product, the firm will do best by swallowing the tax and not attempting to pass it on to its customers. Empirical studies have shown that firms do not understand this but set prices on a cost plus profit basis, including the tax as an additional cost. Hence, taxes may abate the ill effects, if any, of monopolies, but the monopolistic character of an industry does not guarantee that the tax will not be shifted.

(3) *Exclusivity of original incidence.* If the tax originally falls on a few selected commodities or services, as in the case of a selective sales tax, the tax is less likely to be shifted, because including the tax in prices will drive consumers away. The more general the tax, or in other words the broader the tax base, the more likely it is that the tax will be shifted to consumers.

(4) *Mobility of capital.* If a tax is imposed on a given industry, this may affect the transferability of capital to other industries; exactly what happens will depend on the nature of the industries, both that subject to the tax and those to which capital may fly. Capital invested in corporate stock is highly mobile; capital invested in farm equipment is virtually irremovable. The effect of the imposition of the tax on capital in one industry may be to immobilize it by discouraging sales.

(5) *Elasticity of demand for the industry's product.* If the customers of the firms subject to the tax are addicted to the industry's products, the tax can easily be shifted. To the extent that demand is elastic, the tax will be more difficult to shift.

(6) *Is the tax imposed on margin or on surplus?* If the tax increases marginal costs directly, then the short-run effect of the tax will be the same as the long-run effect described above for the lump-sum tax on a perfectly competitive industry.

(7) *Openness of the economy (herein of elasticity of supply).* If the economy in which the tax increase is to be applied is open to the entry of untaxed foreign goods, the elasticity of demand for such goods will tend to be high; the converse is true if the economy is closed. Hence tax shifting is less likely in the case of a state sales tax than in the case of federal sales taxes, because of the possibility of shopping out of state. Openness can affect the elasticity of supply as well by leaving suppliers with markets unaffected by a given tax. Hence, the greater the elasticity of supply, the greater the forward tax shifting. Generally,

$$\frac{\text{Elasticity of supply}}{\text{Elasticity of demand}} = \frac{\text{Buyers' share}}{\text{Sellers' share}}.$$

(8) *The comparative size of the tax.* Smaller taxes are more easily shifted because consumers don't notice or care.

(9) *Proportional vs. graduated taxes.* A proportional tax on profits will affect large and small firms alike. A progressive tax will reduce the attractiveness of investment in a large firm and in the short-run reduce the profitability of larger firms to a greater extent than that of smaller firms; the progressive tax may even be designed not to affect smaller firms. Hence, a progressive profits tax may have less effect on an industry and its consumers than a proportional tax would. A progressive tax directed to the buyer may kill the industry or parts of it, as in the case of the recent curtailment of tax depreciation for luxury automobiles and boats.

(10) *Intermediacy or finality of the product.* If the commodity is a final good, a tax shifted to the consumer will stay there. If the commodity is used in the production of other goods, the analysis should focus on the final producer and its customers, but monopoly and substitutability of components influences the shifting from supplier to final user.[5]

What about personal income taxes? In a perfectly competitive economy, wages would be set in accordance with marginal productivity, and it would follow that income taxes could not be shifted backwards to employers in the form of successful demands for higher wages and salaries. But:

(1) *Taxes may reduce the labor supply.*

(2) *The labor market may not be in equilibrium.* The marginal rate of productivity may be higher than pre-tax wage rates and labor may be able to negotiate compensating wage increases.

(3) *Employers may not be profit-maximizers.* Employers may quite reasonably hope to achieve higher productivity by permitting the tax to be shifted to them, and other motives may affect the decision as well.

A cluster of analyses of the substitution effect caused by taxes on wages have been offered, centering generally on the idea that people work less if the rewards of work are lower. The implication is that a proportional tax leaves incentives in place, while a progressive tax reduces them.[6] Empirical studies suggest that this is true, if at all, only for a small percentage of the working population, at least in the sense that other factors far outweigh the substitution effect for many

---

5. For a more lengthy discussion of these aspects of the general problem of tax incidence, see Edwin R. A. Seligman, The Incidence of Taxation 179–219 (1899). For an authoritative discussion of contemporary tax incidence analysis, see Joseph A. Pechman & Benjamin A. Okner, Who

Bears the Tax Burden? (1974); Joseph A. Pechman, Who Paid the Taxes 1966–85? (1985).

6. See, e.g., Richard A. Musgrave, The Theory of Public Finance 232–46 (1959); Richard Posner, Economic Analysis of Law 481–84 (4th ed. 1992).

categories of wage earner.[7] We shall return to this theme when we consider the problem of analyzing taxpayer welfare.

In brief, a priori solutions to questions of tax incidence are virtually impossible. The assumptions that must be made to yield a result are too strong to permit even mildly reliable predictions. Econometrics, or the empirical measurement of taxpayers' reactions, is the only answer. Unfortunately, there are too few tax changes, and too many difficulties concerning the cause and effect of reactions to tax changes to make measurement easy. A few classic econometric studies of corporate tax shifting tend to show that it takes place extensively in the U.S., India, West Germany and Canada. These studies have been challenged by others who make diametrically opposite findings.

2.3 THE QUEST FOR TAX EXCELLENCE

We turn now to the principal goals for which economic analysis has been enlisted in the design of national tax systems. The selection of one or more of these approaches to the purposes of taxation tends to be the undercurrent in many arguments about more particular tax measures in debate at the national level, especially in debates over the refinement of the federal income tax.

The five approaches to be described are: revenue minimization, national income maximization, tax neutrality, benefit taxation, and taxation in accordance with the ability to pay. The last of these we will discuss only cursorily, because the problems it raises properly belong to a discussion of how taxpayer welfare should be measured, which is discussed in section 3.7 below.

(1) *Revenue minimization.* As we have seen, one contemporary view of the justification of taxation is that it is necessary for the regulation of private spending on goods and services so as to prevent excessive inflation, excessive imbalance of payments, and excessive unemployment. A little reflection will suggest that these excesses may be interdependent. If these are the primary goals, however, then taxes should be devised to minimize the amount of revenue necessary to restrain private expenditure to the desired level.

Nicholas Kaldor made this a cornerstone of his famous argument in favor of an expenditure tax, as a general alternative to income taxes.[8] He called the effectiveness of a tax in reducing private spending its *net expenditure restraining effect* or its *economic efficiency* (E_T), which is defined as

$$\frac{\text{Change in private expenditure, } \Delta C}{\text{Change in revenue, } \Delta R}$$

In this context, C denotes all private spending, both consumption and investment. Obviously, the efficiency of a tax depends on the marginal

7. C.V. Brown & D.A. Dawson, Personal Taxation, Incentives and Tax Reform, Political and Economic Planning (1969).

8. Nicholas Kaldor, An Expenditure Tax (1956).

propensity of the relevant taxpayers to consume. To the extent that different taxpayers have different marginal propensities to spend, so will economic efficiency vary from tax to tax. Thus, a tax change that increased revenue by $100m and induced a fall in private expenditure of $80m would have an economic efficiency of $80/100 = .8$. Inefficiency defeats one or the other purpose of taxation. A greater expenditure restraining effect than that desired will produce unemployment and a smaller expenditure restraining effect excessive expenditure and inflation.

But it is even more difficult to ascertain marginal propensities to consume than it is to determine who bears the tax burden. Moreover, there are some peculiar problems. When the government makes transfer payments, it is not clear what corresponding reduction in private expenditure is appropriate, unless we know what the *net-expenditure-producing effect* of the transfer is. This may be defined as E_G

$$\frac{\text{Change in private expenditure, } \Delta C}{\text{Change in government transfers, } \Delta G}$$

For a properly designed tax measure, $E_G = E_T$.

In addition, taxation and government spending create multiplier effects due to the propensities of the taxpayers and the recipients of government expenditures to save. The change in revenue needed to meet a given government expenditure in a fully employed economy is

$$\Delta R \ E_T \ k_T = \Delta G \ E_T \ k_T$$

All this further assumes that consumption is a decreasing function of income. The less income one has, the less one consumes. Economists who have commented on the work of Keynes and Kaldor have disputed this.[9] It has been argued that some account must be taken of the tendency to reduce savings when income is reduced and to restore savings when income increases, as well as to take expected future income, especially from current assets that have not yet been consumed.

Where all this tends is to the differential treatment of the rich and the poor, or of various classes among them: the burden of tax changes to suppress excess consumption or eliminate unemployment would be placed as firmly as possible on lower-income groups. The gains, however, that would accrue to wealthier or other taxpayers as a result of more efficient taxes would be confined to those uses of wealth that constitute neither consumption nor investment.

In addition, a revenue minimization approach carries with it the negative distributional effects of a growing national debt, with a growing share of the national income going to national creditors.

9. John Duesenberry, Income, Saving   (1949).
and the Theory of Consumer Behavior

(2) *Tax Neutrality.* Taxes on commodities as such tend to produce an "excess burden" corresponding to the distortion of consumers' choices between the commodity in question and other available goods, unless demand is inelastic; the excess burden is greatest if demand is perfectly elastic.[10]

Figure 2 shows how the excess burden arises in the case of an industry (or firm) that faces a declining demand curve, i.e., where the effect of the tax is to curtail production to some extent. The industry loses some "producers' surplus" (ps) and some "consumers' surplus" (cs). This is because the industry (or firm) would have profited from the pre-tax additional sales at a price above marginal cost, and because the consumers who would have purchased at prices between the pre- and post-tax prices would have profited from the lower pre-tax price.

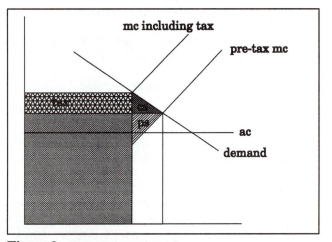

Figure 2 - Consumer and Producer
Portions of Excess Burden

[311a]

Figure 3 illustrates how different elasticity of demand affects the excess burden of a sales tax. Figure 3(a) shows a demand or marginal revenue curve (d) like that in Figure 2. This is typical of industries and firms that can sell greater outputs at lower prices. Figure 3(b) shows a demand curve (d) that would be faced by an industry or firm that cannot sell any of its output above a certain pre-tax price; the tax in this case costs the economy nothing in consumer surplus because the tax cannot be passed on the consumers, but it does cost the industry or firm all the profit that would have been gained by selling a larger output above pre-tax marginal cost. Figure 3(c) shows the demand curve (d) faced by an industry or firm that sells its output to addicts who will buy at any price. The tax is of course passed on to the consumers. It may seem strange to say here that there is no excess

10. John R. Hicks, Value and Capital   *Burden of Indirect Taxation,* 6 Rev. Econ.
(O.U.P. 1939); M.W.F. Joseph, *The Excess*   Stud. 226 (1939).

burden, no loss of consumer surplus, even though the addicts are paying more for their post-tax goods than they did pre-tax, but the idea here is that because they are addicts price really does not matter to them—they are not better off paying less, hence no consumer surplus.

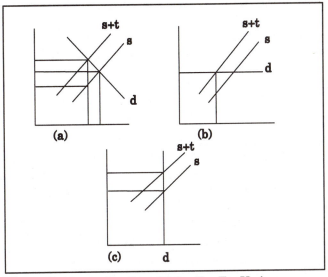

Figure 3 - Excess Burden of Sales Tax For Various Demand Schedules

[312a]

Note that sales taxes on nonaddictive commodities impose an excess burden on the economy only on assumptions of rationality and perfect information. People are somewhat rational and have at least some information, and so sales taxes are perhaps wasteful on the whole.

If this argument convinces you that indirect taxes should be dropped in favor of income taxes, because income taxes do not dictate a re-ordering of the consumer's choices, then note that income taxes may nevertheless have the non-neutral consequence of persuading some taxpayers to work less and enjoy more leisure. A "poll tax", i.e., tax on individuals that does not vary with income, would be preferable from this point of view. So the Hicks–Joseph argument appeared to show. This assumes that the government's goal is merely to raise a pre-determined amount of revenue.

This result is reversed, however, if we acknowledge that government's goal is to minimize consumption, and if consumers will save more under a consumption tax regime. Milton Friedman offered an influential general equilibrium model to show that a poll tax would nevertheless be optimal, even without the assumption of required yield.[11]

11. Milton Friedman, *The welfare effects of an income and an excise tax*, 60 J. Pol. Econ. (no. 1), 1–24.

But these conclusions depend both on unrealistic economic assumptions and on an insensitivity to distributional effects. In real capitalist economies, competition is rarely even approximately perfect, and the demand for the commodities that may be subjected to excise taxes is rarely so elastic as to create excess burdens. Moreover, the anti-progressivity of the poll tax is simply incompatible with the political preferences of all but a tiny minority of most industrial democracies. Thus tax neutrality recedes to the role of a secondary consideration in the design of a tax system.

(3) *Benefit taxation.* It was said at the outset that economists think a principal reason for imposing taxes in the first place is to provide those goods the market would not provide of its own accord, largely because the individuals to be benefitted or harmed by these goods would not have the market motivation to acquire or avoid them. If you think markets are inherently fairer or otherwise morally preferable to charity or government transfers that do not imitate market exchanges, it may occur to you that taxes should be designed to match tax burdens with the benefit of the social and merit goods provided by government. This is usually called *benefit taxation.*

To the extent that government supplies goods whose beneficiaries could be persuaded to negotiate rationally for them, or whose interest in these goods could be determined apart from market transactions, taxation in accordance with benefit has several attractions. Equity is served, because the beneficiary pays for and only for the benefit. Moreover, the benefit approach achieves a simultaneous determination of the tax level and the level of government expenditure required.

Several powerful models for allocating the cost of a shared benefit among a number of beneficiaries have been devised. Their principal purpose is to tax the beneficiary at no greater a level than the marginal utility of the benefit to him or her, but at the same time to achieve a balance between the individual taxpayer's demand for social and for private goods.

Paul Samuelson, a foremost mathematical economist, is famous in the area of public finance for several contributions, of which the earliest was his general-equilibrium "pure theory" of the problem of benefit taxation.

He showed how a benevolent despot might make a welfare-maximizing or optimal choice between a private consumption good like bread and a public consumption good like national defense for a two-person economy. There are an infinite number of ways in which the two individuals' different ways of choosing between competing private and public goods could be reconciled without leaving either individual worse off. (Note this condition: the goal of not leaving anyone worse off is characteristic of optimal strategies that are said to be *Pareto optimal,* i.e., strategies that improve overall welfare without worsening the welfare picture of any individual.) If an individual would be equally happy with 4 units of bread or 3 units of national defense, assuming that the provision of bread (a private good) and national defense (a public good) could be quantified, then that combination of the private and public goods available is a point (4,3) on an *indifference curve* for that individual for the two goods. Similar points of indifference, each of which would have to be established essentially by asking individuals how they feel about tradeoffs, might fall on many non-overlapping curves for the same individual. (This is important because the information to be juggled in solving the problem of optimal benefit taxation in this way could become very complicated fast.)

Samuelson's "solution" of the problem of reconciling two individuals' needs and wants with respect to private and public goods is essentially a method of identifying all the pairs of values, one from each individual's indifference map, which are not in conflict (and which, because they are on the indifference maps, are acceptable to the individuals). The solution, which we will not consider in mathematical detail here, is essentially a mechanical way of picking out the nonconflicting choices for both individuals that add the maximum possible amount to their aggregate welfare, by tacking on some shared amount of a public good.

Samuelson stressed that his "solution" of the problem of identifying tradeoffs of private and public goods *presupposed* accurate knowledge of individuals' preferences as well as the indifference curves of society as a whole. It is of central importance that these social indifference curves correspond to "political" preferences that can vary from society to society. The successful solution of the benefit maximization problem thus underscores the need for extremely detailed and, in the real world, elusive information about society as a whole.

Not all approaches to benefit taxation are as technical as Samuelson's. There is a broad vein of benefit tax theory that aims essentially to condemn other methods of taxation and vindicate the superiority of benefit taxation. Arguments of this sort are now best represented by the work of self-described "public choice" theorists, whose ideas are described in section 4.6 below. For present purposes, however, it is enough to note that like the more technical investigation of benefit taxation, these normative approaches assume the availability in principle of information about how public goods, goods that are essentially shared by large groups of people, benefit individuals within the group. This information is of course hard to get, if it is even theoretically available. Or in the lingo of welfare economics, we may not be able to find out enough about individuals' indifference curves to implement the best advice of the benefit tax proponent.

(4) *Income Maximization.* Since Ricardo and Mill, the goal of increasing the national income, enlarging the pie, has been thought by some to be equal in weight or even to trump other tax objectives.

Income maximization might be achieved by government intervention of various kinds.

(a) *Decreasing average cost subsidies and increasing average cost taxes.* Industries with decreasing average costs may set output at levels dictated by demand that is lower than average cost but higher than marginal cost. In these cases, a subsidy to the industry's cost may increase output to a level at which price is lowered by more than the subsidy, so that there is a net gain to the economy. Similarly, rising average cost industries may yield a net gain to the economy if they are taxed into lowering production, with the result that price is raised by less than the tax paid.[12]

The practical problems this strategy of subsidizing and taxing to increase growth raises are enormous. Cost schedules must be accurately determined for the long and short term, and the form in which the tax or subsidy is levied must be directed squarely enough at the cost difficulty to achieve the desired end. Firms are not uniformly rational enough to respond as governments desire.

(b) *Redistributing demand between products.* A government may increase the national wealth by diverting demand from industries that are working at full capacity to those with idle capacity, and taxes and subsidies may be an attractive means of doing this. But the premium on accuracy is high, and the political costs of intervening in the market, which might itself be achieving the decay of disadvantaged industries, are great. The more flexible the resources of the industries affected, the more likely that government intervention will not be harmful; but to that extent it is also more likely that the market will automatically accomplish whatever is most beneficial to the common weal.

(c) *Redistributing demand between regions.* Job training and relocation for the unemployed can be provided by government in the form of tax subsidies. The problem with direct subsidies and taxes to regions in prosperity or distress is that useful long-term outcomes may be disguised—the kind of economic activity in a region may be right or wrong for the future, and it may prolong the agony or postpone the ecstasy for government to intervene.

(d) *Fiscal reflation.* If there are unemployed resources throughout the economy, fiscal policy may "jump start" the economy, as it seems to have done in 1962–63 with the Kennedy tax cut and as monetary policy may be accomplishing (or may not) at the present moment.

(e) *Growth of income accelerating measures.* The Japanese government is sometimes given credit for identifying important factors inhibiting or promoting growth and acting upon this information by encouraging saving, subsidizing technological advance, rewarding team work and productivity and so forth. In the U.S. and Europe, the closest approximation to this theme has been that of subsidizing saving or investment in various forms (capital gain preference, the investment

---

12. Alfred Marshall, Principles of Economics (1890).

tax credit). Now and then political figures flirt with the idea of exaggerating through taxation or subsidy those market forces that tend to encourage economic efficiency, e.g., through elimination of the double tax on corporate income or by granting a tax credit for research and development.

(5) *Taxation in Accordance With Ability to Pay.* Directly in conflict with the goals of benefit taxation, at least if those goals are inflexible, is the goal of allocating tax burdens in accordance with taxable capacity or *ability to pay*. While taxes on commodities and imports produced most of the revenue governments need, the fairness of the resulting tax incidence received little attention. These *indirect* taxes probably placed the heaviest burdens on those with the smallest disposable incomes. In retrospect, this fact seems to have provided one of the better reasons for which people in and out of government eventually came to prefer *direct* taxes, taxes to be assessed according to characteristics of taxpayers and not according to the characteristics of transactions or goods that changed hands. At any rate, the early advocates of direct taxation pointed to the ability of the individual taxpayer to pay taxes as a self-evidently relevant characteristic on which to base a direct tax. And the history of income taxes followed.

It is still true that many people in and out of government find it overwhelmingly natural and inherently fair to assess taxes by reference to ability to pay, regardless of the benefits to be paid for with those taxes. To the extent that governmental benefits flow untraceably to the entire public, and no individual beneficiary can be singled out as the recipient of more or less than any other, taxation by ability to pay is even more attractive. That is because the spending side of government can be ignored. On the other hand, if government benefits flow in discrete packages to identifiable members of the public, the question arises whether these packages should be taken into account when we measure the individual's ability to pay; or in less veiled terms, the question arises whether these benefits should not be included in the income or consumption of the individual that will serve as the tax base. Advocates of benefit taxation often doubt the value of ability to pay altogether as a guide to proper tax assessment, because they believe that market forces control political decisions as well as private ones, and because they believe that political and private markets tend, whatever appearances may be, to equalize the ability to pay of all members of society. Skepticism about the relevance of ability to pay comes in less radical forms as well. If what is meant by ability to pay is economic income or the consumption of resources that have passed through markets, there are many who question the fairness of assessing burdens on either of these bases because they are not inherently good measures of the total welfare of individual people.

Nevertheless, we will find that the goal of taxation in accordance with ability to pay continues to play a commanding role in thought about taxes, at the highest and lowest levels of sophistication. Under this heading, see chapter 3 and section 9.5 below.

* * *

As has been evident, the foregoing summary of contributions by economists to problems of tax policy and design is based in large part on the works of a few prominent figures. This limits its usefulness as a guide to further interesting results, since in many cases the arguments summarized here have won the day and engender no continuing debate. In some instances, famous though the analysis in question may be, the kernel has borne no fruit but has rotted in its shell. You can't always tell this from my summary. But much of the rest of the story is told in the following chapters.

Chapter 3

HOW TAXES AFFECT PEOPLE'S WELFARE

3.1 WHAT MAKES ONE TAX MEASURE BETTER OR WORSE THAN ANOTHER?

Public policy involves matching means with ends. A policy proposal may clearly aim at goals on which everyone agrees, or the goals may be as controversial as the proposed means. The goals of tax policy, despite the enormous complacency of much public debate, remain controversial. While no one doubts that taxation should finally benefit people, beyond that nothing more definite can be taken for granted. Yet tax policy discussions frequently obscure this, mainly by assuming, as is common in policy discussions, that what is good for people is what maximizes the pleasure or satisfaction or utility of the greatest number of people. That assumption springs from a single strand among many in ethical and political theory. The following discussion first sketches alternative theories of human welfare and then dwells at length on the shortcomings of the customary approach. By focusing on what is left out when the assessment of tax proposals is harnessed to a crude analysis of human welfare, we shall see how other views of the ultimate human objectives of public policy might affect specific areas of tax debate.

3.2 THE MORAL AND POLITICAL BACKGROUND

The inventors of the subject of political economy explicitly concerned themselves with the justice and general moral worth of markets and other existing social institutions. They looked at all public policy as an expression of value-laden goals, and advocated or condemned particular governmental measures, including tax laws, in that spirit. Political economy had of course begun as a branch of moral philosophy. In the works of Adam Smith, John Stuart Mill, and Henry Sidgwick, among others, the subject was treated unself-consciously and consistently as an extension of ethics.[1] Since for many political economists taxation was the least objectionable form of governmental intervention in private decisions, their arguments now stand forth as unusually

1. The way in which Mill, among others, achieved this amalgamation of descriptive and ethical dimensions of governmental policy has been criticized. Mark Blaug, The Methodology of Economics 1–5 (1980).

forthright in championing the assessment of taxation from a primarily moral point of view.

Contemporary tax policy writers, mostly economists, just as consistently seem to avoid all moral and political discussion. Even overtly normative constraints on tax measures—horizontal and vertical equity, for example—are discussed as if they were mere extensions of the uncontroversial principle of treating like things alike, or as if unswerving political reality imposed these constraints on any rational inquiry. By the same token, contemporary defenders of the income tax invoke the touchstone of "ability to pay" with its pragmatic, morally neutral sound, never acknowledging the radical implications of that notion which were the topic of exhaustive, if inconclusive, debate during the last century. Nowadays, some tax policy theorists indeed forthrightly abandon the task of evaluating tax policy measures on grounds of justice or moral propriety altogether. What matters most, however, is that current tax policy thought generally has no clear moorings in moral or political principle, so that when the inevitable value judgments are made, they must either be disguised or treated as extraneous to the real work of the field.

But can this be right? Taxes inevitably affect human well-being and the distribution of satisfactions among people. Many of us, but for the tax systems under which we now live, would end up quite differently situated in the long run. There would probably be greater personal fortunes, if there were a lower maximum rate of income tax. There would certainly be more ignominious losers among entrepreneurs—the economy would be less stable and would experience greater swings from high to low efficiency. Maybe those who are least well off (assuming for the moment that they would also be among the least well off in a state without income tax) fare better under income tax regimes both because government spends more on them out of income tax revenues than it would otherwise, and also because longer and less volatile business cycles insulate them to some extent, as the first to suffer, from economic "misfortune."

Other more subtle effects of taxes are surely just as real, though the comparison between the world with taxes and the world without them can be difficult to formulate. Indeed, some theorists question whether such "before and after" comparisons are at all meaningful. See section 6.6, below.

Whatever the technical problems of determining just how taxes influence our lives, it is clear that they affect and interfere with the workings of the economy, the mechanism whereby good and ill fortune is meted out to those most vulnerable to nonviolent harm—the poor and the market's inevitable victims, unsuccessful entrepreneurs. Tax policy therefore has much to answer for before the tribunal of distributive justice. Taxes, along with talent, education, and inherited wealth, play a part in determining how people fare, perhaps just as large a part as these other, apparently basic conditions.

But whereas taxes obviously change the number of dollars in individuals' pockets, the significance of these changes in welfare terms is neither obvious nor, after considerable exploration, uncontroversial. Indeed, if we know anything about how public policy should be made, it is that attempts to confine the analysis of welfare to a mere technical and subordinate part in the process have failed utterly. In that light, this chapter asks: What must one know about the good things of the world and about human happiness to evaluate the contrasting consequences for individuals of different tax regimes?

The hold of the past on our thinking is nowhere more apparent than in contemporary answers to this question. Broad agreement among economists about the nature of welfare conceals some less than obvious borrowings from ethical theories. Non-economists often start elsewhere, and sometimes do so in conscious rejection of the assumptions economists should discuss but take for granted. In particular, it is useful to distinguish three types of ethical theory that influence the debate about public policy issues generally. They are usually taken to represent the Aristotelian, utilitarian, and Kantian traditions in ethics.[2] In the next section I survey them briefly and call attention to their most commonly cited areas of conflict.

Before embarking on the survey, it may be useful to note that even if what is good for people were not controversial, human welfare would nevertheless pose a basic problem for policy makers. What is good for me can be a factor in how I shape my conduct as well as in the choices others make that affect me. But my perception of what is good for me vis-a-vis my own choice of actions may be quite different from my perception of what is good for me when I call on elected officials to better my lot in life; and both may of course differ from those same officials' perception of what is good for me as they look down on my condition and make decisions for me without consulting me at all. At the most basic level, these perspectives differ because my actions can affect my own happiness in a way that the actions of others cannot. There are things I can get for myself that others cannot give me, although they may be able to deny me these things. They have to do with one's character, integrity, personal attachments, and all the agent-centered features of the life of the individual. These happen to be the things that people care about most deeply and that make people who they are. It is not surprising that the most familiar kinds of moral judgment reflect the agent's perspective. To the extent that ethical theories strive to capture the perspective of the individual agent, they may therefore stress a kind of evaluation that is not possible for the public decision-maker.

3.3 CONSEQUENTIALISM

Of the three ethical traditions mentioned in the last section, the easiest to describe is a form of consequentialism. Consequentialism is

2. See Richard A. Musgrave, *Public Finance Distributive Justice*, in David Greenaway & Graham Keith Shaw, eds., Public Choice, Public Finance, and Public Policy: Essays in Honour of Alan Peacock (1985).

the view that in evaluating alternative courses of conduct as good or bad, not with respect to other goals but as such, we need only consider the consequences of the available choices.[3] Thus, for a consequentialist, the moral goodness or badness of an action depends on the states of affairs it will bring about. Nothing depends on the motives or attitudes that prompt a particular person to choose to act in that way, unless having certain motives or attitudes itself has consequences. In this sense, the "intrinsic" goodness or badness of the consequent states of affairs is what determines the evaluation.[4]

Implicit in this description, and in consequentialism generally, is the premise that it is possible to rank states of affairs on a scale of value from best to worst. This is not to deny that the value of states of affairs is always determined with reference to how these states of affairs are perceived by human beings. But it is to say that potential facts can be evaluated without regard to how they came about on this particular occasion. If human reactions to states of affairs determine the value of these states, and it is assumed that there is a one-to-one correspondence between states of affairs and values—one value per state of affairs—then it is implicitly assumed that the path leading to the occurrence of a given state of affairs is, if not irrelevant, at least not of essential relevance for evaluating it. Thus, the path to an occurrence may enhance or detract from its value but the occurrence itself has a value somewhere on the scale of goodness, whether or not anyone cares how it was brought about.

This assumption is characteristic of utilitarian analysis.[5] Utilitarians offer at once the simplest and the most convincing account of morality: the best act in any situation is that which will bring about the greatest happiness of the greatest number of people. This formula assumes, if not very obviously, that alternative outcomes of our actions can always be compared simply in the light of their content, and this in turn implies that different states of the world can always be ranked from better to worse. What would contradict this? If it were impossible to compare two states of affairs unconditionally, i.e., without basing the comparison on assumptions about what led to these states of affairs, then the utilitarian criterion might simply not be capable of being

3. See Samuel Scheffler, The Rejection of Consequentialism 1–2 (1982).

4. Bernard Williams has made much of the idea that the intrinsic worth of states of affairs is crucial to consequentialist evaluation. Bernard Williams, Morality: An Introduction to Ethics 90 (1972); A Critique of Utilitarianism, in J.J.C. Smart & Bernard Williams, Utilitarianism: For and Against 77, 83–93 (1973); Ethics and the Limits of Philosophy 76–77 (1985). Defenders of consequentialism now sometimes advance this assumption as merely a hypothetical basis for moral theory, see, e.g., Nicholas Rescher, Distributive Justice 10–

11 (1966), or acknowledge that well-being consists in something other than the "welfare" of classical utilitarianism and neoclassical economics, see, e.g., James A. Mirrlees, The Economic Uses of Utilitarianism, in Bernard Williams & Amartya Sen, eds., Utilitarianism and Beyond 63, 69 (1982).

5. It is not, however, always expressed in this way. For a brief history of how "utility" has been understood by philosophers and economists, see John Broome, "Utility", 7 Econ. & Phil. 1 (1991).

applied. It might yield no decision which is the better of two courses of action.

Critics of utilitarianism have often argued that the necessary ranking is impossible or cannot be known to be possible, so that this *nonprocess* form of consequentialism fails. It is helpful to think about other ethical theories in order to see what problems of comparison might undermine the simple calculus of happiness.

3.4 DEONTOLOGY

The essential feature of deontological ethical theories is their insistence on the role of intention or motivation in giving value to actions and, derivatively, to the consequences of action. For motive or intention to be essential, consequences alone cannot ultimately determine the quality of an action. In its simplest form, deontology requires a good intention or good motivation as a condition for finding that an action is good. If this requirement does not collapse on closer examination into the requirement that we know something more about the possible consequences of actions like that in question, then consequences alone cannot have value in themselves, at least not the kind of value that determines or contributes to determining the value of acts.

Deontology—etymologically, an "account of duty"—is at bottom an attempt to explain the role of motive or intent in determining the ethical value of acts. Ethical theories that attribute the goodness or badness of actions entirely to the consequences they produce—consequentialist theories—can only attribute incidental value to motives or intentions. Some acts are more likely to lead to good outcomes if they are done from certain motives. It is the outcome of action that counts. There are powerful traditional reasons for rejecting this feature of consequentialism.

To put the objection into more concrete terms: consequentialism seems to allow nothing to the *integrity* of the individual whose acts are to be guided by its moral precepts. This comes out in several ways. First, it is notoriously a feature of utilitarianism and of other forms of nonprocess consequentialism that everyone bears responsibility not only for what they do but also for what they leave undone and even for what other free agents do or do not do as a consequence of one's acts or omissions. Hence, for example, the utilitarian has no trouble with saying that ceteris paribus one not only may but should kill one innocent person if this is the only way under the circumstances to save the lives of several other innocent persons, even if the reason for the connection between taking one life and saving several more is that a vicious gunman has given one this option. Other moral outlooks would regard the choice as difficult at least, and perhaps as required to come out otherwise. Second, utilitarianism disconnects one's principles from one's own choices for oneself, whenever the situation in which one finds oneself renders those principles moot. For example, a person who is opposed in principle to research on live animals should, on utilitarian principles, engage in such research if the research will go on anyway and if the salary for the job will benefit the researcher or his family.

It may well be that deontology has problems itself in accounting for the moral role of considerations of limited responsibility and integrity, but one of the presumptive strengths of deontology is that it is not plagued from the outset by counter-intuitive consequences like those just set forth.

3.5 PROCESS CONSEQUENTIALISM

Deontology, in turn, has its own problems, one of which is an apparently excessive concentration on moral motivation. If the goodness of an action depends entirely on how I come to choose this action and no other, then the background of the action will have disproportionate importance, from a common-sense point of view. Although Mother Teresa constantly does good works, indeed the same sorts of good works, the moral quality of her conduct could go up and down with the different levels of concentration she devotes to what she is doing. If she is inattentive to her own motivation on Tuesday, her self-sacrificial aid to the neediest of humanity may not count for much on a moral scale, even though it would have if she had begun the day with a little reflection on how this was her moral duty and so forth.

This is of course paradoxical in the light of some of the most constant assumptions we make about the moral value of action. In particular, we sometimes give people *more* credit for doing things habitually than for doing them with great mental effort. The habitually good course of conduct is called virtuous.

A virtue-based moral outlook assigns great importance to the entire past of the individual moral agent. Not only the moral habits of the agent but the opportunities for forming them are important in assessing how good the individual acts of this person are, and how good the person on the whole is. The assessment of habits and actions is consequentialist, in that the states of affairs that acting in a certain way will bring about are central to the agent's moral deliberations. But it is having a certain disposition to act in a certain way, so as to bring about preferable states of affairs, that makes the acts taken from that disposition good—not the goodness of the consequences in themselves. Good consequences can be achieved by people without character, but when that happens, the acts of those people are not as good as the acts of a virtuous person doing the same things.

3.6 COMPARING THE QUALITY OF DIFFERENT STATES OF AFFAIRS

The major differences among deontology and the process and nonprocess sorts of consequentialism have to do with what each theory assumes about the intrinsic value of states of affairs. Nonprocess consequentialism posits that states of affairs have intrinsic value; deontology and process consequentialism both reject this. It is interesting, therefore, that so much of the economic analysis of taxation and governmental action generally should rely traditionally on an assumption that looks very much like the nonprocess consequentialist view.

Neo-classical political economy, represented most explicitly in this respect by Jevons, relied heavily on the apparent truth of utilitarian analysis of human motivation and moral principle. Primarily this was a matter of incorporating utilitarianism into a positive predictive theory of production, but virtually all economists, since they accepted utilitarianism both for methodological purposes and as a true ethical theory, assumed that the notion of utility captured the ultimate good to which human behavior was directed, and that both individual conduct and government policy should be evaluated by reference to utility maximization.[6] In other words, the rational pursuit of the good was identified with self-interest in the somewhat narrow sense of maximizing one's pleasure or happiness, the two terms being used interchangeably.

Economists' borrowings from utilitarianism were fruitful but also dangerously misleading. The advantages of a universal theory of human motivation are obvious for a field in which the important aspects of repetitive transactions turn on such visible indicators of possible motivation as price and profit. On the other hand, as a theory of rationality, self-interest maximization distracted attention from those aspects of group behavior that are self-denying and altruistic and from those aspects of individual well being that relate to character and agency rather than to preference and satisfaction.

The economic paradigm so well stated and preached by John Stuart Mill was one for which description and prescription were usually closely mingled. Later in the nineteenth century the distinction between positive (or predictive) and welfare (or normative) economics began to mark separate fields of inquiry, partly perhaps in response to criticisms of Mill and his contemporaries.[7] At any rate, positive economics has continued to be based in large part on the utilitarian theory of self-interest as the only relevant kind of human motivation, while welfare economics takes into account other limits on economic choice. Unfortunately, as Amartya Sen has recently put it,

> Contact with the outside world has been mainly in the form of a one-way relationship by which findings of predictive economics are allowed to influence welfare economic analysis, but welfare economic ideas are not allowed to influence predictive economics, since actual human action is taken to be based on self-interest only, without any impact of ethical considerations or of welfare-economic judgments.[8]

Economists' view of economics as a science continues, in other words, to rest heavily on a priori assumptions about human motivation that are impervious to empirical or even a priori critique.

---

6. James M. Buchanan, *From Private Preferences to Public Philosophy: The Development of Public Choice*, in Constitutional Economics 29 (1991).

7. See, e.g. Henry Sidgwick, Principles of Political Economy 12–46 (1883).

8. Amartya Sen, On Ethics and Economics 29 (1987).

The theory of taxation, however, belongs to normative or welfare economics. Has this permitted tax policy to breathe a freer air? Only to a small extent. Modern welfare economics depends heavily on assumptions about the essentially self-seeking motivation of human behavior with minimally utility-based criteria of social regulation.[9] Indeed, the move towards normativity within welfare economics may rest on confusion about the problem of interpersonal comparisons of utility. We have no way to measure directly the effect of similar external events on the happiness of different individual people. Hence, we are never in a position to compare changes in one person's satisfactions with another person's as such, but only to compare what each would do in order to enjoy a similar externally identified advantage or avoid a similar externally identified disadvantage. Thus, we may think that an apple is worth more to a starving person than to a well-fed person because the starving person will walk a greater distance for the apple, and so forth.

It was partly in order to resolve the problem of interpersonal comparisons of utility that welfarists embraced the criterion of Pareto optimality, as virtually the sole surviving way of choosing (hence, the normative aspect) between competing social strategies. A social state is Pareto optimal if and only if no person's utility can be raised without reducing someone else's utility. Sometimes Pareto optimality is referred to as "economic efficiency." Note that this slender requirement does not ensure attractive distributional consequences. A state might in theory be Pareto optimal even though some people were subjected to torture while others had every satisfaction. Nevertheless, Pareto optimality is akin to the utility maximization of the utilitarians.[10] It provides a criterion (at least a partial criterion) of choice among alternative social strategies by reference to the ranking of their effect on individual utilities, and it does so by reference to a normative requirement that is arguably necessary, if not sufficient, for social justice.

Criticisms of economists' reliance on utility for this purpose are now the burden of a growing literature on issues of value in ethics as well as on the methodology of economics. Much of this criticism derives from the shortcomings of utilitarianism that have been explored by deontologists and process consequentialists. Briefly, they call attention to the elusiveness of values like personal integrity or character and autonomy in the reckoning of the value of satisfactions.

---

9. Id., at 30.

10. The enormous standing of Pareto optimality in welfare economics ... relates closely to the hallowed position of utilitarianism in traditional welfare economics.... If interpersonal comparisons of utility are dropped, but nevertheless utility is regarded as the only thing of intrinsic value, then Pareto optimality would be the natural surviving criterion, since it carries the utilitarian logic as far forward as possible without actually making any interpersonal comparisons of utility.

Sen, On Economics and Ethics, supra note 8, at 38.

3.7 ABILITY–TO–PAY AS A CRITERION OF TAX EQUITY

How do these criticisms relate to contemporary tax policy? Some debates about tax policy are independent of all welfare judgments. Revenue minimization, benefit taxation and tax neutrality approaches to the design of tax systems may raise distributional problems but these goals themselves are usually presented as independent of welfare effects, so that their proponents typically leave the distributional problems for others to worry about. (This is not always so; recall that Samuelson's general equilibrium solution to the problem of allocating the tax burden in accordance with benefit purported to be Pareto optimal, which is relevant only if we are concerned with welfare effects.)

But the approach that claims the largest following among prominent tax policy experts is one that makes welfare the central issue. It requires that taxes be levied in accordance with taxable capacity or "ability to pay." [11] The basic idea is that people should be taxed with ultimate regard to the effect that paying the tax will have on their welfare, and "ability to pay" or "taxable capacity" thus become surrogates for utility, welfare or well-being. [12] From the beginning of the modern interest in ability to pay, the notion's relevance has depended on its apparent relationship with both equity among taxpayers and the effect of taxes on their aggregate welfare.

A crucial phase of the primordial nineteenth century debate about the design and political viability of an income tax—as that debate developed among European thinkers—concerned how governmental exactions, without regard to corresponding government benefits, should affect the welfare of the taxpayer. In brief, what is the just way of distributing the burden of supporting government? John Stuart Mill set the terms and tone of the discussion with the unargued assertion that tax equity, for income tax purposes, required that each taxpayer should suffer an equal sacrifice *and* that the preferred "mode [should be] that by which least sacrifice is occasioned on the whole." [13] No one seems ever to have questioned the relevance of measuring equity by reference to the sacrifice involved or the importance of minimizing the burden of the tax on society. Indeed, the happy coincidence that both

---

11. See Richard Goode, The Individual Income Tax 17 (1976); Nicholas Kaldor, An Expenditure Tax 21–53 (1956); Alvin Warren, *Would a Consumption Tax Be Fairer Than an Income Tax?*, 89 Yale L.J. 1081, 1092–93 (1980).

12. "Utility" and "welfare" are sometimes, but not always, understood to have different, though closely related, meanings. The earliest utilitarians, represented by Jeremy Bentham, seem to have understood utility primarily as a propensity to cause pleasure or happiness (these two terms being used interchangeably). See Broome, supra note 5. Gradually, the term came to be used freely for the result rather than the cause, i.e., for pleasure or happiness rather than for the propensity to produce them. Finally, with a renewed self-consciousness about the foundations of welfare economics, most economic writers came to think "preference satisfaction" a suitably measurable empirical counterpart of what had been meant by "utility" in either of the older senses. They appropriated the term "welfare" for preference satisfaction, and then replaced "utility" with "welfare" systematically in their discussions of economic distribution.

13. John Stuart Mill, Principles of Political Economy, Bk. V, Ch. II, § 2, at 804 (ed. William Ashley 1909).

concerns could be met by a single criterion for tax design—equal sacrifice—won the day seemingly without contest. And from that point, the debate shifted to refining the meaning of these two key terms.

Before following that process of refinement through a few of its stages, it is vital to notice that ability to pay can only serve as *the* touchstone for spreading tax responsibility if we abandon the goal of making people pay in accordance with the governmental benefits they receive. Ability to pay theories are inconsistent with benefit taxation and with every form of quid pro quo allocation of tax liability. That the political as well as theoretical debate shifted to a consideration of ability to pay, and has scarcely deviated from that orientation since, is worth noting, because it has always signaled a rhetorical victory for the advocates of progressive taxation, as we shall see.[14]

Mill himself favored strategies that resulted in taxpayers at different income levels paying in proportion to the utility of their income for the accounting period. He assumed, as of course virtually all commentators on taxable capacity have, that the utility of money may decrease with the amount of one's income. The principal reason Mill saw for the declining marginal utility of income was that the person whose income is greater need not save as large a percentage of his or her income as the person with a smaller income, in order to provide for future needs. But this observation did not suggest to Mill a clear definition of equal sacrifice as proportionality to income.

Under certain conditions, a proportionate tax rate structure may implement an equal *absolute* sacrifice of utility by all taxpayers; but under other conditions, it may exact only an equal *proportional* sacrifice. A flat rate tax on income forces taxpayers to give up the same amount of utility or imposes on each the same reduction in welfare, if the marginal utility of income declines for all taxpayers at the same rate in relation to increasing income—or in simpler terms, if each taxpayer's last dollar of income does him or her less good than the last just in the proportion that it increases his or her total income.[15] On the other hand, a flat rate tax imposes an equal proportional sacrifice on all taxpayers if every dollar of income does each taxpayer, no matter how great his or her income, the same amount of good. But Mill did not comment on all this. It remained for later writers to clarify how the sacrifice of the taxpayer varies with the amount paid to the government.

For one thing, Mill did not notice that equal sacrifice might mean equal absolute, proportional, or marginal amounts of utility surrendered. The more income one has the better off he or she is, other

---

14. Richard A. Musgrave, Theory of Public Finance 90 (1959); Gunnar Myrdal, The Political Element in the Development of Economic Theory 165 (trans. Paul Streeten 1953).

15. Musgrave, supra note 14, at 99.

things being equal.[16] But the money units in which we normally measure income are not units of the benefit income confers. Defining units of such benefit—units of utility—is perhaps impossible, at least very hard. We measure income in units of money. We suppose, however, that the different dollar levels of income enjoyed by different people often indicate differences in how well off they really are (and not merely differences in how well off they appear to be). If the goal is to impose equal sacrifices on all concerned, we must first decide what we would take from each individual if the utility of his or her total income could be reckoned in common units of some kind. Would we take the same amount of utility from each (given that this might mean taking different amounts of money from different people because the value of money to them differed)? If so, then equal sacrifice would mean *equal absolute sacrifice*. Note that equal absolute sacrifice does not mean equal tax liabilities all round. If on the other hand we would take the same percentage of the utility each person's income gave them, then an *equal proportional sacrifice* would be imposed on each. Finally, to require sacrifice only at the margin of the individual taxpayer's income utility is to levy the tax only on the highest income utility shares. *Equal marginal sacrifice* is just confiscation of the amounts by which the highest incomes differ from the next highest, until the required yield is achieved.

Now reintroduce the measurement of income in money. Equal absolute sacrifice, as we saw, may require different tax payments by people with equal dollar incomes. It will depend on how much a dollar of income benefits the recipient. *If* another dollar added to any person's income makes that person better off to the same extent as it would anyone else, then the marginal utility of money income is the same for everyone. Under this condition, equal absolute sacrifice means equal tax liabilities.

A further condition permits us to equate equal proportional sacrifice with flat rate taxes. Tax rates are set in percentages and are meant to be applied to amounts of income measured in money. If we assume the equal marginal utility of money income (as in the previous paragraph), different levels of income in money correspond to different levels of the utility derived from that income. A flat rate tax is one that requires each taxpayer to surrender the same percentage of his or her money income. This will correspond to the same percentage of the utility of that income to the individual taxpayer only if we know (in addition to the equal marginal utility of money income) that the marginal utility of money income is the same for everyone and is constant, i.e., each dollar of income confers the same amount of utility on whoever gets it, no matter how much he or she already has. Obviously, taking the same percentage of the utility associated with

16. For the moment, it does not matter whether this proposition is a tautology, following from a definition of income in terms of utility added to a person's stock of utility, or an empirical truth, following from some correlation between increases in wealth measured in money and increases in utility.

each person's income does not require an equal sacrifice from each in the same sense that taking the same amount of utility from each would. In other words, equal proportional sacrifices differ from equal absolute sacrifices.

Perhaps the most popular assumption concerning this matter of tax rates and the value of money to people is that the marginal utility of money income is not constant but diminishes.[17] Assuming this, a *progressive* schedule of marginal tax rates is required to exact an equal absolute sacrifice at different income levels. Note that progressive rates, on this rather strong assumption, do not have the effect of reshuffling the comparative order of after-tax incomes. The person with a greater pre-tax income will have a greater after-tax income. Tax liabilities measured in dollars will differ. The person with the greater pre-tax income will pay a higher dollar tax than a person with less pre-tax income. But tax burdens measured in utility will all be the same. Thus, there is no redistribution of income.

Finally, notice that *both* the flat or proportional tax (same rate for all money income levels) and a progressive schedule of marginal tax rates preserve the rank order of incomes, measured in dollars.

Late nineteenth century tax theorists chose from among these positions, mostly in reaction to Mill's powerful arguments for proportional tax rates. Cohen–Stuart analyzed the implications of proportional and progressive tax rate structures, exposing some of the features of these approaches that are restated in the foregoing paragraphs. On that basis, he preferred equal proportional sacrifice because this would leave the relative positions of different taxpayers, in terms of total utility, unchanged.[18] Sidgwick and Marshall considered equal absolute sacrifice the only truly equal treatment, while Carver and others held fast to equal marginal sacrifice, again for reasons of equality.[19] As we have seen, these views did not translate into easy practical solutions, because the task of imposing equal absolute sacrifice and equal marginal sacrifice could require detailed knowledge of the shared marginal utility curves of the population to be taxed.

Among those who proposed variations of these principal analyses of ability to pay, some were also concerned with the effect of income to the taxpayer's life circumstances—educational status, freedom to vary one's employment, mortgages, etc.[20]

Different positions on the nature and implications of equal sacrifice evolved largely on the assumption that tax equity was the primary

17. If the marginal utility of money income declines at the same percentage rate as that at which income increases, a proportional tax is required to achieve equal absolute sacrifice. See Musgrave, supra note 14, at 99.

18. A.J. Cohen–Stuart, Bijdrage tot de Theorie der progressieve Inkomstenbelasting, ch. 5 (1889).

19. Henry Sidgwick, The Principles of Political Economy, 562 (1883); Alfred Marshall, Principles of Economics 135 n.1 (8th ed. 1930); T. Carver, *The Minimum Sacrifice Theory of Taxation*, 19 Pol. Sci. Q. 66 (1904).

20. See, e.g., R. Meyer, Die Prinzipien der gerechten Besteuerung (Berlin 1884).

issue and that individual utility was the proper touchstone of equity. The entire debate took a novel turn when some economists re-examined the distributive problem from the perspective of the overall effects of taxation on society. Mill had claimed that equal absolute sacrifice achieved the least sacrifice of utility in the aggregate. F. Y. Edgeworth, in a paper resoundingly entitled "The Pure Theory of Taxation," was the first to contend that morality alone could not decide the issue whether equal absolute or equal proportional sacrifice was fairer but that only equal marginal sacrifice met the general social goal of least *aggregate* sacrifice.[21] Looking at a society's economy only at an instant, or assuming away changes in the economy resulting from the adjustment of taxpayers' behavior to the effects of taxation as well as other possible structural changes in the economy, Edgeworth's argument amounted to a proof of the efficiency of socialism, because as we have seen equal marginal sacrifice requires the confiscation of the highest incomes and then the next highest incomes until the required yield is achieved. Yet it was also his contention that welfare objectives should control the outcome because it was impossible to resolve the fundamental issue of tax equity among taxpayers.

3.8   UTILITY FUNCTIONS AND INDIVIDUAL WELL–BEING

As the preceding discussion shows, ability to pay took its meaning in these early days of income tax policy from assumptions belonging to the utilitarian tradition in ethics. It was taken for granted that the distributional effects of taxation were to be thought of and theorized about in terms of the utility of distributions of goods among individuals, and in particular, in terms of what would now be called individual utility functions. That is indeed what "utility" meant to late nineteenth century English-speaking philosophers, economists and general public alike, at least for most purposes, and in most contexts today questions of "distributive justice" are assumed to be posed in similar terms. But what exactly are utility functions?

For the first utilitarians, "utility" and "usefulness" were synonyms (as of course in many contexts they still are). Utility was thus a characteristic of things and one that related to human purpose: susceptibility of being used in the service of some end, hence, adaptability to the promotion of some human goal. By extension, events and human acts could be thought of as having utility, since they too could obviously promote a person's goals. The utilitarians were concerned with how much utility things or events or courses of action might have, not for one person only but for groups of people as well, and hence they often had no reason to distinguish clearly between a propensity to advance human goals and the advancement of those goals, between tendency and effect, so to speak. Perhaps for this reason, it became common for utilitarians to speak as if the utility of a thing, event or course of action

21. Frances Y. Edgeworth, *The Pure Theory of Taxation*, in 2 Papers Relating to Political Economy 117 (1925); cf. Alexandre C. Pigou, A Study in Public Finance 61 (3d ed. 1942).

just were the pleasure or happiness occasioned by it, rather than the tendency to produce pleasure or happiness.

It also became common to distinguish between the purely subjective and perhaps idiosyncratic pleasure or happiness a person experienced as the result of some thing, event, or course of action, and the pleasure or happiness that person should have experienced if he or she had known his or her own best interests. The term "utility," in discussions of ethics or policy, came to stand exclusively for the latter and thus might stand for the promotion of one's interests rather than for mere satisfaction of one's conscious, and perhaps ill-conceived, preferences.

Utilitarians also slipped into the habit of speaking as though utility has a number of convenient features that make it suitable for mathematical manipulation. This general assumption about utility manifested itself in various more narrow assumptions: that any state of affairs has a single utility for each individual person, regardless of what else may occur, and that the utility of the combined occurrence of several states of affairs is the total of their separate utilities; that the utility of a given state of affairs for one person does not affect the utility of that state of affairs (or any other) for other people; that the value of those states of affairs that make up a person's life or that figure in the background of a person's life account entirely for the well-being of that person; that the utility of a given state of affairs does not depend on the value of any other state of affairs, for the same person or for others. A central reason for the comprehensiveness of these assumptions that underlay utilitarian analysis was the need for an exhaustive criterion of human welfare, a single and unambiguous measuring rod for the goodness or badness of all states of affairs for all people.

Tax theorists at first took all these supposed characteristics of utility for granted. Closer examination of the distributional effects of taxation in terms of utility so conceived—especially, as evidenced by the work of Cohen–Stuart, Sidgwick, Carver, Edgeworth and other participants in the equal sacrifice debate—eventually led to more critical attitudes.[22]

No one had ever doubted that the utility of a single state of affairs might differ for different people. Tastes differ, if nothing else. Yet much early work in economics and utilitarian ethical theory depended on the complete availability, at least in principle, of the utility for every person of every possible state of the world. Concentration on our obvious ignorance of these individual differences led philosophers and economists to recognize that puzzles abound concerning the very existence of this complete utility information.

In effect, early assumptions about utility amounted to taking for granted that there exists a definite correlation between every possible

22. Professor Samuelson's engagingly irreverent survey of the history of the concept of utility/welfare in welfare economics is among the most accessible. Paul A. Samuelson, Foundations of Economic Analysis 203–53 (2d ed. 1983).

future and some measure of the benefit or harm of that future for every individual person. A possible future must be understood here to be a conceivable unfolding of world history from this moment on; no contradiction among the "contents" of an alternative future is allowed. Slight factual differences between possible futures would register, in this correlation of fact and value for the individual person, as a difference, or no difference, in the utility of the whole future for him or her.

The unexamined assumptions of early utility theory also extended to the compilation of a master reckoning of the utility of possible futures for everyone at once. By the greatest happiness of the greatest number of people, the first utilitarian ethical theorists had apparently meant a simple arithmetic summing up of the utility for all people of alternative events. It was taken for granted that the utility of something that might happen was just the total utility of that outcome for everyone concerned. This required a common denominator of utility and the ability to reduce the welfare effect of a given event for any pair of people to that denominator.

Were all this information known, it would be possible to speak of individual utility "functions." A function is a correlation of a certain kind between two sets of things (or between one set and itself), such that everything in the first set (or domain) has a unique correlation with something in the second set (or range). Utility functions would "map" possible states of the world (or alternatively, particular events that make up possible states of the world) with values. Each person would have a unique utility function, which means that for that person a possible state of affairs would have only one value. The range of utility functions would be the same for everyone, and so it would be possible to compare the utility of the same events for different people, to compare the utility of different events for the same person, and to compare the utility of different events for different people.

It was also customary to assume that utilities could be expressed in absolute values. Not only could one say that one event would benefit a person more than another event, but one could say how great the benefit would be and rank this against all other possible utility values.

With the emergence of microeconomics, as the field came to depend more and more heavily on these assumptions, a broad reaction set in. The exact history of the developing estrangement from utility assumptions does not concern us. But it is useful to know that the critique of utility was basic to the development of what came to be known as welfare economics—the economics of distributional effects. This historical fact is important because economists still rely on the influential work of Lionel (later Lord) Robbins in laying the foundations of specialized work on welfare issues and because the cogency of his analysis is in doubt.[23]

23. Sen, On Ethics and Economics, supra note 8.

Robbins called attention primarily to the apparent problem of interpersonal comparison of utility: how can utility for one person be compared with utility for another? There is no publicly accessible yardstick against which utility for different individuals can be measured, at least not as there are thermometers with whose readings our feelings of heat or cold can be compared and, with the help of neutral-seeming empirical theory, can be compared objectively. Robbins concluded that the quest for objective comparison was futile and that all judgments and theorizing about the common welfare of more than one person must be "normative." By this, he apparently meant that a norm—a utility thermometer—must be chosen on grounds that cannot strictly be traced to what is known about "private" utility. Although thrust upon us by a peculiar theoretical impasse, this norm is of course normative in the usual sense because it represents a range of judgments for which there is no complete empirical foundation, judgments which imply other value judgments of the sort that we usually consider normative, such as judgments of the goodness or badness of individual acts and of public policy.

Despite the widespread acceptance of Robbins's argument, it is not clear that he correctly grasped (or that others correctly grasped his analysis of) the nature of the difficulty about getting from utility for different individual people to shared or interpersonal utility.[24] However that may be, comparing utility for people is not the only problem for welfare economics or for tax policy. At least four other problematic features, taken for granted by early utilitarians, have been noticed by more recent writers. When these are taken into account, the utilitarian account of human welfare, even with the most sympathetic revisions and adjustments, simply is no longer an account of human welfare but is instead at best an arbitrary pronouncement on that topic.

The first problematic feature is the assumed independence of the utility for any person of different states of the world. Or as a leading tax economist has put it, "For it to be possible to introduce numerical measurement of utility [for particular time periods and circumstances of a particular person's life], it is necessary that his preferences regarding what he will be doing at one particular time in one particular set of circumstances be independent of what he may be planning for all other times and circumstances."[25] A utility function that has this characteristic is said to be "separable." It seems odd that utilitarians should ever have taken so sweeping a proposition for granted, especially since people's lives and the plans they make for them resist retrospective evaluation in such piecemeal terms. To quote again from the same economist's appraisal of the theory of utility on this point, "Everything that has to do with life as a connected whole—such as habit, memory, preparation for future action, anticipation, achievement and failure—

24. See Musgrave, supra note 14, at 108–09; Sen, supra note 23, at 30 & n.1.

25. James A. Mirrlees, *The Economic Uses of Utilitarianism*, in Sen & Williams, eds., Beyond Utilitarianism 63, 66, supra note 4; see also James Gorman, *The Structure of Utility Functions*, 35 Rev. Econ. Stud. 367–90 (1968).

seems to have been ignored."[26] Yet it is true that some decisions, especially in the context of a person's plans for future consumption, might plausibly be represented as based on a weighting of preferences for the future that are separable in the required sense. Thus, for the limited purpose of modeling particular decisions, and for representing the interplay of preference strengths and probabilities that seem to characterize these decisions, utility functions may perhaps safely be assumed to be separable.

What has this to do, however, with the overall evaluation of distributional effects of a tax system? Certainly, taxes have an impact on widely separate time periods within one's life, even if the taxes nominally fall on income or transactions from distinct periods. The effect of tax burdens on a taxpayer's welfare, at first glance, cannot plausibly be analyzed just in terms of the period of nominal tax incidence or only with respect to the decisions nominally affected by the tax. For example, a tax on business profits may *gradually* (i.e., over a period encompassing many shorter tax periods) drive an entrepreneur to seek salaried employment; the spectacle of tax benefits flowing to those with high incomes may tip the balance for a youth without education or money towards a life of crime; and so forth.[27] In brief, although we may be able to construct separable utility functions for limited analytical purposes,[28] there is every reason to think that such functions cannot represent a full-blown concept of welfare, such as might ground real-life planning across a wide range of choices.

A second major difficulty about the assumptions typically made concerning utility functions is that in ordinary situations we speak as if there can be a gap between what one wants and what is actually good for him or her. Since preference is not always or necessarily a guide to a person's real interests (let's just define "interests" for the moment to mean what is conducive to one's welfare), an analysis of welfare into preferences requires a strong theoretical defense. There is no commonly accepted solution to this difficulty. One well-known proposal is simply not to think of utility functions as measuring individual preferences at all. Instead, the utility of a state of affairs is deemed to be a measure of the extent to which that state of affairs promotes a person's welfare by reference to objective causation. The idea is that everyone's preferences are caused by the same general causal variables. Differences in preferences could, in principle, be predicted from differences in these variables, arising for example from differences in biological

---

26. Mirrlees, supra note 25.

27. The assumption of independence of utility functions is questionable even for a given moment in time. It cannot be assumed that a person's preferences and interests (assuming that utility, if it is defined, must be a reflection of one or both of these) are unaffected by the preferences and interests of others. Keeping up with the Joneses may be a big issue for Smith, so that Smith's preferences change

when she finds out how Jones will be affected by a given state of the world. See Musgrave, A Theory of Public Finance, supra note 14, at 103.

28. See Mirrlees, supra note 25, at 74–78 (demonstrating in terms of a hypothetical world of individuals with identical utility functions that equal tax incidence does not guarantee economic efficiency).

inheritance and life history. People's preferences do indeed differ, but the differences are to be resolved into these accidental features of their genetic and developmental backgrounds. The argument then goes that in judging how one person's preferences reflect that person's interests, we make allowance simply for these differences, to the extent that we know them. Assessing utility is thus essentially a matter of putting oneself into another person's shoes, by reference to objective features of that person's situation (nature and nurture, again). If enough were known, any such judgments about an individual would boil down to a tailored version of some commonly shared utility function—a gold standard against which personal variations can be explained. This ultimate utility function, which may of course not be any real person's actual utility function, is the common denominator of utility.[29]

This "solution" of course assumes more than we know. We can only speculate about the causal explanation of differences in tastes and values. And even were we to concede on grounds of general principle that all such differences must be causally determined (we *would* certainly think this if we were general causal determinists), it would not follow that the *satisfaction* of a particular person's preferences provided any kind of key to that person's welfare. So the proposed analysis of preferences into objective causal factors relating to welfare does not preserve the thought that what we prefer is, or is an approximation of, what is good for us.

It is far more plausible to say that our most convincing assessments of utility simply are everyday judgments about the relationship between someone's preferences and interests. How do we know what these interests are? By making unscientific judgments about common human needs and wants and the relationship of people's actual preferences to those needs and wants. We informally posit "normal" needs and wants, and interpret the desires people express (in words or through their behavior) by searching for plausible welfare-related goals to which these preferences might relate.[30] Discarding the claim that we could construct a scientific account of how we make these judgments relating preferences and interests, we are still able to capture the everyday essence that makes that hypothesis itself seem plausible. The hypothetical scientific account, if it existed, would inevitably be based on everyday judgments of this sort. Presumably, getting from the everyday judgments to neutral explanatory principles would require that we separate out and acknowledge the normative assumptions we make in assessing what is good and bad for people. So it is not clear that either sort of account really grounds the kind of talk about utility functions that gave utilitarianism and early welfare economics their claims to objectivity.

29. John Harsanyi, Rational Behavior and Bargaining Equilibrium in Games and Social Situations 58–59 (1977).

30. James Griffin, Well–Being 113–120 (1986).

A third problem area concerning utility functions arises even if there were an objective foundation for some interpersonal comparisons of utility (either as suggested in the just preceding discussion or otherwise). It has to do with the possibility that people at the deepest levels have genuinely conflicting values.[31] Jones may prefer, and her welfare may really depend on, altruistic projects to a greater extent than Smith, who on the contrary is more deeply family-oriented. Some events may hold the same utility for Jones and Smith, perhaps even because they satisfy the same sorts of preferences. For, we need not suppose that they do not share each other's values to some extent. But the ultimate weights each attaches to the shared goals differ, and so the utility of some events will not be comparable for them. (Obviously, the possibility of this sort of conflict of values is assumed away by the hypothesis that all differences in preferences can be explained by reference to causal factors.) We do not know that such fundamental differences in values occur. The point is that our shared knowledge of preferences and welfare is not refined enough to establish whether it does. *If* such conflicts can occur, no shared utility appraisal with respect to the conflicting preferences may be possible without recourse to some higher normative standard. Again, if such recourse were necessary, utility functions would not serve the neutral purpose for which they were posited by utilitarians and welfare economists of the past.

Fourth, if utility functions for individuals were known, there would remain (absent some master causal explanation for individual differences) the problem of deciding how differences in tastes and values, expressed as differences in the utility for different people of the same states of the world, should be weighted.

Fifth, utility functions have the attractive feature mathematicians call "continuity" (i.e. they are "continuous functions") only if all people, taken individually, have preferences concerning all combinations of alternative states of affairs.[32] Noncontinuous functions of peoples' preferences may be of interest for a variety of purposes, but they do not allow us to think of welfare effects for groups of people as determined by each person's utility function for particular states of the world. This is because we cannot assume that everyone's utility function will be defined (i.e., will have any value at all) for all the same combinations of goods. One person for example may strongly desire the death of a convicted criminal, while another person may neither have a preference nor be indifferent to this outcome, except in combination with other events, with respect to which our first person has no preference

---

31. John Rawls posits that there are some "primary goods" on which people can be assumed to agree, even if conflicts of values otherwise exist. It is important to recognize that the problem about conflicts of goods is a crucial one for Rawls and provides one of two basic reasons for his departure from the utilitarian tradition in theorizing about justice. See John Rawls, A Theory of Justice 22–27, 90–91 (1971); *Social Unity and Primary Goods* in Sen & Williams, eds., Beyond Utilitarianism, supra note 4, at 159.

32. Kenneth Arrow, Social Choice and Individual Values 17 (2d ed. 1963).

and is also not indifferent, unless yet other events are combined with those of concern to the second person; and so on.[33]

Sixth, utility functions, traditionally conceived, embody the assumption that the situation in which one finds oneself determines one's welfare at that moment. This is a consequence in part of the independence assumption that has already been discussed. But there is another sense in which the situational determinism of the familiar handling of utility functions misses a vital aspect of human welfare. It assumes in effect that everyone is a utilitarian—that the good or bad of an outcome for one is independent of considerations about how one got to that point, about the process by which the person's own decisions as well as the decisions of others contributed to what happened. Not only does process often matter very much in our valuations of states of affairs in which we find ourselves, but we are also capable of debating how process should matter. We are capable of being converted from utilitarianism to a process form of consequentialism or to deontology, or from these views to utilitarianism. As one critics of the use of utilitarianism in economics puts it:

> The general point then is this: it seems plain that utility consequences of social actions are highly relevant to the evaluation of such actions. But there is, in general, no unique way in which these consequences can be aggregated and even if there were such a unique way, it seems simply wrong to assert that these consequences are the only relevant criteria for evaluating social actions.[34]

In summary, it cannot be taken for granted that utility or any other measure of human well-being has the convenient characteristics that were taken for granted by early utilitarians and economists. Although no one seriously defends a contrary view, and although serious students of the subject consistently point out that well-being is more complicated than this, a good deal of writing in the tax policy area seems still to rely on the availability of a utilitarian approach to welfare considerations and distributive justice. Indeed, these feet of clay weaken many of the more sophisticated approaches to current tax policy issues.

3.9 IS "DISTRIBUTIVE JUSTICE" A WELL–DEFINED ASPECT OF JUSTICE AS A WHOLE?

It matters for our purposes that there is great difficulty about utility comparison and about the equation of welfare with utility, conceived either in the manner of the original utilitarians or in more recent revisions, because the whole point of analyzing welfare in terms of utility presupposes that the foundations of this approach are secure, even if particular applications remain sketchy or highly simplified.

33. We need not assume continuity in order to consider the problem of getting from the preference or choice functions of various people to a single collective (or "social") choice function. Arrow, supra note 32, at 9–23.

34. Frank Hahn, *On Some Difficulties of the Utilitarian Economist*, in Sen & Williams, supra note 4, Beyond Utilitarianism, at 187, 188.

We have seen that when economists discuss and compare tax burdens, they most often take for granted that these burdens are to be measured in dollars or their equivalent. This of course presupposes that the burdens in question, no matter how they are experienced, can be translated into market terms—in short, into money received or expended. Is this an assumption about facts or is it a judgment that whatever resists translation can properly be ignored? By going along with this way of comparing tax burdens, do we make a controversial assumption? Do we miss anything important?

These are questions that real people may well ask about the effects of taxation. Somehow they don't occur to tax policy commentators. Their complacency is a symptom that something big has been resolved by implicit argument and that the argument has been forgotten by those who take it for granted.[35] What is the argument? What is the problem?

Making comparisons among the effects of taxes on particular people is one of the inevitable and recurring tasks of legislators. Like other basic tasks for the legislator, this one is influenced by tradition— not a tradition concerning the best public policy decisions for a particular area of legislation, but a tradition concerning how the wise legislator should view his or her task. The tradition stems from the magnificent convergence of philosophy and public policy that is called utilitarianism. It has been and remains attractive to experts because it posits a separation between aggregate measures of social goods and the individual or distributive measure of the same goods. From the foregoing discussion, however, it should be clear that this very distinction stands in need of defense.[36]

3.10 OTHER APPROACHES TO WELFARE

The respects in which traditionally conceived utility functions miss the point, or may miss the point, provide a focus for extensive contemporary debate among economists, political theorists and philosophers. Although the mainstream of writing by tax economists and tax lawyers has yet to take that debate into account, the outline of a different approach and style is already discernible.

One ingredient in the alternative assessment of human welfare is the recognition that economic behavior, which can be and usually is viewed as a concatenation of discrete decisions, provides a weak reflection or no reflection at all of what matters most to people's lives from a less piecemeal perspective. "Quality of life" has come to connote background rather than foreground aspects of how we live, and usually

---

35. It has not been forgotten without trace. Richard Musgrave's masterful treatment of the proposition that taxes should accord with ability to pay is perhaps in the background of contemporary economists' more casual acceptance that only dollar effects need be taken into account.

36. See Sen, Economics and Ethics, supra note 25 (proposal that a more complex measure of welfare be devised in the light of criticism of old-fashioned consequentialism).

such shared aspects as the general social climate or environmental health or sheer variety of experiences available.[37] The quality of an individual's life, however, is easily capable of triumphing over the limitations of the society in which he or she lives, just as a life can easily go wrong or sour despite the most favorable circumstances. Our understanding of human welfare, to say the least, cannot leave out these obvious facts. The principal flaw of traditional utilitarian analysis and of more modern welfare analysis based on the assumption of homogeneous, continuous, separable utility functions is that they cannot easily accommodate the larger perspective that matters most. They are myopic.

Thus, for example, it is argued that welfare economics has traditionally shortchanged, and should take account of, the basic measure of individual welfare provided by comparing the situation of the individual with an acceptable standard of living that happens to be shared by that individual with others in the same society.[38] This is advisedly a measure of welfare that varies from society to society. But it amounts to more than simply admitting the effects of sympathy and envy (charitable impulse or keeping up with the Joneses) on how well off people feel themselves to be. (Introducing sympathy and envy effects on welfare is already difficult enough, from a computational point of view, for mathematical welfare economics: interdependent utility functions, as they are called, greatly complicate and may defeat the definition of aggregate welfare functions.) What else is included in the relevant measure of deviation from an acceptable standard of living? An acceptable standard of living must make some ordinary human life plans possible: feeding and clothing oneself, living in security from physical violence, raising a family, and so forth.

So far tax experts have not rushed to adopt standard-of-living welfare notions. It is easy to imagine the difficulties facing any empirical investigation of welfare in this untraditional and less myopic sense. One must have much more information about people than tax returns typically provide. On the other hand, the elusiveness of information does not make it irrelevant. Much of the information old-fashioned welfare analysis assumes to be available in principle is practically beyond our reach—one need consider only the most heavily investigated of factors, such as cross elasticities of labor and leisure.

37. Tibor Scitovsky, The Joyless Economy: The Psychology of Human Satisfaction (2d ed. 1992).

38. Amartya Sen, John Muellbauer, Ravi Kanbur, Keith Hart & Bernard Williams, The Standard of Living (ed. Geoffrey Hawthorn 1987).

Chapter 4

THE POLITICAL JUSTIFICATION
OF TAX POLICY

4.1 THE POLITICAL PROBLEM OF JUSTIFYING TAX MEASURES

The idea that the state is within its prerogative in adopting and enforcing *almost* any beneficial measure, including any tax, accords well with most traditions in political theory. The big exception is anarchism, which has always been on the margins of discussions about what government may do because it denies government all legitimacy. But even liberalism, in any formulation that has been seriously defended, does not authorize completely unrestrained tax policy or even tax policy restrained only by the requirement that it be beneficial. Indeed, a chief ingredient in liberalism is a priori restraint on the legitimate scope of government action, regardless of its utility. We might therefore expect tax theory to renounce some types of taxation, or taxes with certain effects, on general political grounds. But we would be disappointed.

Most tax policy discussions of the classical period, including of course the work of John Stuart Mill, took for granted that the principal addressee of tax policy arguments was a perfectly benevolent but unrestrained despot (omniscience was sometimes, if not always, thrown in for good measure).[1] That tradition survives. It probably owes its momentum to the prevailing influence of utilitarian assumptions in economics. As we have seen, the utilitarian tradition in moral philosophy supplies key assumptions of most tax economics. Chapter 3 dwelt

---

1. Criticism of this assumption is often associated with "public choice" theory. See James M. Buchanan, *From Private Preferences to Public Philosophy: The Development of Public Choice*, in his Constitutional Economics 29, 30 (1991). The point is basic to any recognition of the difficulties posed by the quest for a welfarist solution to the issue of tax justice. For, if majority voting cannot be assumed to maximize welfare fairly, decisions *de haut en bas* may be better (and of course may also be worse) than is realistically possible in a democratic society. Cf. Richard A. Musgrave, *Public Finance and Distributive Justice*, in David Greenaway & Graham Keith Shaw, eds., Public Choice, Public Finance and Public Policy 1, 13–14 (1985).

on those concerning human welfare. This chapter moves on to consider political assumptions.

It is not at all a necessary feature of consequentialism or, more particularly, of utilitarianism that policy analysis should proceed as if the state has supreme authority to adopt and enforce tax measures of any sort it chooses. An assumption to that effect, however, grew naturally out of the circumambient nationalism of the early nineteenth century, when the assumptions of modern tax policy coalesced. Nationalism seems to have shaped utilitarianism by default: there simply were no respected rivals to the view that nations were natural units and that within their bounds national governments were sovereign for all purposes. This view is nonetheless incompatible with the liberal tradition in politics, which is built into this country's fundamental political documents, and genuinely seems to capture the mainstream received wisdom of the people. The incompatibility is straightforward. Utilitarianism recognizes no rights—they are "nonsense on stilts," as Jeremy Bentham proclaimed—and that means that there are no inherent limits on valid government action.

If we take this conflict between utilitarianism and other political theories into account, much of tax economics appears to be politically eccentric. Utilitarian political theory, which assigns only a contingent place to civil and political rights, has few contemporary advocates who are not quick to argue that utilitarianism can account for all the individual freedoms and prerogatives that liberalism holds dear. If many government officials and their advisers habitually regard something like the utilitarian calculus as the primary tool of their trade, they may do so on the assumption that *prior* limitations on the legitimate power of the government render it unnecessary for them to consider whether utilitarian measures transgress rights or other politically necessary constraints on legitimate government action.

It is worthwhile to examine the political basics of tax policy for two reasons: First, we have seen that utilitarianism in general may be radically flawed, precisely because it makes the assumption that has rendered it so attractive to governments and their advisors—the assumption that all people have utility functions that are closed under addition, or in more common terms, that human welfare is determined by the benefits and burdens individuals experience and that these are capable of being netted, without further normative assumptions or knowledge about individual people. A lively recent body of thought in ethics questions this assumption, as we have seen. Therefore, it may simply not make sense to base anything on the assumption.

Second, we should examine the political basics of tax policy because some political theories undermine standing arguments in the principal tax policy debates about the design and purposes of taxation. The more stringently limited theories of natural rights, which are today associated with political conservatism and have a historical link with classical liberalism, imply draconian limits on government spending and taxation. A version of mild anarchism, which is not associated with any views about human rights, can have similar consequences. Even less restrictive views of government action such as are advanced by those who place the ideal of communitarian good above that of individual autonomy seem indefensible without some restriction on the proper scope of government action; in particular, the communitarian model inserts goals related to justice into the framework within which individual as well as collective action is to be appraised morally and politically, and these goals may require more of tax policy than economists have meant by tax equity; indeed, the communitarian ideal of justice may require more than government can coherently aim at, if taxes are an inevitable expedient.

This last possibility points to another reason for re-examining taxation in the light of political theory. On the most unfettered analysis of what is required for the public good—i.e., even on a purely utilitarian analysis—the purposes of government cannot be carried out unless taxes are imposed. This is because borrowing would cause inflation and disturb the balance of payments between the taxing state and other parts of the world economy.[2] If taxes are inevitable, they also intrude on individual choices and world-views. We are not free to make our choices as if there were no taxes, at least if high levels of taxes must be imposed, because taxes may have a radically disturbing effect on the circumstances we take for granted in framing our aspirations and decisions. If the utilitarian conception of human motivation, moral and otherwise, were correct, this would not be as much of a problem. Indeed, some approaches to taxation are designed to assure that taxes do not disturb our moral and intellectual autonomy, but as we have seen, these approaches have traditionally been built on the loaded assumption, borrowed from utilitarianism, of individual utility functions closed under addition.

In order to get at these problems, simplified versions of some main theories of political justification will be of use. In the following, I shall summarize several broad political perspectives: anarchism, Hobbesian necessitarianism, and the forms of liberalism that descend from Locke and Kant respectively. Other political philosophies are of course in the air, but none raises distinctive problems for our subject or has caught the fancy of both the public and public officialdom. Each of the four political theories to be discussed appears to influence much actual tax policy analysis some of the time, although utilitarianism is the common language of the field. After this survey of grand theories, we will turn

2. It is worthwhile to note here that a permanently endowed government is a theoretical alternative of sorts; if the source were taxes, this would not truly be an alternative, but if the source were piracy from others or voluntary contributions from the citizenry, the government might simply be another player in the economy and confine itself to actions that could be supported by its success in the market. This would no doubt be a politically unstable arrangement, because it would place citizens' property rights in the hands of a guardian that would not only have a motive to infringe those rights but would perhaps be thrown constantly into a position to try.

to more recent studies of social choice theory and to the special orientation towards social choice that calls itself "public choice."

4.2 FOUR POLITICAL PHILOSOPHIES

It may be helpful briefly to describe the four basic theories of political justification. The first of them, anarchism, is better thought of as skepticism about the peremptory character of political authority.

A somewhat technical definition of political authority is in order. When the state or political officials on behalf of the state claim the right to adopt measures in the name of society, they usually do so on the implicit grounds that any duly promulgated command of the state imposes an obligation on the members of the relevant community to obey or at least to defer within limits to the state's preference for a certain standard of behavior. This claim for obedience or deference is what I mean by political authority. Obviously, a state without the power to enforce its commands would not be in a position to assert the legitimacy of those commands, but political authority is by definition a matter of legitimacy and not of de facto ability to make things happen.

This prepares the way for a careful definition of skepticism about the peremptory character of political authority. I am skeptical about political authority in this fashion if I am not convinced that a political command or preference deserves my obedience or deference simply because it issues from an authentic state source. The mere fact that Congress has made it a crime to sell food that the FDA hasn't approved does not seem to me to make it immoral or irrational to do so. Such skepticism does not imply that the state's choices on my behalf among alternative courses of action are always wrong. I may even be well advised to consider the state's choices as inherently more probable to be right than my own, at least if I am no expert on the facts relevant to the courses of conduct that are in question. But the fact that the state has spoken does not stop me from thinking further about the matter.

It is easy to extrapolate from this form of skepticism to a general distrust of the state. The modern national state invariably speaks with the voice of unfettered and unlimited authority to direct its subjects' conduct. If the state is never entitled to such authority, its preferred mode of expression is misleading and distasteful. More importantly, the absolutism with which the state expresses itself may confuse the well-intentioned individual in what would otherwise be his or her own responsible attempts to exercise autonomy in life-shaping decisions. Hence, the rancor of anarchism.

The polar opposite of skepticism about the peremptory character of political authority is the view associated with the name of Thomas Hobbes. Hobbes argued that we are morally obligated to obey the commands of any state that happens to be in power, if it is able to exercise power effectively in certain ways, no matter what the content of those commands may be. The expedience of the state is so overwhelming of other goods, in Hobbes's view, that it pre-empts any question as to the wisdom of the particular state and its actions.

We may not, however, need the state, regardless of its character. John Locke and others who influenced the framers of civil government in the United States strongly believed that government had nothing to contribute to certain kinds of decisions, and that it indeed had no business interfering with those decisions. On this view, the justification of the state depends crucially on the role of the state in preserving and promoting individual welfare and freedom in certain key respects— liberty and property, roughly in the sense in which these are referred to in the fourteenth amendment of the Constitution. The state exists in order to advance these human interests, and the implicit consensual authorization of the state to do just that disappears if the state hinders or destroys those interests. In this context, I do not so much want to stress the part assigned to consent in the Lockean justification of the state, but only the balance of interests that supposedly entails the rationality of going along with the state. Civil and political rights are assumed, in a sense, whether the individual is subject to a state's authority or not, because individuals come equipped with a broader panoply of rights than those that survive membership in civil society, and this broader panoply never disappears without trace but is preserved in a modified form when the individual consents, explicitly or implicitly, to membership in civil society.

It may strike you that the balance of interests—the comparison of where we would be without the state and how our lot is improved by the existence of the state—presupposes the artificial possibility of living apart from any ordered human community, of living in a "state of nature." Rousseau and Kant and a tradition linked with their names argue that community is essential to being human, but that being human is also essential, and that what this requires is individual autonomy. Preserving individual autonomy works out to much the same thing as protecting liberty and property, but its rationale is not one of natural right (as was the case for the classical liberalism of Locke); the rationale is instead a theoretical analysis of human welfare. Human welfare is not just a matter of the isolated experiences or involvements that benefit us or cause us to suffer, but also depends on the social framework within which isolated experiences and so on occur. In a word, a just society is a prerequisite for complete humanity. The details of the autonomy-based account of political justification follow from this essential human need. A justified political authority, however, is obviously going to be one that works within the limits of its calling: that of preserving and enhancing individual autonomy.

4.3 TAX POLICY AND THE DEMANDS OF JUSTICE

What assumptions need one make about the justification of political authority or the justifying scope of political activity before addressing tax policy issues? Can the resolution of such political issues have a substantive influence on tax policy?

Some of the answers are obvious, once the questions are posed. If there is no justification for deferring to political authority, taxes as a species of governmental activity that cannot take place without authority are also indefensible. If skepticism about all forms of governmental authority is reasonable, it is unreasonable to defend any scheme of taxation.

(1) *Anarchism.* Skepticism about the peremptory character of political authority, however, is not necessarily equivalent to skepticism about the justification for every form of coercive governmental activity. Even if we should think for ourselves in spite of laws that direct us to act in one way or another, it may not be wrong for the elected or customary government of a society to *try* to minimize consumption. As we have seen, although taxation is in some ways the preferred way to minimize social consumption, borrowing can be equally effective. When government borrows, it may act coercively without asserting a monopoly on coercion. Government can perhaps borrow without special justification, simply as the agent for those in society who approve of the governmental programs to be financed with the borrowed funds.[3] The point here is that government borrowing, which is equivalent to taxing under some circumstances, poses a superficially different problem of justification. But let's relax the assumption of special circumstances. If government were to attempt to capture a portion of society's wealth for itself by borrowing without taxing, it would surely run into trouble in the long run, and perhaps even in the short run. Hence, the anarchist who thinks all coercive action by government is wrong leaves government no visible means of support.

What about milder forms of anarchism? The anarchist may believe that collective action, whether by society as a whole or by smaller groups within society, can give rise to practical authority that is not peremptory. A group of people acting together as a guild, for example, to further the manufacture of some special product (stained glass, let's say) may make themselves collectively so valuable to their common pursuit as to give themselves the right to veto choices by nonconsenting individuals who share that pursuit. It may be immoral, for example, for a non-member of the guild who wants to be a stained glass worker to produce cheaper goods if the result will be to bring stained glass into disrepute and thereby destroy the market for it and the culture of its practitioners. The sort of immorality involved is like that of deliberately shooting oneself in the foot. Obviously, the value of the activity will

---

3. When a government borrows, it arguably exercises a Hohfeldian liberty rather than a Hohfeldian right, just as an individual person exercises a liberty and not a right when competing economically with other individuals. If individuals may justifiably act in concert to achieve otherwise permissible ends, then surely a government that is the genuinely consensual agent for any segment of society can surely act for those ends as well, and this would presumably include such activities as borrowing to further the ends in question. Compare this view of limited government action with the "minimal" government Robert Nozick envisages in his argument in justification of a somewhat broader governmental authority. Robert Nozick, Anarchy, State and Utopia 31–48 (1968).

have everything to do with the seriousness of going against the established practice.

If there are cases of small-scale authority—my example may or may not be a good one—then there may also be society-wide pursuits that similarly justify rule-making and legitimate authority to prescribe conduct for the society generally. I am stacking hypotheticals on hypotheticals, I know, but if all this is granted, then it may also be the case that government is justified *for specific social ends that are in fact generally shared* to levy taxes. Indeed, since legitimate governments cannot exist without the right to tax, this would be the only explanation an anarchist might accept for putting up with (limited) taxation.[4]

If this is how taxation should be regarded, then the inventory of authorized governmental goals for the particular society has everything to do with the proper scope and technique of taxation. A traditional society might not authorize a government to seek to maximize aggregate income, on the grounds that economic growth is corrupting. A religious society might not authorize any government debt, and hence require that any permissible tax be as certain as possible as to the revenue it produces, so as to be sure to cover government expenditures for the relevant period. A highly developed society might require taxes to further environmental protection, even at the cost of imposing a considerable excess tax burden on affected economic activities. The list could go on indefinitely.

(2) *Lockean Liberalism.* Lockean and Kantian liberalism are akin to the limited anarchism I have been describing in this respect: although each recognizes broad political authority, each also holds that some governmental conduct is absolutely illegitimate, regardless of the particular society's preferences. Civil and political rights, generally, must be upheld at all costs.

As regards the proper role of taxes, Lockean liberalism may differ importantly from Kantian liberalism. If the former variety is strongly grounded in a theory of rights that are independent of the existence of society—absolute property rights, for example—there may be limits to governmental coercion to achieve the ends of taxation. On the simplistic view that taxation is necessary merely to secure support of governmental activities, Lockean liberalism arguably implies that benefit taxation should be the norm.[5] Thus, in a sense, property rights would

4. I suspect that this is in fact how some people think about the political justification of taxation. Hence, the current "tax rebellion" which consists in part of individuals who dispute the justification for specific governmental projects and refuse to pay taxes for those ends in particular.

5. An important dictum of Locke has quite different implications. Although whatever a person takes out of a state of nature and mixes his or her labor or other property with becomes his or her "own", the owner may only retain the produce of *land* (because of its scarcity) "where there is enough and as good left in common for others." John Locke, Two Treatises on Government 328 (Peter Laslett ed. 1960). This proviso "became the foundation for a long succession of authors who viewed land as the prime, if not the single, source of taxation." Musgrave, *Public Finance and Distributive Justice*, supra note 1, at 2.

not be disturbed; what is taken away in taxes is restored in benefits conferred. On such a view, government would not be justified in levying a tax whose incidence was uncertain or unknowable, such as the classical corporate tax. Moreover, it is not clear that government would be justified in levying any tax without obtaining the specific consent of the taxpayer/beneficiary, even though the tax was a just price for a benefit conferred. This is really just another form of the objection that has always plagued the Lockean argument for political authority, and that many writers have considered fatal to the argument: real consent can always be withdrawn, even if it is unreasonable to do so. It has been argued that, to the extent that taxes are coercive, they may be conceived of as liens on property that is otherwise absolutely protected against government interference.[6] But this metaphor presupposes governmental authority to impose benefits on the unwilling recipient and then collect their value, as it were, to prevent unjust enrichment. The core of Locke's justification cannot support such overreaching by government.

Indeed, even if the Lockean argument is recast along the severe lines suggested by Nozick, there is, as Nozick himself observes, an inevitably redistributive element in the very conduct of government.[7] Severe Lockean liberalism really cannot find room for taxation and hence does not justify a nonvolunteer government. (Note that the justification of political authority to proscribe and prescribe might succeed, even though coercive action could not be justified.) This is just another reason, added to many already noted by political philosophers, for preferring the more sophisticated Kantian defense of liberalism to the rights-based approach linked with Locke's name.

(3) *Autonomy–Based Theories of Political Justification*. Kant and contemporary heirs to his thought take a seemingly easy route to solving the problem of political justification. They assume that ideals associated with the community outweigh ideals associated with the individual, and that is that. There is no need to argue from the position of the isolated individual to that of the individual bound by communal obligations. The isolated individual simply has no priority; there is nothing about this form of autonomy that needs to be defeated in order to justify the state.

By negative implication, however, the Kantian view has no attraction unless it can point to requirements of morality that presuppose organized society. The theory of justice is the key to this sort of analysis. I will follow the custom of the day in regarding John Rawls'

---

6. Richard Epstein, *Taxation in a Lockean World*, in Philosophy and Law (ed. Jules Coleman & Ellen Frankel Paul) 48–74, at 57 (1987).

7. Nozick, supra note 3, at 25–30 (Nozick recognizes that virtually any governmental provision of public goods is redistributive because society's members are likely to derive different levels of utility from the same public goods and yet pay equally for them; he attempts to justify this result by reference to the nonredistributive purposes of a minimal state, but the explanation rings hollow).

Theory of Justice as the best representative of the core of the Kantian tradition in this regard.

In Rawls' view, justice is a complex concept that needs to be "constructed" or analyzed by reference to a range of alternative rules that might define just treatment for individuals in a society of the sort we live in. He does not address the question whether we will regard justice as morally valuable but presumes that we will. In that light, he argues that the principles of justice are "the principles that free and rational persons concerned to further their own interests would accept in an initial position of equality...." [8] The initial or original position is one in which the persons who are adopting the principles of justice do not know their places in society, their class positions or social status, or their talents, strength, and so forth. But they do know enough about what society is like, how markets work, and so forth, to appreciate realistic constraints on institutions like those with which we are all familiar.

Given this hypothetical problem—what principles would a plurality agree upon behind the carefully constructed veil of ignorance—Rawls argues that the problem has to be understood by reference to what he calls the "circumstances of justice." The individuals must be understood to live in a world that provides them with enough in common to wish to regulate matters amicably, but not such an abundance of natural resources and goods or other advantages that there is nothing for them to compete about. In addition, it has to be assumed that the persons making the initial position agreement do not know themselves to be so benevolent by instinct that conflicts among them are impossible or unlikely. It is not taken for granted that everyone will place the same relative values on the same human goods. One of the features of Rawls' theory that sets it apart from utilitarianism (and from what I have called nonprocess consequentialism generally) is that it is designed not to assume a narrow identification of goods for humankind. On the contrary, it assumes some variety of goods, though it also assumes that everyone values some basic goods to roughly the same extent—these would be the goods associated with subsistence, family life, and perhaps other preoccupations of human beings.

By leaving a question mark over the entire range of goods people may pursue, Rawls avoids assuming a utility function that is closed under addition. His notion of welfare is therefore not the traditional one of welfare economics. It is apparently a sufficiently broad concept of welfare to accommodate virtually any range of incommensurable goods.

We need not consider in detail the principles of justice Rawls goes on to derive from his analysis of the original position. It is enough to note that he thinks justice requires that no governmental allocation of advantages make anyone worse off—an echo of Pareto optimality in a world devoid of well-behaved utility functions. Interestingly, Rawls

8.   John Rawls, A Theory of Justice 11
(1971).

seems to think that some general features of taxation are required by principles of justice that can be identified in the original position. Most importantly, he argues that taxes should be designed to prevent too great an accumulation of power in the hands of any individual or group within society. He therefore argues for a strong estate and gift tax regime and for a progressive income tax. Could even such broad features of a tax system as these actually be required by justice; in other words, could it be unjust to impose income taxes on a proportional rather than a progressive rate schedule? We should recall that the debate over equal sacrifice purported to be about the minimum requirements of justice as well. What about the taxation of savings? Rawls thinks this too is a matter that requires analysis from the standpoint of the original position.

It seems to me, however, that Rawls' analysis of the role of taxes in a just society is obviously conditioned by familiar features of the twentieth century United States and that it falls back on the assumptions about utility that have constantly been cited in support of an income tax based on the ability to pay. It is not obvious that income always confers power, although it normally does in the society we know. (In many developing countries women are discriminated against in virtually every power allocation and yet women are the principal entrepreneurs and the primary earners of income.) Moreover, even in a society in which income and power are closely associated at some income levels, an income tax that is progressive through all income ranges may artificially create more power blocks than it disperses. It might do this, for example, by discouraging workers at certain low income levels from joining unions, but encouraging workers at other income levels to do so; this would be the natural result of income taxes that allow a deduction for union dues and also allow a high standard deduction (again, this is the case in the United States). Further, in a society that imposes both income and excise taxes and whose government borrows in order to achieve full employment, the effective progressivity of the entire tax system cannot be inferred from the apparent progressivity of the income tax. In brief, this aspect of Rawls' analysis seems superficial to me.

On the contrary, it would seem that the "circumstances of justice," which give the original position a glimpse of strife and hence a need for order, are affected by the structure of the taxes that government relies on to achieve its goals. If taxes were very high but everyone were provided with all his or her wants, as might be the case in a supremely successful command economy, the circumstances of justice would arguably be absent. Yet there would be issues of justice and at least issues concerning the justice with which taxes were imposed. Or to turn our attention to our own society, many of the broad facts of welfare distribution that we think of as constant, if not inevitable, are highly conditioned by the structure of our tax laws—the strong preference for owner-occupied housing, the preference for large houses, the preference for private education, the preference for certain forms of saving over others, and so forth.

What follows from all this is, I think, that even at the level of abstraction to which the original position is devoted, the justice of tax laws is elusive. The point of the original position is to determine what the principles of justice *for all purposes* should be. Yet the perspective of persons in the original position must be conditioned by the welfare distributions that tax laws themselves influence to a very great extent. If we must assume, in addition to the broad assumptions Rawls specifies, that taxes will not have too great an effect on welfare distributions and the related aspirations and attitudes of the populace, what exactly are we assuming in the original position?

If Rawls is right in thinking that principles of justice presuppose "circumstances of justice," then because these circumstances could be influenced by taxes, constraints on taxes derived from consideration of the circumstances of justice may alter whatever was assumed about taxes as part of those circumstances and hence undermine the analysis. In this respect, Rawls' original position analysis is circular with respect to taxation. I think it follows, not just that Rawls' analysis is inadequate on the narrow topic of tax equity, but that it is inadequate overall, precisely because taxes so greatly influence the general features of society that figure in conflicts to be avoided or settled by principles of justice.

There is, however, a way of defending Rawls' analysis, and he emphasizes it. The task of formulating and justifying principles of justice, Rawls argues, must take place within a "reflective equilibrium." The equilibrium he has in mind balances our first hunches about what justice requires with the working out of their consequences. We begin, for example, with the idea that justice involves treating everyone alike and see where that leads in terms of the content of possible laws. Similarly, Rawls would surely maintain that any circularity in discovering the principles of tax justice is not at all pernicious. We may well have to build information about the social world we inhabit into the original position, including such things as our expectations about availability of education, nongovernmental consequences of class differences, and so forth. If particular tax laws influence what we consider to be reasonable expectations about life styles and alternative life plans, we must reach reflective equilibrium in assessing the pros and cons of those laws.

What this process of weighing and balancing would produce in concrete terms remains for some Rawlsian tax theorist to show us. Clearly *in*consistent with Rawls's methods and goals is the rigid translation of first-approximation principles of justice into simplistic constraints on all future tax policy. For example, Rawls calls one of his own first-approximation principles the "difference principle." It says roughly that government should not confer or condone a greater benefit for some than for others unless the policy in question will benefit everyone to at least some extent. If the consequences of tax laws were limited to effects on individual income, and these effects in turn were straightforwardly comparable for all people, the difference principle might be thought to say that government *may* adopt tax laws that grossly enrich a small number of people if the result is to increase each individual's income.[9] While Rawls himself has not commented on the application of his ideas to tax policy, it is doubtful that he would accept so controversial a consequence without reflecting further on the principle and its apparent implications and adjusting the principle to achieve a new equilibrium.

(4) *The Expedient State.* Of the four political theories we have considered, only the Hobbesian theory raises no special problems about taxation. If the state deserves our respect and deference, no matter what its policies, then tax policy too is completely unfettered.

In effect, most tax policy today assumes the expedient state.[10] That is, tax policy usually acknowledges no limit to the state's prerogative to adopt revenue raising and spending policies, with the exception of an unspecific concern for equal treatment. Is there any justification for proceeding on this assumption?

No one surely will argue that the modern national state accomplishes the tasks that seemed to Hobbes to make the state's asserted monopoly on violence and coercion expedient. Principal among these tasks is the objective of guaranteeing the physical security of the members of society. But physical insecurity is now an accepted feature of large industrial democracies. And even if actual states could do what Hobbes thought expedient, it is not clear why they must also have the power to do everything else. That is the point of liberal theories that deny the state's prerogative in various ways.

If this is correct, the agnosticism of tax policy concerning the elementary assumptions required for tax justice cannot be justified as such. Is this agnosticism defensible as a working assumption, with the proviso that the fine tuning of tax design must ultimately alter tax measures to achieve whatever justice requires? Isn't this approach vitiated by the same considerations that make Rawls' original position analysis circular where taxes are concerned?

There is a possible solution to the problem, at least in principle, in the approach to issues of justice that Rawls himself advocates. He

---

9. Some "optimal tax" theorists translate the difference principle in this way. Implicit in the translation is the assumption that income correlates with utility or well-being in the same way for all individuals and that individual utility functions are not interdependent. See section 14.5, below. These assumptions are probably false.

10. See, e.g. James A. Mirrlees, *The Theory of Optimal Taxation*, in Kenneth Arrow & Michael Intriligator, eds., Handbook of Mathematical Economics (1986) (dictatorship is a basic assumption of problems in optimal tax theory); Richard Goode, The Federal Income Tax (1977) (assumption that the state may choose freely among alternatives); contra Musgrave, *Public Finance and Distributive Justice*, supra note 1, at 13 (just distribution of income is prior condition for voting to approximate to just public choices).

emphasizes that *any* analysis of the concept of justice is to be tested from the standpoint of what he calls "reflective equilibrium."

4.4 NEW "THEORIES" OF PUBLIC DECISION-MAKING

Other approaches to the foundations of public policy have emerged in the last few decades from theorizing about the problems of voting. Since the problems of taxation in a sense include all public policy problems,[11] how we view the mechanisms by which society chooses its strategies is of peculiar importance to the justification of tax policy.

As chapter 3 indicates, the traditional consequentialism of economists has bred great curiosity among economists concerning the relationship between the common weal and the welfare of the individual. Economists, like their utilitarian colleagues among social philosophers and moralists, appear to have assumed for quite a long time that the welfare of the individual, traditionally conceived of as the individual's utility function, could be aggregated with other individuals' utility functions to yield a single social utility function. It is now generally recognized that aggregating individual utility functions may pose basic theoretical problems. Some still think of these problems as posed by the conceptual impediments to the interpersonal comparison of utilities. The view developed more fully in Chapter 3 is that what utility functions tell us about different individuals, even if that information were presented in the same coin or units, does not necessarily permit all packages of alternative goods (or courses of action) to be evaluated for these individuals with a definite outcome. Perfect knowledge of the wants and needs of the people who make up society, in other words, might not imply a straightforward ranking of alternative social policies from best to worst. This is so for several reasons.

Individual utility functions may be interdependent, i.e., the value of an outcome for an individual may depend on its value to other individuals. They may be "inseparable," i.e., they may not yield values for particular outcomes at all, but only for whole trains of consequences, valuing the same rewards and detriments quite differently in the light of the process that produces them. They may be "discontinuous," i.e., for any pair of outcomes that are related to each other for the individual as better to worse, there will not always be another outcome that is better than one of these and worse than the other. They may not even be "transitive," i.e., for any set of three outcomes, it need not be the case that if an individual prefers one to another, and that to the third, he or she must prefer the first to the third. This last possibility is of course not guaranteed if people are allowed to be irrational, but examples suggest that even rational utility functions may be intransitive.

If individual utility functions can turn out, when we know all the facts, to be intransitive, then it will be no surprise that a society-wide utility function—one designed to reflect everyone's preferences at

11. Mirrlees, *The Theory of Optimal Taxation*, supra note 10.

once—can turn out to be intransitive as well. Surely, the idiosyncracies of the individual utility function can be carried over to the social utility function.

If we postulate that individual utility functions must exhibit a certain minimum of rationality, then it seems natural to postulate too that they must be transitive, if not necessarily continuous. One of the more interesting conclusions about the *political* justification of public policies flows from asking whether separable, transitive, but not necessarily continuous individual functions (dubbed "choice functions" by Professor Kenneth Arrow, who first systematically investigated them) must necessarily be transitive. A rigorous proof shows that they need not be.[12]

This has several implications. One of them is that even an ideally democratic procedure designed to reflect the preferences of everyone in a society (of more than two persons) cannot be counted on to set priorities among alternative courses of action, without arbitrarily discounting someone's preferences. It is not possible to design a social welfare function that will necessarily be consistent with the preferences of the individuals who make up the society. This is Arrow's famous "impossibility" theorem, sometimes described as proving the impossibility of democracy. A related proof has been offered to establish the impossibility of the Paretian liberal, i.e., the impossibility of respecting even some individual rights while requiring the social welfare function to satisfy the principle of Pareto optimality.[13] As important as these, and other impossibility theorems, is the recognition that individual choice functions and collective decisions cannot regularly be harmonized as some dominant traditions in political theory had hoped.

There are two more or less openly political reactions to the groundbreaking results of social choice theory. That which goes under the name "public choice" insists that the inconsistency of private interests with the common good can only be dealt with fairly or in an acceptable way from a peculiar moral point of view if constitutional constraints fetter public decisionmaking. This perspective, closely associated with the writings of James Buchanan, interprets the puzzles that have arisen concerning the translation of individual preferences into a single collective preference as proving something more than the impossibility of accommodation. They see the "supergame" of pitting the private preferences of some members of society against others as a generic political problem that can only be overcome rationally and morally by a constitution, which is in effect a rule for settling conflicts that may work to the disadvantage of some.[14]

---

12. This is not the usual characterization of the famous "Arrow's theorem," but it is equivalent to Arrow's own formulation. Kenneth Arrow, Social Choice and Individual Values (2d ed. 1963).

13. Amartya Sen, *The Impossibility of a Paretian Liberal*, 72 J.Pol.Econ. 152 (1970).

14. James M. Buchanan & Gordon Tullock, The Calculus of Consent: Logical Foundations of Constitutional Democracy (1962); James M. Buchanan, The Demand and Supply of Public Goods 101–25 (1968); *From Private Preference to Public Philoso-*

The argument for a constitutional solution to the paradoxes of social choice echoes attempts to base a moral requirement of co-operation on the possibility of "prisoner's dilemma" effects in multi-person "games." A prisoner is given a choice between some reward if he informs on another prisoner to that prisoner's disadvantage or no reward if he refuses to inform on the other. The other prisoner, however, is given the same alternatives. If both prisoners inform on each other, the rewards they would receive for doing so will be more than offset by the additional punishment each will receive. Thus, if one informs and the other does not, the informer will enjoy the best of the possible outcomes; but if both inform, they will be worse off than if they had done nothing. Each prisoner knows that the other has the same choices. What is the rational choice under the circumstances? Those who believe that reason dictates a solution to the prisoner's dilemma usually prefer the "cooperative" and certainly safer alternative of not informing on the other prisoner. It has long been recognized that the big difficulty is to defend the rationality of this sort of cooperation, given the fact that it can only be expected to produce a benefit if all decision-makers behave well and cooperate. Hence, the rationality of cooperation depends on whether others will follow the same policy.

Co-existence within a community poses a prisoner's dilemma if choices are interdependent and all individuals know the results of others' choices. To some extent, no doubt, these conditions—let's call them "interdependence" and "transparency" of individual decisions—do obtain. But to some extent they do not, and to that extent, the analogy between constitutional constraints and cooperation in a prisoner's dilemma setting breaks down. In particular, if we cannot tell whether others are going along with the game, and choosing the less disruptive course, we cannot know whether cooperation is paying off even after we have made our individual choices, and to that extent we cannot rationally go along with the game. Further, even if we can determine whether others are cooperating or not, it is essential that we know their cooperation makes a difference to us, for if it does not, there is no point in cooperating. Matters are also complicated by the opportunity within a community to cooperate in many ways on many occasions, and to benefit from cooperation both immediately and more remotely, even through the effects of others' cooperation on one's friends and relatives.

The argument that it is rational to "bargain" with others in the peculiarly open-ended way that is characteristic of the prisoner's dilemma requires careful evaluation with reference to the particular sort of community in which the bargain is to be made. Frustration with this complexity may be one of the motives for the view that an authoritarian state is expedient, no matter what the benefits and burdens. Unfortunately, the argument that cooperation is rational and the argument

phy: The Development of Public Choice, in
his Constitutional Economics 29–45 (1991).

that cooperation is expedient because the details are too complex to be grasped are sometimes presented as if they were a single argument. This of course undermines the force of both arguments because it suggests that the truth of their premises is not very important, and that a higher logic confirms the authority of the state, whether we subjects of the state can see that this is so or not.

Another problem for the prisoner's dilemma is the now-familiar problem of community perspective. People belong to many communities at once. With which other individuals should one cooperate, assuming that the conditions for a prisoner's dilemma are present? If cooperative behavior came in a single flavor, there would be no difficulty. Cooperating with the members of a small community would amount to the same thing as cooperating with all the members of the largest community to which one happened to belong. But communities can find themselves in conflict, especially with overlapping communities. Whatever the prisoner's dilemma tells us about the rationality of cooperation, it does not tell us *how* to cooperate. The impossibility theorems of social choice theory suggest that even within a single community, determining what counts as cooperation is problematical.

Finally, however, note that the lessons of the prisoner's dilemma and the entire approach of the public choice school are only persuasive if we think democratic decisions are inherently better than social decisions forced on the members of a community by a despot, by tradition, or otherwise without regard to the preferences of individual community members. Some political traditions—notably, anarchist and totalitarian traditions—specifically deny any normative value to democracy in this sense. Liberalism, to the extent that it fears the tyranny of the majority, places limits on the moral or political authority of individual preferences.

The implications of theories of collective choice are still emerging. Research along these lines serves at least to underscore the variety of political principles with which democratic traditions are compatible in theory. Tax theory is just beginning to take these developments into account.

Chapter 5

THE STUDY OF TAXATION
BY NON-ECONOMISTS

5.1 CONFLICTING SOCIAL SCIENCE METHODS AND THE STUDY OF TAXATION

Tax policy writing often seems to ignore the historical forces that condition and constrain the design of our tax laws. Sometimes tax experts openly refuse to take politics into account, but more often they pass over aspects of process in silence. Human irrationality as manifested by a range of bureaucratic and taxpayer foibles, often on a grand scale, is almost absent from the phenomenon of taxation as it is analytically viewed. Why?

The answer is itself partly historical and irrational. As we have repeatedly seen, professional economists hold the high ground in tax theory. One consequence, discussed in Chapter 3, is the general acceptance there of a certain view of human well being, which translates into assumptions about distributive fairness. Another is the indifference of most tax theory to the admittedly unique aspects of the political process through which each country's peculiar tax system is created. This indifference is no doubt a direct reflection of the way in which economists view their discipline as a whole. They typically aspire to produce simple, elegant, strongly explanatory, and in brief, highly general theories of the phenomena with which they deal. But a corollary is that cultural, partisan, and irrational elements in actual tax systems seem to the economist uninteresting and irrelevant. As a result much of the best work on taxation, done by economists, seems to pay no attention to how tax policy is made in real life. People find this apparent lack of realism puzzling.

While economics commands the field, though, other armies are in attendance. Other disciplines examine taxation as a social phenomenon, analyze particular episodes in the history of taxation, or attempt to generalize about the behavior of taxpayers and tax collectors, at least partly in the hope of deriving practical lessons for the design and improvement of tax systems. Would anyone delve into tax history, for example, if the subject matter implied no appraisals of the goodness or badness of past events and held no lessons for the future? Is political science, when it surveys the politics of taxation, not somewhat concerned with current or prospective tax problems? And why would anyone collect data on taxpayer behavior if he or she were not ultimately thinking this might change our attitudes towards the design of tax systems?

Unlike economists, however, the proponents of other social studies of taxation are ambivalent about drawing lessons from their investigations. Cautious historians make no claim of authority in practical matters. Political theorists, psychologists and sociologists who pattern their work on any of several emerging models of the ideal behavioral science steadfastly deny that they are offering advice when speaking as scientists. Since much of the work of non-economists claims to be descriptive, one might reasonably (if wrongly) take for granted its neutrality with respect to prescriptive problems like designing a tax system. Yet the whole point of the more historical, more concrete approaches to taxation must at some level be to raise relevant issues that are typically absent from economists' view of the field. Political theorists, historians, and sociologists who write about tax realities naturally cannot refrain from speaking in admiring or minatory tones as they marshall the tax phenomena. Does their expertise contribute anything of importance to tax policy?

Broad questions about the relevance of social studies are usually also questions about methods of theory testing and structure, questions not at all peculiar to tax policy. While the professedly different social disciplines share areas of factual inquiry, they do not communicate well with each other. Political theorists have come late to the problems of taxation and are loath to borrow much from the earlier cultivators of the area. To do so, they seem to think, would cast doubt on the possibility of distinct political insights into tax issues. Historians of taxation have their own reasons for avoiding any serious engagement with economic thought or even empirical economic studies. Quantitative methods have always raised peculiar questions for historians, no matter what the subject matter, and have indeed led to fundamental disputes among them over their mission. Moreover, while all three are social studies, economics, political science, and history also define themselves in part by reference to different explanatory ideals.

Of the fields of study under discussion, economics is easily the most enigmatic. It originated as a variety of armchair speculation that has only lately begun to consider empirical research relevant to its task. It has traditionally sought to explain already recognized facts about economic behavior by reference to a special kind of hypothesis about human motivation. Economic hypotheses generally purport to show how apparently unrelated aspects of possible human behavior patterns could after all interact and indeed be mutually influential. The competition of individuals for scarce commodities can, under the right conditions, increase the supply for everyone. But it does not matter if the circumstances that would produce these interesting correlations ever actually occur. That is because the economist only claims to show us how the world works apart from idiosyncracies of time, place, and individual personality. The well recognized oddity, and perhaps part of the charm, of economic models lies in their ability to aid understanding and yet distract us from their lack of predictiveness. By keeping models simple, economics abandons the goal of foretelling the future or even of unravelling the past. Not in principle, of course. There is always the possibility of "specifying the model", of including more factual determinants of the real, so that economic generalizations might yield predictions and retrospective explanations of concrete occurrences.[1] But again, the style of the discipline has been to treat such empirical concerns as marginal to its real work.

Next in elusiveness, history too has what may broadly be considered a disciplinary style. It concentrates on narrative, or in some contemporary guises, on statistics or brute facts in all their particularity. It is typically unfriendly to simplification. This may seem an inevitable concomitant of the historical obsession with details of the social process, but if it is, then other disciplines are off on the wrong foot. History, to the extent that it has this controversial edge, this disdain for generalization, is at odds with other supposed methods of understanding social phenomena. What sort of understanding does it offer then? Isn't all understanding a matter of showing how the general subsumes the particular, and hence of generalizing and simplifying the model? Historians struggle with this paradox, and produce schools of historical study. Rarely, however, do they flirt with the methods that characterize the self-proclaimed social sciences.

What are these "methods"? They are not, as some may think, well-defined techniques of any sort, or standards for testing theories or hypotheses, but instead a range of investigative ideals borrowed from the more highly developed physical sciences—physics, chemistry, geology, and so forth.

These fields have prospered. Their success seems closely linked with the way their practitioners frame hypotheses and test them. Of course, what has made this apparently methodological bias of the physical sciences sustainable is their subject matter. Mechanical phenomena, for example, fortunately lend themselves to the drastic simplifications of first Newtonian and then relativistic mechanics. It would be wonderful if other phenomena would similarly bow to our efforts to understand them. So powerful is the wish for simplicity and explanatory success that those who have tried to say what makes a science

---

1. See Paul A. Samuelson, Foundations of Economic Analysis 3–6 (2d ed. 1983) (contending that the empirical foundations of economic analysis are secured by operational definition of theoretically embedded terms); but see Mary Hesse, The Structure of Scientific Inference 8–44 (1974) (the now prevailing view among philosophers of science is that the empirical character of theories is not explicable in terms of the correspondence of theoretical statements with nontheoretical ones).

authoritative, and what distinguishes science from pseudo-science or confused common sense, is a method.

A few years back this would have been called the hypothetico-deductive method. Its proponents supposed that scientific activity essentially consisted in formulating hypotheses (with no prior restriction on content) that could be tested decisively by comparison with objectively ascertained facts, and rejecting the false hypotheses; the rest of what scientists do was either not authoritative or not very important to the scientific status of their work.[2] The hypothetico-deductive model was supposed to capture all the really important aspects of scientific practice. After a while, however, the weaknesses of this model became apparent. A testable hypothesis had to be one that could be falsified or found to be consistent with objectively determined facts. But doesn't all fact finding presuppose laws of nature—those that govern the collection of data? It was soon widely recognized that scientific observation was inexorably theory-laden. There is no way to isolate a particular hypothesis from the empirical and equally falsifiable assumptions on which a test is based. No test is decisive. The method of science cannot be described as that of comparing hypotheses directly with the facts and rejecting hypotheses that are falsified.[3]

Philosophers of science no longer pretend to be able to give as strong an account of what distinguishes good from bad science. Nevertheless, the culture of the social sciences has been fixed for the time being by the methodological aspirations of an earlier generation. Some social scientists therefore still strive to frame hypotheses and theories comparable to those of the physical sciences; this is what being scientific means for them. Other investigators of the same phenomena, who never embraced the hypothetico-deductive model or any other conscious view of the scientific method, strive for a very different product.

This partly explains why economics, history and fields of study that proclaim themselves social sciences have different aims in the most general possible sense. It may be that all attempts to gather empirical information and understand it must ultimately use the same methods, and that the valuable results of these three fields must therefore be susceptible of comparison, at least by an ideally well-informed reader. Superficially, though, comparison is hard indeed.

5.2 POLITICAL INERTIA AND TAX LEGISLATION

An illustration is in order. Written by two political scientists, an ambitious recent contribution to the political theory of taxation surveys the tax policy of the expanding British government since World War

---

2. Carl G. Hempel, *The Theoretician's Dilemma* in Concepts, Theories, and the Mind–Body Problem: Volume II, Minnesota Studies in the Philosophy of Science 37 (eds. Herbert Feigl, Michael Scriven, & Grover Maxwell 1958).

3. Hesse, The Structure of Scientific Inference, supra note 1, at 8–44; Willard Van Ormand Quine, *Two Dogmas of Empiricism*, in his From a Logical Point of View 20 (2d ed. 1961).

II.[4] We consider their argument and conclusions in some detail here because they are interesting in themselves and because they highlight the methodological problem. The study contrasts its aims with those of economists, whose work the authors criticize for treating "the concerns of politicians as exogenous variables ... that is, influences outside the theoretical calculus of economic policy."[5] They themselves consider not only concerns of politicians but also public response to tax issues to be crucial aspects of the phenomenon of taxation.

In a variety of ways, and with detailed illustration drawn from the recent British experience, the authors contend that only a "public policy model" of taxation permits us to break down the barriers that separate the various specialized studies of the subject. They propose to model real-life taxation as a *function* of laws, administration, and economic activity. Indeed, they translate this aspiration into mathematical symbols, asserting that tax policy is a function in the mathematical sense of variables that include inertia, public satisfaction with the status quo, and so forth. But the model is in fact specified only in qualitative terms, by long discussions of the intricacies of the legislation, tax planning, tax administration, and taxpayer reaction to the entire tax system of a particular country. The gap between concrete detail and generalization is never bridged.

Does this mean that the whole effort comes to nothing? On the contrary, the authors strategically add to our understanding of government finance by sticking to a historical or evolutionary perspective. The size of the tax bite and of government spending are relevant to political decisions, because they are of course relevant to taxpayer reactions to taxes, and the authors stress how rapidly the period since World War II has transformed that relationship. Since this change occurred without conscious political decisions either at the polls or by politicians in office, for this phenomenon of unheeded metamorphosis they coin the description "inertia." It is, in their view, by political inertia that the most pressing current problems about the design of tax systems have arisen.

The study simply asserts, though, that for politicians the problem of taxation is that of balancing gross amounts of government spending with the requisite gross amounts of government revenue, given that on taking office politicians inherit massive popular spending programs and also inherit massive unpopular tax systems. Despite their campaign promises, and perhaps sincerely held partisan views about the role of government, politicians from both parties in Britain have regularly left the inherited system more or less alone, changing the scope of spending or taxing only in marginal ways both as to amount and incidence. Hence, the authors conclude that:

> The political problem of taxation is easily stated but hard to resolve: how can elected politicians maximize spending on popular

4. Richard Rose & Terence Karran,   5. Id. at 3.
Taxation by Political Inertia (1987).

programmes while minimizing the political costs of paying for these programmes?[6]

And the solution they impute to most politicians is equally streamlined:

> Whether or not the existing tax structure is optimal in economic theory, from a politician's point of view it can be viewed as the least worst that is available. Compared to the alternative of taking responsibility for introducing new tax measures, a politician may decide that doing nothing and relying upon existing taxes is preferable. If keeping out of trouble is a basic law of politics, then not making decisions about taxes is one way to avoid trouble—in the short run at least.[7]

Nor does it follow that inertia favors one set of partisan preferences to another. Although identifiable constituencies among the taxpaying public bear larger and smaller parts of the tax burden, those who bear the largest burden also receive, not surprisingly, crucially large parts of the government benefits that taxes pay for (at least in Britain, according to these authors).[8]

If all this is so, then how did "big government," in the post-World War II sense, come about? The authors' answer is that among all the wealthier nations, it has happened by bracket creep—the gradual, imperceptible shifting of taxpayers from lower average tax rates to higher average tax rates resulting from inflation and a progressive marginal tax rate structure without indexation for inflation. One way of demonstrating that inflation has been responsible is to track the "tax effort" made by the relevant governments during the period in question. Tax effort is the ratio of tax revenues to gross domestic product. It therefore stays constant if taxes claim the same proportionate part of the national accrual-income pie from one year to the next. With minor fluctuations that is what has happened among the OECD countries, although there is some divergence between countries in which tax effort has constantly been greater than average, e.g., the Scandinavian countries.

Other political scientists have stressed many of the same factors affecting the tax policy process. For example, they often stress that the ratio of public spending on large politically popular programs to tax revenues that must be raised to finance these programs is roughly constant for most countries. The inertial thesis is an immediate corollary of this brute fact. It also follows that party politics has had little effect, despite party platforms, on the real scope and content of the tax laws, except at the politically least sensitive edges.

This may shed a negative light on the nonhistorical approach to tax policy that characterizes tax economics. It suggests that irrational considerations crucially affect the design of tax systems. But

6. Id. at 3–4.

7. Id. at 5.

8. Id. at 11; contra Peter Bachrach and Morton Baratz, Power and Poverty: Theory and Practice (1970).

it does not indicate that change is impossible or even unlikely. So where do we plug in these large irrational patterns? Are they properly part of the theoretical analysis of tax alternatives or should they be taken into account only when we begin to try to apply theory to practice? We may be inclined to draw conclusions about what ought to be from what is inevitable. But it is not always reasonable to respect historical forces, any more than it is always reasonable to disregard them.

Obsessive attention to method may make these questions harder rather than easier to answer. The role that traditional (and now heavily qualified) views about the logic or structure of scientific reasoning assign to "theory" or "hypothesis" on the one hand and to "initial conditions" on the other has no useful implications for our problem.

The supposed structural relationship of these two sorts of ingredient, on the traditional view, is simple. The more general propositions that make up a scientific hypothesis or theory are conceived of as axioms or basic propositions in a deductive system. (The idea of a system here is ultimately borrowed from the way in which mathematicians and logicians understand the structure of self-contained areas within their respective fields; the seminal works in symbolic analysis of number theory, for example, showed that theorems could be generated from a very few elementary propositions about numbers by means of a few elementary principles of inference.) The deductive systems to which scientific hypotheses are compared rigorously distinguish between the propositions of the theories that are about the theoretical subject matter, e.g., mechanical or electro-magnetic phenomena, and the means by which these propositions are made to yield other propositions. The means in question, principles of logical inference, are common to all kinds of subject matter. Ideally, they can be formulated symbolically so that the content of the propositions from which and to which they authorize inferences need not be filled in. To return then to particular theories, it is natural to think of any small set of propositions from which all the rest can be deduced by subject-matter-neutral principles of logical inference as the highest propositions in a hierarchy, with propositions that can be inferred from these occupying lower places in the structure.

The lowest-level propositions of the theory, however, those that come closest to predicting observable occurrences or explaining them ex post facto, still do not connect with observation and hence cannot guarantee the possibility that theories are testable. The empirical character of any theory, on this view, depends on statements of "initial conditions", which together with one or more deductive consequences of the theory yield concrete predictions or explanations of things that have already happened.[9]

9. Philosophers of science have long since abandoned this model of scientific theory structure in its strongest form, i.e., as providing a non-circular account of what makes a scientific theory empirical. See Hesse, The Structure of Scientific Infer-

Suppose, for example, that our theory of thermal energy has as a deductive consequence the proposition that "Copper expands when heated." On the hypothetico-deductive view, what makes this an empirical proposition and makes the theory vulnerable to experience are the further statements that link the general proposition about copper's behavior with particular experimental circumstances. In a laboratory, an experimenter must provide the further proposition that "This is a piece of copper" and "Heat is being applied to it", in order to arrive at the prediction that "This will expand." Although it may seem strange to dignify this rather simple framework by calling it a model of theory structure, it does seem to do a good job of separating the roles of general theoretical statements, subject-matter-neutral rules of inference, and particular observations of fact. But does that framework help us answer the question of the mutual relevance of disparate approaches to tax theory? Should information about the political sphere figure in theorizing about the economics of taxation as part of the theory proper, or should such information serve only as statements of initial conditions that shape the application of tax policy to the peculiarities of the world as we find it?

Tax theorists have to address these questions by deciding for substantive, i.e., not merely formal, reasons whether there are any inexorable facts about public attitudes, the functioning political system, or other contingent circumstances, that must be factored into tax policy. They must decide whether tax policy should accommodate or attempt to subvert those facts. Public insistence on low taxes and high government benefits, for example, may be more or less universal. Incompatible demands cannot be satisfied. Should tax measures therefore be designed to disguise the disappointment or should they make the incidence of taxes and their connection with government benefits more apparent, in an attempt to educate the public? Unfortunately, any answer to these questions must represent value judgments that academic disciplines inevitably avoid or import without discussion. Reluctance to make value judgments is a chief source of the friction among disciplines with which this chapter is concerned.

Before commenting further on it, a further sampling of work on tax policy by non-economists is in order.

5.3 NON-ECONOMIC STUDIES OF TAX POLITICS

(1) *Political Science.* Consider first the politics of taxation, as examined by political theorists. It is inevitable that the study of politics should extend to the ways in which tax policy is made and implemented. Taxation is a central, even a defining, characteristic of government, and a well documented sphere of state action. The work

---

ence, supra note 1, at 8–44; Nicholas Jardine, The Fortunes of Inquiry (1991). But in the present context, the model still captures the problem of the relationship between conspicuously "theoretical" propositions, such as those entertained by the economist as model-builder, and non-theoretical statements that do not presuppose any theoretical knowledge.

of professional political scientists, however, often aims not to show how or to what extent political factors influence the course of political decisions, but only to identify those factors in very broad terms.

For example, the political scientist may devote much attention to voters' general dislike of tax increases—conducting empirical surveys of these attitudes perhaps—and investigate how elected representatives avoid calling attention to legislation that produces an overall tax increase.[10] But how does such general reporting on the political process help us to decide on the most equitable, efficient and rational way to raise an essential amount of revenue, revenue that must be raised whether voters like it or not? It may be tempting to brush aside information about the awkward, irrational, and bruisingly recalcitrant aspects of political life, on the grounds that imperfections cannot and should not influence our views about what tax systems should be like. But what do we learn when we survey these uncooperative political realities with special reference to the problems of taxation?

What may strike us first about the work of political scientists in this area is the relatively loose relationship among the topics or themes they explore. Finding a place for self-evidently important facts is perhaps the first task of the scientific inquirer. As such, the political studies I refer to are resolutely scientific. They have identified features of political life that have a bearing on taxation and that are salient in one respect or another—often for reasons that we cannot easily articulate—and they gather further information about these features. The results, however, remain largely helter skelter, as it were, variables waiting for a formula to unite them. Here are some examples.

(a) *Taxpayers' self-contradictory attitudes towards taxation.* Virtually everyone who has written about the politics of taxation is struck by the brute fact that taxpayers typically say they love the effects of government spending and hate the collection of taxes that is necessary to finance this spending. We are talking about the stuff of opinion polls, the comparatively raw information about taxpayer attitudes that can be skimmed from a large sample of taxpayers by means of a tolerably brief questionnaire. The apparent irrationality of the crowd, which seems to surface in the tables that summarize such surveys, may be a reality. It certainly *is* a reality to some extent and with some degree of relevance to a rational approach to taxes. But everything depends on the strength of the reality and on how we decide it is relevant. Empirical studies of the phenomenon in question usually do not delve into either of these issues.

There is perhaps a different kind of lesson in the stubbornness with which taxpayers' attitudes resemble each other from one country to the next. Comparative studies of what taxpayers in states with strikingly

10. See B. Guy Peters, The Politics of Taxation 152–66 (1991); Rose & Karran, Taxation by Inertia, supra note 4.

different tax systems say about taxes yield surprisingly similar results. The studies, however, are all recent, i.e., they deal with attitudes towards taxes in the mid- to late-twentieth century, and they all deal with attitudes in prosperous countries, most of which have close cultural ties. Still one cannot but feel that the homogeneity of these taxpayer attitudes holds some implications for what we should think about the design and purpose of tax systems.

(b) *The politicians' quandary.* Closely related to the theme of taxpayers' contradictory attitudes is that of politicians' reluctance to advocate significant change in the tax laws. Though taxes are often a headline issue in election campaigns, circumstances rarely permit a candidate who advocates fundamental tax reform or repeal to win at the polls; it is just as rare for an elected official to win re-election on a record of basic tax law revision. Politicians therefore seem fated to let the tax system take care of itself in all essential respects—concerning tax incidence and the bottom-line of revenue raised. But to satisfy that part of the public who do demand change, a little tinkering always goes on at the margins: tax law revision that looms large but affects few dollars can be politically advantageous. The phenomenon of political inactivity where the basics of the tax law are concerned has justly been labelled "taxation by inertia."

To be reminded of the fact of political inertia may be useful, especially if the writings of economists have lulled us into the assumption that problems of "public choice" can be solved by political processes in a rapid and frictionless manner,[11] but what sort of fact is this really? The electorate does, from time to time, seem to want and get fundamental tax law change. Politicians sometimes spend their hoarded political clout in backing such changes. Balanced budget laws, shifting the burden of taxes from the middle class to large corporations, the simultaneous elimination of a wide range of tax preferences have all been achieved in a single wave of tax reform enthusiasm, and it cannot be said that their joint effect has not been fundamental, even though it may have been packaged for the public in the claim that the new tax legislation was "revenue neutral", i.e., did not threaten existing governmental spending programs.

(c) *The infrequency of decisions about tax issues.* Implicit in the theme of inertia is the reality that most wealthy countries have by now structured their tax laws so as not to require re-enactment of the tax laws at frequent intervals. Revenue measures are designed to stay in force indefinitely. Proposing a "sunset" provision in a legislative tussle over tax measures is almost always a rhetorical device, not intended to be taken very seriously, precisely because no politician would lightly accept the future prospect of having to re-encounter the voters' wrath over the imposition of a new tax. Instead, tax laws are usually in place

---

11. See Peters, The Politics of Taxation, supra note 10, at 156–57, *and sources cited therein*; Rose & Karran, Taxation by Political Inertia, supra note 4; Rolf Hadenius, *Citizens strike a balance: discontent with taxes, content with spending,* 5 J. Pub. Pol. 349–64 (1985).

when legislators take office and can be allowed to do the work of supporting government activities, even if no new taxes are imposed and no old taxes are revised or repealed.

(d) *Constancy of "tax effort" during the growth of "big government."* It appears to be a fact that the twenty or so major industrial democracies have, with few exceptions, taken about the same fraction of gross domestic product in taxes throughout the twentieth century or longer. As we have seen, so-called tax effort obviously provides a convenient measure of the tax bite in one interesting sense of that colloquial expression. If tax effort has remained more or less constant during the growth of the contemporary welfare state, and if the tax laws of most countries have been revised only around the edges, then the greatest change in the relationship of taxation to modern political issues has taken place without the active participation of the electorate or for that matter of the political elite. For, despite the constancy of tax effort throughout the period of the greatest governmental growth, the result of that growth has been a new political order.

Sameness of tax effort does not imply that all taxpayers have been touched to the same extent by the growth of our tax systems. Another important political truth about the growth of most big tax systems is that the tax burden has been borne more evenly by a steadily increasing fraction of the population. This outcome is not primarily due to overt political decisions to spread the tax burden to progressively more people but to inflation and "bracket creep." Most of the countries whose governments spend a large fraction of total private income have progressive income tax laws, that is to say, the tax rate is higher for taxpayers whose income is greater. Tax rates have also been set by reference to currency units, such as dollars, that are not automatically adjusted as the currency loses value due to inflation. Thus, a taxpayer whose income remains unchanged from year to year, apart from the effects of inflation, will pay higher rates of tax and may not even notice that the rate is increasing in real terms.

As we noted earlier, political investigators of the phenomenon of taxes emphasize that taxpayers approve, almost unanimously, of the biggest public spending programs such as national defense, Social Security, health benefits, and education. "Political reality" seems to insulate all these spending programs from significant change.[12] If this

12. Obviously, this assumes no change in some familiar features of the world, an assumption that need not prove true. The collapse of the Soviet Union will inevitably curtail defense spending in the United States, and a majority of taxpayers will presumably be delighted. Philosophers are fond of pointing out that when the laws of physics or other natural sciences are stated subject to the condition *ceteris paribus* (other things remaining equal or remaining unchanged), they normally assume vast unexamined bodies of information and even of physical relationships that are open to correction. The dependency of the validity of formulated hypotheses on unexpressed hypotheses renders the content of the former peculiarly blurry. The same is obviously true of the political relationships discussed in the text. All are true ceteris paribus, and the removal of the Soviet military threat is just the kind of change that can happen despite our hav-

is true even to a degree, then the most important aspects of our tax systems, their size and general public finance objectives, have been and are likely to remain beyond the political process. They have simply happened, like a change of climate that cannot be reversed once it is noticed.

Finally, a trend away from constancy of tax effort may be developing. Dating from the recent international wave of tax reform initiatives, the more prosperous countries, those whose public spending programs constitute large and entrenched parts of their national budgets, have begun to scale back these programs *and*, perhaps surprisingly, tax effort as well. Explaining this datum and determining whether there really is a trend, and if so, whether it is short- or long-term, will certainly be a major item on the agenda of the political scientists who study taxation.

(e) *Tax avoidance and evasion.* Retaining the good will of the taxpaying public is not only morally important, as Mill noted, but practically important, as surely every politician has always known. Unlike some of the themes just enumerated, the significance of voluntary tax compliance is not lost on tax economists.[13] But political theorists have paid greater heed to the specter of taxpayer rebellion as a recurring political nightmare. Any sort of social rebellion is of central importance to political theory. What is special about taxpayer rebellion or contentment is the frequency and, for most taxpayers, the painlessness with which the obligation to pay taxes tests the social compact.

What can be said at a theoretical level about the problem of taxpayer compliance? Is it just a matter of culture, as popular opinion (often repeated by economically sophisticated tax policy commentators) has repeatedly declared? Gathering and classifying empirical information on this topic offers helpful if sketchy confirmation of this popular notion. But the main result of efforts by political scientists to probe the extent and nature of tax avoidance and evasion is to underscore the extreme difficulty of defining the problem in a way that lends itself to the collection of hard data.[14] There is reason to distrust polls in which taxpayers are asked to comment on conduct of their own that may be illegal. But even if this were not a problem, defining tax avoidance and evasion in a way that can be grasped rapidly in a poll presents a communication hurdle that has so far defeated most opinion surveys. There may well be a fundamental problem of expertise as well, since few political scientists can be expected to possess the knowledge of the tax laws that may be necessary to identify significant tax dodges. Even accountants and lawyers find it hard to keep abreast of the latest

ing thought it so unlikely as to be virtually impossible.

13. See Charles M. Allan, The Theory of Taxation (1962).

14. Peters, supra note 10, at 210–16.

tricks; that is how some parts of both professions make their fortunes.[15]

(2) *The Political and Bureaucratic History of Taxation.* Historical writing, by virtue of its subject matter, defies summary. But this is of course partly a matter of style as well. Historians prefer, as against broad hypotheses, the concreteness of details that refuse to resolve into larger patterns. Hence, no gross account can be given of what historians who have studied tax systems have had to say about them. It must be said, however, that some historical work seems not only vitally important for the perspective it offers on how the problems of taxation have arisen, but also calls into question categories and assumptions with which we present-mindedly approach current tax policy issues.[16]

Two landmark studies in tax history may serve as illustrations. Shehab's *Progressive Taxation* and Brewer's *The Sinews of Power* both deal with vital stages in the development of the British income tax system. Brewer examines the peculiar growth in Britain of effective tax collection, largely in response to the huge budgetary demands of eighteenth and nineteenth century military ventures, and the intertwined, gradual institutionalization of a substantial national debt, as well as the cultural differences between Britain and other European powers that made the British people more receptive to a greater tax burden and lenders more confident in the British government's ability to fund its debt. Shehab's study sets forth the evolution of public argument in Britain for progressive taxes generally and for the progressive income tax in particular.

What is most striking about the two books is the revelation of now familiar institutions in their infancy and the remarkable currency of the terms in which these institutions were perceived by the politicians and intellectuals who invented them. For example, the transition between the Glorious Revolution (1688) and the American Revolution from reliance on land tax revenues to firm and open reliance on various excise tax revenues, which of course helped foment the second Revolution, was clearly the result of professional planning and implementation by forceful and ingenious bureaucrats, who knew how to take the public pulse, both urban and rural, with great accuracy. And oddly, the British government's credit-worthiness—a rare attribute in centuries characterized by the venality of most governments—reinforced the need for taxes instead of taking pressure off that instrument of fiscal intervention. Britain was indeed the first nation to borrow successfully

---

15. American Bar Association Section of Taxation/American Bar Foundation, *Report of the Second Invitational Conference on Income Tax Compliance*, 42 Tax Lawyer 705, 710, 730–31 (1989) (Michael C. Durst, Reporter) (alluding delicately to the need for tax professionals to serve as models of acceptable behavior to their clients).

16. The politics of taxation is often illuminated by historical writing that historians would not classify as "political history." If the latter is concerned more cen- trally with politicians, parties and political movements than with the social history of periods in which tax systems have undergone significant evolution or have otherwise flourished, or with the intellectual history of taxation (whether made by politicians or not), then political history as such is not even a primary source for the politics of taxation as that term has been used most often by political scientists and others.

on a vast scale, with the advertised recognition that it was going to be in debt for very long periods.[17] So significant was the relative permanence of the British debt, and the acceptance of it as such by the British public as well as by foreign lenders, that nineteenth century political opponents of new-fangled income taxes could seriously propose that debt rather than taxation should at long last be made the counterpart of military spending—with the idea of course that the country would eventually triumph in its wars and pay off all government obligations without the need for a permanent direct tax.[18]

The high repute in which tax collectors were held in eighteenth century Britain makes the story more vivid. One excise man, Thomas Paine, the author of *Common Sense*, gained credibility with his audience in the British colonies by virtue of his professional standing as a tax collector.[19] Generally, the profession was known for its rigor and even-handedness, and the plurality of excise taxes—most familiar to a contemporary American audience from their role in the background of the Boston Tea Party—seems to have struck some positive chord with the public, perhaps because of the censorious and redistributive implications of taxes on luxury items, which were not yet clearly perceived to be regressive.

Tracing the principle of progressive taxation through eighteenth and nineteenth century pamphlets and parliamentary commissions, as Shehab's work does, is a powerful way of demonstrating that the goal of vertical equity, as it is now more comprehensively called, has deeper roots in a variety of political and social concerns than one would ever glean from the more abstract debate among economists that largely grew out of this vital series of episodes in tax history. Again, it appears to have been in Britain that the ground was fertile for the adoption of a more comprehensive tax base than those of the hitherto very productive excise and customs taxes. However that development may be explained, Shehab takes it for granted. Since taxes on commodities and transactions were well established, the big alternative was some sort of exaction based on the wealth or (very broadly understood) income of individuals. What he demonstrates is the rapid and articulate establishment of opposing views about the attractions of a broadly based tax on individuals that made some allowance for differences of station in life, wealth, role in the economy, and a variety of other factors. Out of all this emerged a handful of persistent landmarks of tax policy: the British schedular tax (embodying more or less deliberately John Stuart Mill's arguments for a *non*-self-assessing *consumption*-based tax), the search pioneered by the mathematical economist Francis Y. Edgeworth for an "optimal" analysis of the ability to pay, and reliance on mathematical models of the economy to justify and explain the expected operations of the new income tax. Other, later

17. John Brewer, The Sinews of Power 88–134 (1989).

18. F. Shehab, Progressive Taxation (1954).

19. Brewer, supra note 17, at 105–08.

debates in other countries over the merits of income taxation were truncated. For example, in the United States there was virtually no debate about many aspects of the justice or economic efficiency of taxing income, and only a mild debate about the definition of "income" among rival academic proponents of an essentially British-style income tax.

The leading events and paradoxes of the past, however, are not easily evaluated. Do the differences between our political culture and that against which the rise of national debt and systematic tax collection occurred so effortlessly tell us how to design our own tax systems, and if so, what sort of advice do we get from these historical sources, Machiavellian clues about how the mob may best be handled or insights into the true well springs of social utility?

(3) *Other Social Sciences and the Politics of Taxation.* Psychologists and other social scientists have contributed to our knowledge of the politics of taxation primarily by discovering certain of the areas to which political scientists now also devote their attention: taxpayer attitudes towards taxing and spending measures, and tax evasion and avoidance. Opinion polls are the primary means by which social psychologists collect data on these topics. Since opinion polling is a notoriously hazardous business—the results being open to criticism on so many fronts but primarily failure to exclude biased questions and to elicit what subjects really think—it is not surprising that a good deal of the effort that has gone into this sort of research is concerned with the design of questionnaires. Very little, as yet, concerns the relationship of taxpayer attitudes to broad issues of tax policy.

The resulting data, however, point to two interesting conclusions. One is that taxpayer attitudes towards taxes and elected political officials' tax agenda do seem to move together. If taxpayer responses to opinion polls indicate stronger disapproval of the current level of taxes than at previous times, politicians in office also move effectively to lower taxes; and when taxpayers have favored government spending programs that necessitate higher taxes, politicians have raised taxes.[20]

Since no general empirical studies of this sort were conducted before the mid–1960's, the correlation of taxpayers' and politicians' attitudes is relatively precarious. It may well be that some parallelism should be expected simply because politicians, in the countries for which data exist, now customarily attend to opinion polls, and because the political elite are able to educate the public effectively through press coverage of their views. Since the data only show at best that there has been parallel movement, they cannot of course hint at a causal link or demonstrate that it was the electorate or the elected official that caused the other to hold certain opinions.

Similarly, the results of questionnaires about tax avoidance and evasion point to mildly interesting, mostly predictable conclusions at

---

20. Peters, The Politics of Taxation, supra note 10, at 159; Alan Lewis, The Psychology of Taxation 108–20 (1982).

best. Taxpayers disapprove of tax avoidance and evasion unless they are well placed to engage in it themselves. Wealthier taxpayers under progressive tax systems are more inclined to avoid or evade taxes than are poorer taxpayers. On the other hand, attempts to find correlations among other factors promise to permit a more deliberate manipulation of taxpayers' propensity to comply with the tax laws. Using figures collected by an international economic organization, researchers have found some support for a range of hypotheses relating tax rates, the visibility of taxes, the prosperity of the country, benefits of the political system, and the ability of taxpayers to express their dissatisfaction with the political system.[21]

5.4 MAKING INTERDISCIPLINARY SENSE

Several questions about the relationship of the politics of taxation to conventional tax policy have accumulated in the course of this survey of non-economists' approaches and results. It is useful to consider these questions in two groups.

(1) How do the alleged facts about the politics of taxation that are uncovered by social scientists transform tax policy? Tax policy, though worthless if not grounded in fact, is after all a matter of advice and prescription. Economics has claimed the higher ground of prescribing, and not merely describing. Where does purportedly empirical research, using other models of human behavior, fit in?

(2) Do the methodological concerns of the academic disciplines under discussion stand in the way of combined use of their contributions to our understanding of tax matters?

In response to (1), the first cluster of questions, we should dismiss, as based on methodological confusion, two possible answers. The first is the view that the descriptive results of non-economic social studies belong to tax policy as statements of initial conditions—circumstantial information that when coupled with the general law-like statements of economic models yields practical applications of the economic theories.[22] The second is that non-economic theories of tax politics are general theories that achieve a more comprehensive explanation of essentially the same facts.[23] Neither way of looking at the social disciplines'

21. Peters, The Politics of Taxation, supra note 10, at 208–23; Lewis, The Psychology of Taxation, supra note 20, at 155–60.

22. Alan Lewis, a social psychologist, seems to take this view when he says

The biggest differences [between economics and the social psychology of taxation] arise from the fact that economics is largely a deductive science and psychology an inductive one. While economists make assumptions about rational economic man, and predictions based on those assumptions that can be tested by

empirical observations, psychologists tend to derive their model of man from the observations that the make.

Lewis, The Psychology of Taxation, supra note 20, at viii. Professor Lewis's own subsequent survey of economic and psychological views of taxpayer motivation, however, suggests that there is considerable methodological distance between the fields, and a fair degree of confusion about that distance. Id. 20–35 ("Some Methodological Issues . . .").

23. Margaret Levi, Of Rule and Revenue 7–9 (1988).

markedly different handling of tax policy acknowledges the obscurity that shrouds the methods of behavioral studies, including economics.

Economics, political science, history, and social psychology, which may be harnessed to the ends of tax policy, are not comparable to the advanced physical sciences. In particular, the goal of unifying separately developed scientific theories, which is unexceptionable in the physical sciences, has so far eluded social studies. Economics and empirical psychology, to mention two of the fields with which we are concerned, not only speak different languages, but there is also nothing like consensus about the knotty task of comparing the hypotheses they entertain. On the whole it is not possible to say whether these hypotheses are even consistent with each other, much less to determine which is better confirmed by the known data. Since the fields are incommensurable in practice, it is idle to speculate whether their results are comparable as those of physics and chemistry have turned out to be.

A good part of the difficulty is due to the double nature of economic thought. Economists traditionally contrast the "positive" and "normative" parts of their specialty. Positive economics is supposed to be purely descriptive. It is supposed to seek general principles that do not express value judgments of any sort, and to deduce from these principles more particular propositions about economic behavior. "Normative" or "welfare" economics explicitly makes value-laden assumptions. These are intended to be such as everyone would assent to, but they are nevertheless open to dispute. Unfortunately, theories allegedly belonging to positive economics make assumptions that are essentially like those of welfare economics. This has led other economists to argue for the convergence of the two, although they do so in terms that seem to announce another separate field of inquiry—public or social choice. In fact, the supposedly descriptive, positive parts of economics have regularly made normative assumptions about the kinds of decisions it is rational for a person to make, given certain information. And so the field as a whole has what has been called a "value-oriented bias." [24]

Well-informed, neutral observers today still consider the empirical status of economics to be doubtful, in part because of its confusion of a normative bias with descriptive aims.[25] Thus, from the neutral standpoint of an outside observer, the strong position of economics in relation

24. Henry Sidgwick, Principles of Political Economy 12–29 (1883). There is still nothing like agreement about the matter. Economists have struggled for well over a century with a supposed division of their field into "positive" (descriptive) and "normative" (prescriptive) subfields. Jevons, Sidgwick, and others tried scrupulously to separate the purely empirical and testable theory of economic behavior from the theory of taxation in particular, since it was taxation in particular that had led earlier economists, especially Mill, to build ethical and political values into arguments that seem continuous with the mere description of economic behavior. See William Stanley Jevons, Theory of Political Economy, chapter 2 (1871) ("Theory of Pleasure and Pain").

25. Ernest Nagel, The Structure of Science 485 (1961).

to other disciplines that concern themselves with taxation is not explicable in terms of method, explanatory simplicity or predictiveness.

It does not follow that insights and information from economics, history, and other areas of social research cannot be joined together in a single approach to tax policy. The point is just that there is no hierarchy of scientific authority among the disciplines in question. It only makes sense to evaluate what each has to say on its own merits. Methodological problems of course make it harder to evaluate what each has to say than is the case in some other areas of research. We have no choice but to seek to know something about what these fields *cannot* tell us.

The second set of questions formulated at this beginning of this section concerns the methodologies of disciplines relevant to tax policy. Do these methods or concerns about method actually impede our understanding of tax matters?

Not really. At bottom, it is a matter of style and, negatively, of the stylistic intransigence of some exponents of the fields in question. Economists should certainly forget the claims of micro-economics (or neo-classical economics) to provide the only correct account of human rationality and well being. Economists already do so in most specialized areas. Those engaged in econometrics collect empirical data that often point to the inadequacies of neo-classical economics. On the other hand, political theorists should drop their adversarial approach to synthesizing self-consciously anti-economic theories of tax politics. In brief, mixed analysis of tax phenomena already exists, and it should be the norm. There is no higher authority.

The methodological problems of social inquiry remain. They are a reason for some barriers to communication among rival specialties that deal in one way or another with taxation. To conclude that none of these specialties deserves greater respect than any other is not to dissolve the problems that made them competitors in the first place. In fact, new efforts that attempt to synthesize the more compelling insights of economics, political theory, and other social studies are not uncommon.[26] Some of these are discussed in sections 4.4, 10.3, and 13.4.

---

26. See, e.g., Walter Hettich & Stanley L. Winer, *The Positive Political Economy of Income Taxation*, in The Personal Income Tax: Phoenix From the Ashes? 265 (ed. Sijbren Cnossen & Richard M. Bird 1990); John A. Kay, *The Interrelationship Between Tax and Benefit Systems*, in The Personal Income Tax: Phoenix From the Ashes?, supra, at 187.

Chapter 6

PARADOXES OF DEFINITION: "LABOR," "CAPITAL," AND "INCOME"

6.1 THE PROBLEM

Since the beginning of the great debate over income taxation in the last century, it has been thought not only fairer to tax income than wealth, transactions, or other things, but easier to measure income for this purpose than some alternatives. The technical advantages of the income tax base still make it attractive, though not perhaps more attractive than cash flow and net sales. We do, however, live with the income tax, and much more is known about its theoretical and practical features. This chapter is devoted to fundamentals that have both theoretical and practical implications.

6.2 CAPITAL AND LABOR IN THE STATUTORY INTERPRETATION OF "INCOME"

The American common law of taxation draws attention to a dichotomy between labor and capital. The Supreme Court observed in an early tax decision that capital and labor or their combination are the only sources of income.[1] Later the Court changed its mind and said that income for tax purposes can include receipts not traceable to either capital or labor or the two combined.[2] Why should this seemingly abstruse issue about the composition of income seem important to a court charged with interpreting the Constitution or a statute? Are the sources of income relevant, for that matter, to the rationale of taxation? Putting the question somewhat more technically, should income be viewed as the sum of the individual's "factor payments"—payments for contributing one or another factor of production such as labor, loans, capital, and so forth?

---

1. Eisner v. Macomber, 252 U.S. 189, 40 S.Ct. 189, 64 L.Ed. 521 (1920).

2. Commissioner v. Glenshaw Glass Co., 348 U.S. 426, 75 S.Ct. 473, 99 L.Ed. 483 (1955).

The answer is not simple. On a common understanding, income is the collective product of society.[3] Production sometimes uses up previously available wealth or "economic resources." It does not always do so. When people actively produce new wealth without using up resources, their labor alone must be the source of the product. By implicit definition, production uses capital if it employs and exhausts anything apart from or in addition to labor. It seems to follow that an apparent benefit that cannot be traced to capital or labor cannot be income.

When the Supreme Court first broached the issues concealed in these simplistic observations, it was dealing with a realization issue. The taxpayer before the Court had received a new possession—a stock dividend—not as a gift but as an incident of previously owned wealth— the stock on which the dividend was paid. The new possession was valuable in itself; it could also be sold separately from the original stock; but its value was only part of the value of the original stock, as it stood immediately before the distribution of the dividend. Hence, new wealth? Hence, income? After deciding that the ostensibly new increment in wealth was actually part and parcel of the old wealth, the Court decided no change in wealth had occurred when the ostensibly valuable new possession was received. The Court seemed to stress that the production and severance of wealth from some source can be crucial in deciding whether *new* wealth has been created by a given transaction or event.[4]

Generally, though, the "factors" view of income is not only abstruse; it is contrary to our intuitions and sometimes downright misleading. Things of value often come to us by means other than our own effort or ingenuity. For example, you may be so lucky as to find money on the sidewalk and by operation of law become its owner. You may also be awarded noncompensatory damages for someone's misconduct of which you are the victim. You may get a benefit from your employer's pursuit of its business ends, as when a night watchman is provided with a place to lie down on the job. In all these cases, formal reference to the source of the putative income seems to point to the wrong answer or merely to restate the question.

How, if at all, is the labor/capital distinction useful? Consider for a moment the task, very different from the judicial one, of designing a system of taxation in the first place. Basic policy preferences affect the design problem. We are concerned with the effect of taxation on the

---

3. See David Bradford, Untangling the Income Tax 18 (1986); Alvin Warren, *Would a Consumption Tax Be Fairer Than an Income Tax?*, 89 Yale L.J. 1081, 1085 (1980).

4. The holding is usually said to have announced a constitutional "realization" requirement: the Sixteenth Amendment permits an increase in wealth to be taxed as income only if it has been realized. Presumably, realization here is to be un-derstood, at least generally, in the accounting sense of the term that was developed for other purposes before income taxes became common. Scholars now think the Supreme Court has abandoned or, if asked to, would abandon the view that the Constitution limits income to realized gains. See Joseph T. Sneed, The Configurations of Gross Income 63–68 (1967).

political stability of society and on the improvement of social relations. We insist that the tax system be fair. We are also concerned that taxes should not kill the golden goose—undermine the social conditions needed for the production and enjoyment of new wealth. A clear view of product and its sources—the "factors of production"—may be crucial.

Newly produced wealth sometimes owes nothing to existing economic resources and sometimes does. When it does, it is the net product that may be taxed (or so it seems at first glance) without hindering the production process itself. It may be useful to see the world through labor/capital lenses, if this helps us net new product against the contribution of the old. But by naming the sources of new product we merely underscore the importance of distinguishing new product from old. Since the point is to contrast previously available economic resources with newly created ones, we actually put great pressure on the concept of economic resources. What are they, anyway? Tangible goods and raw materials are easy examples of economic resources. All the hard cases have an intangible element.

6.3 HUMAN CAPITAL

Inventions, know-how, product image, trademark recognition, and so forth, are economic resources of an intangible sort. They are well within the category of economic resources that have traditionally been called capital. But to say that they are intangible is to say that they reside, in a way, in people's minds or muscles (know-how may be a question of muscle memory, as in knowing how to perform a ballet). And as we turn to human beings, the problem of deciding what is and what is not an economic resource becomes tricky. Is there human capital as such? Certainly people are used up gradually in their labors—if they do labor. Industrial accidents are naturally regarded as imposing costs on their victims that should be regarded as costs of the industrial process for some purposes. Some productive activities benefit more if the person performing them is equipped with an education, training, or muscle that has deliberately been acquired for productivity sake. Moreover, some productive activities take more out of a person emotionally or spiritually than do others, quite apart from injuries and unforeseen events. In brief, there are lots of respects in which productive activity consumes not only labor but the laborer as well. We might therefore quite reasonably think of human beings as capital from which new wealth is produced.

But "human capital" is *not* like other capital in important ways. It does not "accumulate" in quite the way gold, housing stock, and factory equipment does. We do not regard squandering it as unfortunate in every instance. We regret an Einstein who is kept from producing by adverse circumstances; but we do not think it a pity that the economy does not manage to squeeze the last drop of effort from everybody; quite the contrary, we would regard that as an abomination.

There are other differences. Human capital rarely undergoes "wear and tear" in the way a brick kiln or printing press does. Other sorts of capital such as computer software that lose their value over time more in the fashion of putative human capital also pose difficulties for the normal conception of capital. In particular, software and the education of a worker both promise to contribute to the future earnings of any business operation to which they are committed. But as they are used up year by year, the cost of the revenue-generating capacity for that year ought to be computed by reference to the revenue-generating capacity that is left, and the whole point about these intangibles is that we usually cannot predict their remaining useful lives because they become obsolete unpredictably. We can rarely estimate the value of software (and this would be a way of anticipating its earnings) through a market transaction, and we cannot do so for human capital because we do not countenance slave markets.[5]

Not surprisingly, income tax systems generally do not tax individuals on accumulations of human capital until it is converted into marketplace receipts. Various reasons for this tax exemption have been cited. To tax people on their earning ability would be to guide their life plans in a manner that is incompatible with shared principles of individual autonomy. Moreover, if the object were to tax all income from human capital, it would be necessary to tax individuals on the increase in present value of their future earnings from the exploitation of their talents and education as those earnings draw closer in time. Consistency would perhaps also require tax allowances for the recovery of the costs of creating human capital—deductions for education costs, for "improving" cultural experiences, and so forth. These are of course mere inconveniences, which do not preclude a tax treatment of human capital paralleling that of physical and investment capital, but they are such substantial hurdles that they undermine the very idea of human capital.

Of course the basic question concerning the tax treatment of human capital is whether the analogy between human endowments and the accumulated wealth that is sometimes employed in creating new wealth should guide tax policy at all. We might instead decide that *everything* that distinguishes individuals from each other (except their labor) should be kept from influencing the design of tax measures. (The principle might be limited so as to exclude labor, which of course distinguishes people from one another, on the grounds that labor is an *expression* of a person's individuality, rather than that individuality itself.) We might think abstention from tax discrimination among individuals appropriate on various grounds. Respect for the individual,

---

5. As one tax theorist recently commented, "Purchased human capital presents a situation at the opposite end of a spectrum from nondepreciable assets such as land or wasting assets such as an annuity contract (with a fixed revenue stream) or a machine (producing expected revenues that are taken into account by an efficient market that sets a price for purchase or resale of the machine)." David S. Davenport, *Depreciation Methods and the Importance of Expectations: Implications for Human Capital*, 54 Tax Notes 1399, 1401 (March 16, 1992).

for example, has a prominent place in our ethical and political traditions. A dedication to treating people as ends rather than as means could therefore prompt us to stand militant against the entanglement of tax law in matters of human difference, even though a divorce might require that we disregard the effects of investment choices by which individuals acquire different abilities to contribute to society's wealth.

To illustrate: The possessor of a rare blood type can earn large sums by regular donations of blood. Giving blood, for such a person, is an activity that resembles production but also does not resemble production. The relevant internal organs of the talented blood donor can be compared with the physical plant of a factory. They produce the blood that is sold for profit. In this respect the blood is a product. The production of blood might therefore be considered closely analogous with the production of other things that require labor alone and no financial or nonhuman, physical capital. On the other hand, a person's blood is a proper part of him or her, something that is not ordinarily shed or even replaced in such a manner as to produce an excess (like a sheep's fleece). It is a fundamental asset from which others are produced. One's blood is therefore human capital in a different, and perhaps more compelling, sense than other endowments.

Should the earnings of the donor be thought of as income and taxed as such (assuming that the jurisdiction has an income tax)? I have suggested that we might consider a person's blood to be part of his or her capital. Even as such, it would still be subject to tax if sold, unless our conception of an income tax excludes income from capital. (Although some theorists did once believe that capital gain should not be treated as income, the view has no contemporary defenders and has begun to seem rather obscure even to intellectual historians.[6])

But arguably, respect for individual autonomy, for the individual's control over the aspects of himself or herself that confer individuality, argues against taxing these intimate products. The fact that the donor earns money by giving blood, something uniquely his or her own, for which there would be no bounty if the blood type were common, would therefore be a reason for *not* taxing the proceeds. Taxing people differently because of who they are, because of their physical or mental endowments, should not be permissible. Taxing the profit from a sale of blood would therefore be as improper as taxing physical height or waist size.

If this analysis is not wonderfully convincing, surely that is because the capital/product distinction does not fit the human factory at all well. One might conclude from examples like this that everything people produce without nonhuman input should be regarded as labor, including such things as the effort involved in giving blood of a rare type. Since blood donation is virtually the only troublesome case

---

6. See Marjorie E. Kornhauser, *The Origins of Capital Gains Taxation: What's Law Got to Do With It?*, 39 Sw. L.J. 869, 886 (1985) (citing Malthus and E.R.A. Seligman).

involving a physical product of the human body—body parts not being in most cases alienable—we could also decide to say nothing about how this case fits into the categories provided by the labor/capital distinction, and say instead that proceeds from the sale of blood are income because they are not exempted from that category by any defensible application of the concept of capital. In effect, we would just be admitting that the division of production into labor and capital is not illuminating, at least for the present purpose.

Unfortunately, other recalcitrant types of human endowment demonstrate the same point, though not as dramatically. The most important in practical terms is education.[7] Should the costs of education be treated on a par with the costs of materials used in productive activities? Education is sometimes used productively. It wastes literally, given the frailty of human memory. Substantive change in information renders it obsolete. Educational qualifications sometimes add a measurable market value to a person's labor. Note though that the deterioration of one's education rarely makes one less marketable. The process of acquiring an education involves some postponing of consumption, just as the accumulation of physical or financial capital usually does.

On the other hand, the tradition of liberal education emphasizes the *general* benefit of study and the difficulty of distinguishing "practical" from "impractical" intellectual pursuits. Even if we limit our attention to professional and vocational education, the correlation between gaining credentials and exploiting them may seem too weak to support treating educational costs as costs of production. A license to practice law or medicine *can* go unused. And if used, the state of accomplishment the license represents nevertheless requires constant refreshment through practice and occasional study. (United States tax law does not allow amortization, or gradual recovery of costs, with respect to some intangible assets, e.g., certain types of customer lists, because they are constantly being renewed while being commercially exploited.[8])

Although, as has just been suggested, the concepts of labor and capital themselves contain no solution to this and similar problems of taxation, we can deepen our understanding of what is at stake by comparing different perspectives on the concept of *taxpaying* capacity. Defining "economic resources," we have seen, is important because net product is important. But what net product is obviously depends on a stark contrast between what was available before and what is there after some interval of effort. How do we ascertain the pre-effort

7. John K. McNulty, *Tax Policy and Tuition Credit Legislation: Federal Income Tax Allowances for Personal Costs of Higher Education*, 61 Calif.L. Rev. 1 (1973); Brian E. Lebowitz, *On the Mistaxation of Investment in Human Capital*, 52 Tax Notes 825 (August 12, 1991); Davenport, supra note 5.

8. But see, Donrey, Inc. v. United States, 809 F.2d 534 (8th Cir. 1987) (subscriber list held depreciable); Newark

resources? The value of manufacturing equipment is determined exclusively by the productive use that can be made of it. We can look at other things in similar fashion.

One plausible way of looking at taxable capacity focuses on the taxpayer's *ex ante* ability to appropriate things of value. For example, a newly licensed surgeon may have the ex ante ability to earn $5 million over the course of a long career. She may also fail to earn that much by opting to become a concert pianist or a medical school professor. Generally, income tax systems are designed not to tax people on what they can earn but only on what they actually earn after making available choices. This amounts to taking an *ex post* view of taxable capacity—it assesses what could have happened by the safe benchmark of what actually did happen.

Whether to view taxable capacity ex ante or ex post is an issue that has both practical and pure policy dimensions. The universal preference manifested in existing tax systems for the ex post perspective has been explained as a "libertarian *constraint* on the tax system that prohibits the government from forcing people to work or to maximize income simply to meet their tax obligations."[9] But it has also been defended as a plausible response to the difficulties of estimating future income. "One might obtain information about a man's income-earning potential from his apparent I.Q., the number of his degrees, his address, age or colour; but the natural, and one would suppose the most reliable, indicator of his income-earning potential is his income."[10] It should be stressed that the practical problem relates not to what a person *can* earn but to what he or she *will* earn. Nevertheless, we may have information about whether individuals or groups of people are inclined to exploit their earning capacity, which will tell us how well actual earnings reflect ex ante capacity.

The significance of human endowments in determining what should count as economic resources for the purpose of defining the net product of the individual or society may therefore depend on which point of view we choose for reasons of policy and/or feasibility. One perspective harks back to the autonomy rationale for not taxing blood donation proceeds. It seeks not to tax away the freedom individuals have to make choices and instead highlights what they actually chose. Hence, the unexercised capacity to earn is not to be taxed, but earnings are. The other perspective would counsel that we tax people on the capacity to earn, penalizing the failure to exploit whatever endowments they possess. Excess leisure (by some objective standard of what is excessive) would be taxed as if the individual had worked instead. At first glance, it may seem that this is clearly incompatible with respect for individual autonomy, since it appears to tax the individual's most basic life plan decisions concerning whether and how much to work.

Morning Ledger Co. v. United States, 945 F.2d 555 (3d Cir. 1991), cert. granted, __ U.S. __, 112 S.Ct. 1583, 118 L.Ed.2d 303 (1992).

9. Mark Kelman, *Time Preference and Tax Equity*, 35 Stan. L. Rev. 649, 654 (1983).

10. James A. Mirrlees, *An Exploration in the Theory of Optimum Income Taxation*, 38 Rev. Econ. Stud. 175, at 175 (1971).

Extreme respect for individual choices, however, would prevent any restriction on human behavior for the common good. To the extent that even limited social authority is justified, there is redistribution of initially held rights and options.[11] And fair redistribution must obviously focus on the individual's income-earning *potential*. Otherwise, a fair redistributive scheme could be frustrated by the refusal to work of those who believed themselves likely to be adversely affected.

Obviously, this is a messy problem. By far the more convenient and hard-headed approach is that adopted by most tax systems—ignore taxable capacity and only take results into account. Implicit in this approach is a refusal to classify educational and other accomplishments as human capital.[12] Arguments to the contrary are of two kinds. Some advocates of tax relief for educational costs contend that it is simply unfair not to allow deductions for outlays that benefit production.[13] Others argue that it is good tax policy to create a tax break for tuition because education is valuable, quite apart from any traceable contribution to the social product.[14] In the light of the foregoing discussion, it is plain that whatever strength these arguments gain by invoking the phrase "human capital" is spurious. What lies behind the labor/capital dichotomy is the maxim that we should not repeatedly tax the economic resources that contribute to new social wealth, but that maxim has no clear application to things as intimately connected with human beings as education and physical attributes. This means that the maxim cannot decide all relevant questions and should not be expected to do so. The decision whether to provide tax relief for the cultivation or accidental possession of certain human endowments, namely those that have a notable influence on market values, should be recognized as a separate policy issue.

6.4 THE SCHANZ–HAIG–SIMONS DEFINITION OF "INCOME"

Difficulties, like ours, in taking the idea of income as product seriously led three economists (Schanz, Haig and Simons) to propose a definition of income that makes no reference at all to production. Instead, they drew the conclusion that income must be understood in terms of receipts. Thus, they stressed what the phrase "income tax"

11. See Robert Nozick, Anarchy, State and Utopia 25 (1974).

12. To be precise, ignoring the human-capital approach has two implications. First, it implies that the tax laws should neither allow the student to deduct educational costs as they are paid nor later, as they benefit the former student's career. Second, although for some, at least, the lazy days of college and graduate school are days of disproportionate enjoyment, which might from an absolutist perspective be regarded as a drain on social wealth, earnings foregone during school years should not be taxed to the student. Subsidies for education—whether of the direct variety or through tax deductions for gifts to educational institutions—should also be ignored, even though they arguably benefit students to a measurable degree.

13. David S. Davenport, *The "Proper" Taxation of Human Capital*, 52 Tax Notes 1401 (September 16, 1991); McNulty, *Tax Policy and Tuition Credit Legislation: Federal Income Tax Allowances For Personal Costs of Higher Education*, supra note 7.

14. Douglas A. Kahn & Jeffrey S. Lehman, *Tax Expenditure Budgets: A Critical View*, 54 Tax Notes 1661 (March 30, 1992); Lebowitz, *On the Mistaxation of Investment in Human Capital*, supra note 7.

itself suggests: that income is an attractive tax base because it succinctly homes in on what gives a person taxable capacity but avoids questions about how the capacity arises.

In Simons's formulation, income is the sum of the increase (or decrease) in a person's net worth over an interval of time added to the person's consumption during that period. One's income for a given year is a total comprising the wealth consumed during the period and the wealth kept or accumulated. (N.B., accumulation can be negative, as when the individual consumes but gains nothing with which to defray this.) Thus, current tax policy is often framed in terms of effects on accumulation and consumption. It should be noted here that early income tax theorists disagreed about whether accumulation belonged in the equation. John Stuart Mill and Irving Fisher, to mention only two of the most prominent income tax champions, always assumed that income meant only the consumption component and that accumulation should not be taxed.

Whether Schanz, Haig and Simons meant their definition of income to solve puzzles like those about human capital is not obvious from the historical record. Simons seems almost to have missed the importance of the issue. He clearly thought the equation of income with the sum of accumulation and consumption captured the idea of income as product. As he put it, "[t]he *sine qua non* of income is *gain* ...." [15] But he definitely thought that market transactions provide an adequate yardstick for the measurement of both. Income for him included unrealized gains, but these would be measured "by appeal to market prices." [16]

It is fairly clear that on the SHS definition of income the sum of individual incomes does not equal the total product of the society. Consider a day of rest from productive activity on which members of a community gamble with their previously accumulated wealth. The winners would enjoy an increase in net worth for the day. But what the winners gained would not be subtracted from the income of the losers because they have merely consumed previously taxed wealth. [17] (Following Simons's definition, the losers have positive consumption and negative accumulation that net to zero.) The gambling society would thus have positive income in the aggregate. The same result occurs if nothing is produced but some individuals make gifts to others. Those making the gifts apparently consume the value of what is given and suffer a corresponding reduction in net worth, again producing no change in income. The net worth of each recipient, however, is increased by the amount of the gift. Taken as a group, the donors and donees would have positive net income.

---

15. Henry Simons, Personal Income Taxation 50 (1938) (emphasis in original).

16. Id.

17. This would indeed be the result under the Internal Revenue Code. A net gambling loss is not deductible. I.R.C. § 165(d).

It may be objected that gambling and giving gifts should not be classified as consumption or, in the alternative, that new wealth really is produced when someone gambles or gives something away because the gambler or donor extracts full enjoyment from the value of what they give up and so does the winner or donee. Remember, though, that the whole point of the formal definition of income is to isolate those situations in which there is product or "gain," to use Simons's term. Hence, the point of the definition is in large part to offer an account of "economic resources" that will permit us to distinguish between previously available resources and those added to the common store by productive effort. The definition is wholly inadequate for this purpose if it must be applied on an individual basis not by reference to market prices alone, but by reference to some more nebulous standard when the aggregate of individual incomes is computed.

Again, it may be thought that the anomalies of gifts and gambling can easily be reconciled with the otherwise relentless market orientation of the definition if it is acknowledged that the market value of what is received in some transactions should be deemed to equal the value of what is given up. If these deemed receipts increase the social product, the transaction causes no discrepancy between social product and the sum of individual incomes. But this *ad hoc* rule does not restore the value of the SHS definition. Its purpose was to resolve such puzzles in advance, and it is worthless if it must be saved piecemeal by ingenious supplementary rules.

It may be objected that human capital is too limited a puzzle to use as a fundamental test of a proposed definition of income. There are other similar problems. Determining whether there is income when economic resources are shared poses another sort of puzzle, and it takes a variety of forms. Hospitals provide sleeping areas for interns who are on call for periods as long as twenty-four hours. Though surely no luxury to the interns, the accommodation provided is a supplement to their regular abode. The use of a bed and minimal privacy are perhaps not worth much, but they are worth something. The interns enjoy a small benefit. The employer, however, insists on the arrangement and derives, let us assume, a greater benefit. Under current United States tax law, the benefit would either not constitute income in the first place or would be excluded from income under a special provision of the tax law.[18] The SHS definition, however, does not justify the exclusion. It would have to be asserted, again in an *ad hoc* manner, that there is no cognizable gain to the interns, or a special rule would have to be invented to prevent the employer from netting the cost of the sleeping quarters against hospital revenue.

Benefits shared by employers and employees range from those in which the employer absolutely must provide the benefit and the em-

18. Benaglia v. Comm'r, 36 B.T.A. 838 (1937); I.R.C. § 119.

ployee absolutely must take advantage of it, or the job will not get done—the case of a sleeping arrangement provided to a night watch-man—to cases in which the benefit appears to be a disguised payment of additional compensation to the employee—a private jet for a corporate executive allegedly provided for security purposes, or free luxury accommodations provided to a hotel manager.[19]

We saw that the problem concerning the blood donor and education costs is part of the very basic problem of delineating economic resources and social product. If we cannot say in general what counts as an increase in the wealth of the society in question, we cannot say whether it has enjoyed income. This is relevant because aggregate income ought to equal the sum of individual incomes. Here, the problem concerns aggregate income or product, but a clear delineation of economic resources would not help much. Whether the benefits provided to employees are considered to come out of previously available resources or not, the difficulty is whether the employer and the employee can benefit simultaneously from the same events or activities, without decreasing the benefit to either. Some clever lobbyist no doubt grasped this point in proposing the current exclusion from income for "no-additional-cost" fringe benefits to employees.[20] The premise appears to be that the employer incurs no additional cost in providing the fringe benefit, but there is nevertheless a net benefit to the employee—net of the contribution the outlay makes to the employer's business. (Whether this is really ever true in practice is debatable; free rides for airline employees no doubt cost the airline something because every pound on board adds to fuel costs, yet these are the paradigm case of "no-additional-cost" fringe benefits, according to the legislative history.) Even if the benefit to the employee is not necessary for the employer's business, the equation of social product with aggregate individual income seems to tell us that the employee derives no income from the arrangement.

6.5 INTANGIBLE AND EPHEMERAL ADDITIONS TO THE SOCIAL PRODUCT

Other complex economic phenomena pose further difficulties for the simple view of social product as gain on previously existing economic resources. Assets like land and corporate securities fluctuate in value without any traceable offset elsewhere in the economy.[21] There are several possible explanations for this. For one thing, markets today are to an ever larger extent affected by the availability of devices that permit the risks of business and investment strategies to be shared

---

19. The case of the night watchman was first noted in an English case. Tennant v. Smith, H.L. (1892) App. Cas. 150, III Brit. Tax Cases 158. The private jet is undecided. The luxury accommodations for the hotel manager were excluded from his income in *Benaglia*, supra, note 18.

20. I.R.C. § 132(a)(1).

21. See Warren, *Would a Consumption Tax Be Fairer Than an Income Tax?*, supra note 3, at 1089. Warren concludes, however, that the equivalence of social product with the sum of individual incomes under the SHS definition nevertheless holds "but is obscured by the complexities of our economy."

in novel ways by those who supply the financial, physical, and intangible capital.

We can glimpse the effect of risk shifting within capital markets as follows. It is no longer the case that a shareholder in a corporation, for example, must own a share of the corporation's potential losses and gains in equal proportion. Shares now come in a variety of forms that separate certain kinds of risk from others in order to appeal to investors who either have objectively different needs or simply hold different subjective views of the risks involved. When a corporation has issued both common and preferred shares, the preferred shares are by definition entitled to a fixed level of dividend before any dividend at all can be paid on the common shares; but the common shares in the aggregate can claim a higher proportion of any upside gain on the capital invested in the corporate venture. Thus, the common shareholders have chosen to trade their chances of a higher short-term return for a chance of higher long-term returns. The corporation's motive for issuing the alternative stock choices may in many cases be to attract additional capital.[22] If this happens, and the net assets of the corporation are increased, the net worth of the corporation may be increased by an even greater amount, because the influx of capital puts it in a better position to take advantage of existing opportunities, goodwill, and so forth.

The shareholders, common and preferred alike, may in turn benefit from the appreciation in the value of the corporation. To the extent that this occurs because of the way in which shares in the corporation divide the risk of corporate investment, the marketing device in question resembles insurance, because it turns the shifting of risk into an above-normal return on invested funds. Similar insurance effects probably pervade today's sophisticated capital markets.[23] And if investments that promise insurance gains of this kind sometimes succeed, others most assuredly fail for the investors, but reward promoters instead.[24]

Profits from insurance operations may measure real increases in social product, viewed as the addition of valuable though intangible resources to those previously at the disposal of the society in question.

22. Sometimes, a corporation is capitalized or recapitalized to replace previously held common shares with preferred shares merely for the convenience or other economic advantage of the current shareholders. As tax advisers are well aware, controlling shareholders sometimes compel a corporation to recapitalize, and in the process exchange their common shares for preferred shares, in order to "freeze" the value of the controlling block of stock to current value for estate tax purposes. See I.R.C. § 368(a)(1)(e), 2701–2704; Senate Finance Committee, Revenue Reconciliation Bill of 1990, S. 3209, at 58–60.

23. See Stephen Utz, *Partners in Crane: Partnership Investment and Economic Risk*, 31 Tax Notes 827, 838–39 (May 26, 1986); *A Comment On Disproportionate Partnership Loss Allocations and Other Matters*, 49 Tax Notes 1025, 1028–29 (November 26, 1990).

24. This appears to be the consensus view of what happened to large parts of the enormous market for real estate limited partnership interests in this country during the late 1980's.

Whether this is so depends on the success with which the insurance arrangements *spread* losses associated with risks more evenly among the individuals and firms that face these risks and spread the losses over longer periods of time than those in which they would otherwise be felt. While risks are thus not eliminated, the negative effects of sudden and unforeseeable losses are.

Profits from ill-planned or unplanned insurance arrangements, on the other hand, are merely gambling profits. Instead of spreading losses among larger numbers of people and over longer periods of time, bad insurance schemes merely shift risks from some people to others, and often shift losses without achieving the benefits of spreading them. To the extent that the capital market is beset by such imperfections, it merely transfers wealth from some pockets into others but manages to show a paper gain, which in the short-run may make loanable funds more widely available. Nevertheless, retrenchment seems inevitable in at least some instances. The losses are realized and the results are like those of the gambling society described in the previous section. As a result, individual incomes under the SHS definition may temporarily, though for relatively long periods, provide a very inaccurate measure of gain on economic resources, if the notion of an ultimate measure of social product has any application at all in an economy whose capital market is as complex as this. Arguably, there simply is no way of getting at the difference between true and apparent social product.

The "announcement effects" of putting tax laws in force also cause changes in prices than cannot be accounted for as nominal in relation to a bedrock of "real" values. Sometimes this is due to what economists call "tax capitalization." It occurs when sellers of goods react to the announcement of a tax preference (deduction, credit, or other tax benefit) associated with owning such goods by raising prices, in order to take advantage of buyers' willingness to pay more because of the tax advantage; by raising prices, they capitalize the tax advantages. Hence, the term "tax capitalization." The phenomenon can also occur when buyers react to the imposition of a tax on goods of a particular kind by seeking a discount and refusing to pay the old higher prices.[25] While there is some temptation to suppose that tax capitalization merely alters the prices of goods and services in relation to their "true" market values, it is not obvious what conditions would define a noncapitalized market—is it just the current actual market adjusted by altering prices to remove tax effects, or is it the market that would exist if taxes had never been imposed? (Tax capitalization is only one kind of announcement effect. Others include changes in market prices in response to the imposition of a tax on business activities that are henceforth shunned by those who would otherwise have engaged in them.)

25. John A. Kay & Mervyn A. King,   1990).
The British Tax System 10–12 (5th ed.

These are a few specific forms of the problem of defining social product for a complex economy. A large literature exists concerning the practical problem of *measuring* even gross national product (GNP) and gross domestic product (GDP). The measurement problem is of course complicated by the problem of definition.[26] But we should also consider the well recognized difficulty of unscrambling broad effects of taxation on economic values from hypothetical underlying values.

6.6 MEASURING SOCIAL PRODUCT AGAINST NO–TAX AND PRE–TAX WORLDS[27]

The greatest difficulty in defining income for tax purposes springs from the effect taxes themselves have on what is produced and how it is produced. It is of course a truism that taxes *can* affect economic behavior both in more or less obvious and direct ways and also in less obvious ways. Ronald Reagan's 1980 presidential campaign relied significantly on a crude analysis of the indirect effects of taxes. His supporters stressed the theoretical claim that there is an ascertainable ceiling on how high taxes can go without damping economic growth and reducing the social product, and that the previous administration had allowed taxes to exceed that limit (a certain point on the "Laffer curve"). The idea was not that the economy shrinks when taxes get above a certain level just because, e.g., top executives refuse to work as hard as they might, but that higher taxes have this and other effects that interact to discourage economic activity. Most economists remained skeptical of the Laffer curve largely because the detailed analysis of how taxes interact with economic behavior was left to the imagination.

Taxes affect economic behavior in a variety of ways, most of which are easy to understand, if not to measure, when considered in isolation from other ramifications of the taxed economy. For example, it makes sense that income and payroll taxes, which account for the vast majority of federal tax revenues, might constitute so great a burden on work that some people choose leisure, which is not taxed, over gainful employment, which is. How many people are deterred from working by taxes on earnings is another matter. Economists have tried to measure the extent of tax-induced substitution of leisure for labor, never reaching complete agreement about the correct models and econometric technique, but sharing at least the goal of abstracting tax effects on labor from information about actual economic systems.[28]

26. See R. Stone & G. Stone, National Income and Expenditure 31–32 (10th ed. 1977) (both interpersonal accounting and direct measurement of social product are necessary perspectives for measuring income in a complex society).

27. The discussion of "pre-tax" and "no-tax" "worlds" in this section is prompted by Professor Jeff Strnad's analysis of these worlds and criticisms of his analysis. Jeff Strnad, *Taxation of Income From Capital;*

A Theoretical Reappraisal, 37 Stan. L. Rev. 1023 (1985); *sources cited in notes 35–36 below.*

28. See, e.g., Hall, *Wages, Income, and Hours of Work in the U.S. Labor Force*, in Income Maintenance and Labor Supply 102 (eds. Glen G. Cain and Harold W. Watts 1973); Jerry Hausman, *Labor Supply* in How Taxes Affect Economic Behav-

Similarly, the deductibility of contributions to charity would seem to encourage such contributions, at least in some cases (perhaps less in the case of most contributions to religious institutions); there have been careful and persuasive studies of the extent to which changes in the tax rates, which alter the tax benefit of charitable contribution deductions, may increase or decrease the aggregate amount of charitable giving.[29]

The economic analysis typically applied to these questions about tax effects, whether the discussion remains a priori or makes use of empirical data, concentrates on how tax incentives or disincentives affect behavior in one market or type of transaction, e.g., the labor market or the "market" of charitable giving. An almost universal feature of such analysis is that it also *ignores* the simultaneous indirect effects of taxes, the ramifications of the effects that are under scrutiny, when those effects have other effects in other markets. The contrast is one between *partial equilibrium analysis* (the analysis of economic behavior in a single market or a few markets) and *general equilibrium analysis* (the analysis of economic behavior in all relevant markets, including interdependent behavior phenomena). For example, a decrease in charitable giving that is induced by lower tax rates might be compensated for by increased employment, also as a result of lower tax rates, with the ultimate effect that less charitable giving is needed. Although the analytical practice of disregarding the interaction of markets in assessing tax policy has frequently been criticized,[30] efforts to extend the power of general equilibrium analysis to cope with indirect tax effects are just beginning.

This is directly relevant to the definition of income because the values we place on economic resources cannot easily or uncontroversially be corrected to remove the influence of old or new tax laws. In other words, the tax system that was in effect yesterday directly or indirectly produced a variety of changes in the values of available economic resources; the tax system as it existed at earlier times affected earlier resource values, thus leaving traces that were carried forward by the more recent tax effects, and so on. Not only resource values but past political and moral views and their consequences picked up something at least, and perhaps a great deal, from the economic conditions thus shaped by the tax systems in effect. British tax policy not only increased the value of colonial land holdings in the eighteenth century, it enabled Britain to out-borrow Continental rivals in the newly emerging government bond market (see section 5.3(2), above); it also fomented rebellion and contributed to this country's fundamental constitution-

---

ior 27 (eds. Henry Aaron & Joseph Pechman 1980).

29. Charles Clotfelter & Eugene Steuerle, *Charitable Contributions*, in How Taxes Affect Economic Behavior, supra note 28, at 403; Watkins, *Institutions Dependent on Charity Brace For the Effects of the Tax Bill*, Wall St. J. p. 23, col. 4 (August 25, 1986).

30. See Carl S. Shoup, Public Finance 12–15 (1969); Boris Bittker, *Effective Tax Rates: Fact or Fancy?*, 122 U. Pa. L. Rev. 780, 798–802 (1974); Jeff Strnad, *Taxation of Income From Capital: A Theoretical Reappraisal*, 37 Stan. L. Rev. 1023 (1985).

al and ethical culture.[31] The massive and highly intrusive tax systems of modern industrial democracies must pervasively affect culture as well as the values of economic resources from year to year, and they do so cumulatively: tax law reform and fine-tuning is never directed to restoring the status quo ante but only to improving on the present.

These observations support several conclusions that challenge the foundations of income tax theory. Given a consensus as to the meaning of income—agreement to embrace the SHS definition, say—the general equilibrium effects of taxes imply that the pre-tax base in a world *with* tax is not the inevitable benchmark for measuring tax fairness, because the existence of taxes will already have affected both the valuation and composition of pre-tax wealth. This applies not only to judgments about the fairness and effects of an income tax but to such judgments about any sort of tax. It applies with particular force to an income tax because the imposition of such a tax apparently changes interest rates which then affect the net wealth term in the SHS definition.

Unfortunately, the difficulty is not simply to carry out a general equilibrium analysis with respect to the measurement of net wealth in a *no-tax* world. (Recall that such an analysis, though theoretically possible, is currently unavailable.) Given the post-tax moral and political decisions that have shaped the world with tax, why should it now be appropriate to annihilate this input in assessing tax fairness? The layers of tax effects that contribute to the current values of economic resources and that have helped determine what those resources are include responses that are the only preferences individuals and groups of individuals have formed on some issues; these responses may even play so fundamental a part in people's lives as to affect the character and identity of those people. Devout libertarians and bleeding-heart liberals in large measure are who they are, in their respective ways, because of their visceral responses to a world with tax.

There may be much broader, comparable tax effects. The widespread belief that the kind of education that is open to all can enable children without the advantages of social class to achieve those advantages for themselves and their own children depends in part on the characteristics of our current mix of public and private institutions of higher learning. Private universities and colleges, if one is to believe their fundraising officials, would not have grown as they have if it were not for property and income tax exemptions and the deductibility of contributions to them. Public universities and colleges largely emulate the accomplishments of private institutions. The result is a sliding scale of aspiration and accomplishment across the range from elite to more modest institutions. Whether it was a good idea to assign such a large role in educational policy to the de-centralized device of tax incentives and subsidies, we nevertheless are used to the idea, and

---

31. Gordon S. Wood, The Radicalism of the American Revolution 325–38 (1992) (describing the mutual reinforcement of mini- mal government expenditure and a market-dominated culture in the years following the American Revolution).

arguably base thereon to some extent our willingness as a society to regard class differences as inoffensive to the ideal of equality.

The no-tax world is therefore a world without many of our cherished or at least familiar value judgments, while a pre-tax world represents a mix of high aspiration and mundane compromise in light of the seeming inevitability of taxes, as they happen to be imposed under current law. To illustrate: Suppose that the current income tax has induced people to choose more leisure than they would in a no-tax world and this provides fertile soil for a variety of tastes in entertainment. As a result a given pop star earns twice what she would in a no-tax world. The choice between the no-tax world and the pre-tax world as a benchmark determines the fairness of the total income tax the pop star pays. If the no-tax world governs our fairness appraisal, the pop star could be made to pay at least 50% without being thought to suffer the loss of anything properly hers. If the pre-tax world sets the standard for fairness, then the pop star's income should be taxed without regard to her gains from tax distortions elsewhere in the economy, in particular, without regard to the distortion that gives her pre-tax twice the income she would have in a no-tax world. If the draconian treatment suggested by comparison with the no-tax world seems all right because pop stars exploit the shallowness of public taste, then let her be instead a poet, an athlete, or a TV evangelist. The point is that the no-tax and pre-tax worlds suggest quite different views of what is fair.

Recall that this discussion began by taking the SHS definition of income for granted. But now we should ask whether that makes sense after all. We have seen that the no-tax and pre-tax worlds have different implications for tax fairness. Although these basic perspectives must be defined somewhat differently for the more basic purpose of defining income, they are nevertheless relevant to that purpose, because they affect the value and supply of economic resources, which must provide the ultimate point of reference for distinguishing new product.

The pre-tax world, i.e., the world as we know it except that income tax liabilities are added back to all taxpayers' net worth, is made up of certain economic resources with given values. These values are fixed by markets subject to the effect of taxes on economic behavior. Thus, for example, since oil-drilling equipment is subject to accelerated depreciation, which produces a tax benefit to the owner, it will be priced somewhat higher than it might otherwise be; but since some mobile oil-drilling equipment is subject to an excise tax on heavy truck sales, its price is influenced *both* by the tax advantage of accelerated depreciation and by this price-depressing excise tax. Its price may also be influenced by tax advantages and disadvantages of oil exploration as a type of business venture. For example, the at-risk rules apply to prevent the purchaser of oil-drilling equipment who uses nonrecourse financing from obtaining any deductions with respect to it,[32] but passive losses from oil *production* can offset passive income in contrast with passive losses from other types of endeavor.[33] Nevertheless, what we mean by the pre-tax world is the hypothetical world in which a piece of mobile oil-drilling equipment has its current market value, except that no one gets the depreciation deductions, pays the excise tax, or is influenced by taxes in any other way.

The no-tax world would probably value the same equipment somewhat differently, and perhaps quite differently. Removal of the excise tax alone might affect the mix of oil-drilling equipment that manufacturers produce. Since off-highway vehicles are now exempt from the excise tax on heavy trucks, some special-purpose mobile oil-drilling equipment that is not adaptable to normal highway use has a market advantage over similar equipment that is adaptable. Since the excise tax on heavy trucks is 10%, it probably affects manufacturers' decisions about how much equipment of each kind is produced as well as the pricing of that equipment.

Other differences between the pre-tax and the no-tax world could influence the course of economic development in the society, career decisions, sports, the arts, and so forth, as has already been suggested. This is important for the definition of income because the values of things in the pre-tax world presuppose whatever tax regime participants in the economy were expecting to be in force for the foreseeable future. If tax reform suddenly undermined these expectations, what is available would not change but the values of particular resources would (so-called "announcement effects"). On the other hand, people must cause tax reform to happen; if it does, current market values will already have been influenced to some extent by probable changes in the tax laws, and so the announcement effects may be greater, the more unexpected the content of the change in tax regime.

Since current economic resources are thus influenced in several ways by expectations about future taxes, it would be plausible, for the purpose of defining new product, to take those resources as we find them: available in just the present assortment and valued as the market now values them. Thus, seeking to measure the income of a wildcat oil producer for next year's income tax, we might define his or her net worth by reference to what currently owned equipment is worth under last year's tax laws. But we might also try to wash the distorting effects of taxes out of the definition by referring not to current market values and availability but to no-tax world market values and availability.

In favor of the pre-tax world perspective, without any adjustment for the windfalls and huge unexpected losses that some types of tax reform could cause, is the difficulty of deciding which past tax effects were distortive and which were "normal" or inevitable under any

---

32. I.R.C. § 465(a).   **33.** Id. § 469(c)(3).

reasonable tax regime. The tax laws could have affected economic resources in a wild variety of ways, but some tax regimes would have been politically impossible under any plausible set of assumptions. Some politically possible tax regimes nevertheless distort markets considerably (the real estate market of the late 1980's, for example). Then again, the political impossibility of the no-tax world—every government must take economic resources by taxing, borrowing, or random confiscation—strongly undermines its relevance to the definition of income.

Whatever perspective we choose—pre-tax, adjusted pre-tax, or no-tax—as the starting point for measuring product, the choice will be open to criticism. The problem is therefore not how to make a definition of income that focuses on individuals equivalent to a definition that takes the entire society and its economy into consideration. The choice of a perspective for determining what economic resources there are affects both sides of the hoped-for equivalence. The real problem is to decide in a principled way how much of the influence of taxes on past production and the values of existing resources should be taken for granted in measuring new product.

6.7 FAMOUS SEMI–FINAL WORDS

This conclusion brings our discussion of labor and capital full circle. We saw in Section 6.2, above, that it is difficult to separate labor from capital; some apparently unassisted human contributions to production are ambiguous—they can be regarded as using pre-existing capital, if we countenance *human* capital. Our discussion found no bedrock on which to base a decision about the merits of the human capital question. Now we find that there is no bedrock on which to base even a reckoning of nonhuman capital. Of course, the usual response to these highly elusive puzzles about the definition of income is to forget the whole thing. Some commentators are inclined to offer as a reason for doing so their hunch that the differences between the pre-tax and the no-tax benchmarks for measuring social product are not very significant or that allowance can properly be made for the differences through partial equilibrium analysis.[34] One commentator has noted that the problem of choosing among these perspectives is not essentially one for economists but instead one for the political philosopher, since the differences are largely the result of important individual preferences and collective decisions.[35] That is obviously correct, but in these terms the problem is no less radical.

34. Louis Kaplow & Alvin C. Warren, Jr., *An Income Tax By Any Other Name— A Reply to Professor Strnad*, 38 Stan. L. Rev. 399 (1986) (discussing the problem of perspectives with reference to judgments of tax fairness alone).

35. William Popkin, *Tax Ideals in the Real World: A Comment On Professor Strnad's Approach to Tax Fairness*, 62 Ind. L.J. 63, 71–72 (1986) (discussing the perspective problem with reference to judgments of tax fairness alone).

Chapter 7

TAX EXPENDITURE THEORY AND PERSONAL DEDUCTIONS UNDER AN INCOME TAX

7.1 INTRODUCTION

We saw in the last chapter that to define income either in terms of social product or in terms of the receipts and uses of individuals poses difficult, and perhaps insoluble, problems. On the one hand, to delineate social product we must be clear about what are the economic resources to which production adds; we must also agree on what constitute real additions to pre-existing economic resources, given that there may be value in such things as insurance and risk-allocation arrangements over and above the goods and services these arrangements serve.[1] On the other hand, to define the income of the individual in terms of receipts, or alternatively in terms of uses, is possible only if we can solve both the problem of identifying new economic resources—a version of the problem facing the definition of social product—and the problem of assigning uses of resources to the individuals who may benefit from them. Unfortunately, but not surprisingly, these problems about the definition of income did not present themselves to the economists who first framed and popularized the prevailing definition of income in terms of accumulation and consumption. Their focus was elsewhere and is today largely unrecoverable.

Later theorists, who were lawyers by training, took over the Schanz–Haig–Simons (SHS) definition of income as a tool for analysis but also for polemics. They saw, resourcefully or perversely, that the SHS definition does not really capture the concept of "gain" that Henry Simons thought essential to it, and they played on this defect to expose other issues and directions for tax policy. Stanley Surrey's powerful idea of "tax expenditures" set the ball rolling. Professor Surrey, who both trained two generations of tax lawyers at Harvard and served as Assistant Secretary of Treasury for Tax Policy in the Kennedy and

1. See Alfred L. Malabre, Jr. & Lindley Clark, *Productivity Statistics For the Ser-* *vice Sector May Understate Gains*, Wall St. J., page A1, col. 6 (August 12, 1992).

Johnson administrations, advocated that the standard by which specific tax measures should be tested is a comprehensive income tax, proceeding from the SHS definition of income, and that the large number of tax provisions that do not obviously pass that test should be evaluated as if they involved direct government expenditures corresponding in amount and distribution to the revenue reduction they cause.[2] The phrases "comprehensive income tax" and "tax expenditures" were the buzz words of most tax policy writing for a decade or so. They tended to simplify debate over tax issues drastically. Naturally, this prompted a reaction, focused especially on what seem to be the most vulnerable of tax expenditures, the so-called personal deductions; advocates of these deductions purported to justify them with reference to intrinsic income tax goals.

This chapter surveys the deductions themselves, as they stand today and as they stood in the not so distant past, and goes over the arguments for and against them, prompted by tax expenditure analysis. In large part, this serves as a critique of the concept of tax expenditures, but since that concept embodies a blind adherence to the SHS definition of income, it also serves as a critique of that definition, from a slightly different angle than that of Chapter 6, above.

7.2　DEDUCTIONS BELOW THE LINE

Many income tax systems provide something like the deductions from gross income, permitted for U.S. tax purposes, that are called "personal" or "itemized deductions." [3] "Natural persons," as opposed to entities that have legal personality and that may also be classified as persons under the tax laws, are eligible to benefit from a range of tax provisions that do not extend to corporations, partnerships, trusts, and so forth. Not all of these are called personal or itemized deductions. For example, most taxpayers are entitled to reduce gross income, in computing tax liability, by a fixed amount (currently, $2300), just for being a human being. The amount does vary with income tax bracket, and so not everyone who must pay tax benefits from it. But this personal exemption establishes a threshold for tax liability. Interestingly, taxpayers are allowed to benefit from the exemption for dependents as well as for themselves. This is one of few respects in which the current structure of the tax laws recognizes the family (or housekeeping units) as the proper taxpaying unit.

These personal allowances are not what are usually referred to as personal deductions. The personal deductions reduce gross income, *after* personal allowances and a variety of exclusions from income are

---

2. Stanley S. Surrey, *Federal Income Tax Reform: The Varied Approaches Necessary to Replace Tax Expenditures with Direct Governmental Assistance*, 84 Harv. L. Rev. 352 (1970); see also M. White, *Proper Income Tax Treatment of Deductions for Personal Expense*, in 1 House Comm. on Ways & Means, 86th Cong., 1st Sess. Tax Revision Compendium 365, 369–70 (Comm. Print 1959).

3. For a brief history of the personal deductions, going back to the 1861 income tax, see William J. Turnier, *Evaluating Personal Deductions in an Income Tax—The Ideal*, 66 Cornell L. Rev. 262, 264–69 (1981).

taken into account. And the personal deductions produce tax saving only if they exceed a threshold amount, that is sometimes called the "standard deduction." (Few taxpayers could benefit from the personal deductions before the late 1940's because the standard deduction reduced taxable income to zero for the vast majority of taxpayers.) The personal deductions are for medical, interest, state tax and miscellaneous employee and other expenses, and for casualty losses. Restricted in various ways, the taxpayer's expenses or losses under each of these headings are summed and compared with the standard deduction; if the total is greater, the taxpayer is allowed to reduce gross income by more than the standard deduction. Thus, a person with high medical and interest expenses for a given taxable year pays less tax than a person with the same receipts and other expenses but with low medical and interest expenses.

The deduction for medical expenses has always been subject to a special limitation—prior to and in addition to the overall limitation to amounts in excess of the standard deduction. The limitation is now very strict, since only non-elective medical expenses in excess of 7.5% of adjusted gross income (gross income refined by all permissible deductions and exclusions except the personal deductions) can be claimed. In this connection, it must be noted that employer-provided health benefits or insurance is, within broad limits, excluded from an employee's income.[4] *This*, rather than the explicit personal deduction for medical expenses, might be thought the primary expression of public policy in the matter of health and medical benefit income. More of the consolidation of the two later in this discussion.

Only interest paid to purchase first and second residences, with a cap on the amount of the mortgage obligations, can now be deducted; formerly, all interest, including interest on consumer items, was deductible. Thus, for example, credit card interest is no longer deductible, but until 1986 it was. Buying a house to live in and buying a TV set to watch for enjoyment are both acts of consumption. Hence, the current distinction between home mortgage interest and other interest on borrowing for personal consumption strikes many as peculiar. It is difficult to say whether Congress intended anything by the distinction. It first considered repealing the personal interest deduction altogether, then restored the mortgage deduction in response to perceived public opposition and intense lobbying from the construction industry.[5]

The charitable contribution deduction is available only for contributions to approved organizations (not for charity to individuals) and is

---

4. For the fiscal year 1990, revenue losses from the exclusion of employer-provided health insurance were estimated at $29.585 billion and from the deduction of medical expenses at $37.255 billion. U.S. Office of Management and Budget, Budget of the United States Government, Fiscal Year 1990, Special Analysis G, Table G–1, at page G–43 (1990).

5. Staff of the Joint Committee on Taxation, Analysis of Proposals Relating to Comprehensive Tax Reform (Pamphlet JCS–35–84) (October 8, 1984) (proposing the elimination of home mortgage interest deduction).

subject to two percentage limitations. If the contribution is to a private foundation (as defined in the Code), the donor can deduct the full amount up to 20% of his or her adjusted gross income. Otherwise, the maximum is 50% of AGI. Generally, the deductible amount is no greater than the taxpayer's basis (roughly, the already taxed or tax-exempt investment) in the gift. So, for example, the contribution of one's own personal services to a charity is not deductible, because the services have no basis. On a contribution of appreciated property, only the taxpayer's basis is deductible, unless the property is a capital asset and will be used by the recipient in its tax-exempt activities, in which case the deduction is the full fair market value. This last oddity has been under steady attack for some years on a variety of policy grounds, as will be discussed briefly below. Primarily, however, the charitable contribution deduction is interesting because it allows the tax on new income to be avoided (or allows the tax on already taxed income to be recovered) at the election of the taxpayer.

State taxes, now with the important exception of most sales taxes, are deductible. These include state income taxes (federal income tax is not deductible for federal tax purposes) and real estate taxes, both transfer taxes and ad valorem or annual assessments. By special provision, sales taxes on unusually large items are deductible, though sales tax on run-of-the-mill purchases is not. Until 1986 all state taxes were deductible with the exception of sales taxes of limited application. (It is worthwhile to recall in this connection that interest paid to holders of state government obligations, usually referred to as "municipal bonds," is exempt from federal tax. The deductibility of state taxes and the exemption for state interest paid are sometimes said to evince a deference on the part of the national government toward state governments.)

Although the foregoing are the principal itemized deductions, and the only ones that are usually called "personal deductions," certain other deductions must also be itemized, in the sense that they are given no tax effect unless their total, when aggregated with the personal deductions, exceeds the standard deduction. (Since 1986, these "miscellaneous" itemized deductions have also been limited to the excess of 2% of the taxpayer's adjusted gross income.) The deductions in question include some sorts of employee business expense, deductions linked with the rental of nonbusiness property, expenses incurred in investment activities like maintaining a stock portfolio, and a few others. Since all are closely tied to income production, they differ pointedly from itemized personal deductions. There is no principled reason for limiting their deductibility, as current law now provides, apart from the arbitrary decision that the standard deduction is an adequate substitute for them. They are otherwise not relevant to this discussion.

7.3 THE ISSUES

The powerful grip of the SHS definition of income has long shaped American thinking about tax matters, both in and out of government.

At times, indeed, it has seemed to some that the equation of income with the sum of personal accumulation and consumption is both unrivalled and self-justifying. Nevertheless, there have been rivals and the arguments are not all one way. Moreover, the arguments advanced in favor of the definition by its authors and current champions do not fully explain its pervasive and continuous appeal.

It is not surprising that alternatives to the SHS definition have much in common with it and identify many of the same items as income. This presumably reflects taxpayers' and voters' widely shared sense of the economic facts that should be taken into account in designing any personal tax. That shared sense, however, is of recent date, and may well have been inculcated by developing tax laws that embody it. As we have seen, the great nineteenth century legislative debates that led to the invention of the income tax in Britain proceeded from a much more diffuse collective sense of tax fundamentals. Radically inconsistent conceptions of "income" were mooted. No consensus ever won out, to judge by the fragmentary character of the early schedular tax and the discord among its advocates. In Germany and Italy an amazing array of differing views about the ostensibly unitary notion of income claimed adherents and influenced early income tax laws. (Medieval people were just as sure that the relevant characteristic of people as taxpayers was their wealth.[6]) It is perhaps only an accident, due in significant part to the way in which the income tax was popularized here, that Congress and the American public have found the broad concept of an income tax so straightforward, and the SHS definition capitalizes on the seeming self-evidence of the underlying tax base.

Nevertheless, the rough idea of income the American public and its elected representatives take for granted is not at all interchangeable with that captured by the SHS definition. On the contrary, the early advocates of income taxation in this country successfully tapped a widespread familiarity with accounting practices to help put over the image of a tax based on income. This intuitively recognized tax base included receipts regardless of most sources but excluded government transfer payments, unrealized gains, gifts and various other kinds of SHS income.[7] Both the general inclusiveness of our notion of income and the treatment of capital had been controversial among the Europeans. Of these, indifference to source is the important central suggestion taken up and magnified in the SHS definition.[8] But just as

6. Edwin R.A. Seligman, Essays in Taxation, chapters 1 & 2 (1921) (discussing the concept of "faculty" or "ability" as used in the Elizabethan poor law and in the early legislation of the American colonies).

7. See Edwin R. A. Seligman, The Income Tax: A Study of the History, Theory and Practice of Income Taxation At Home and Abroad (1911); F. Shehab, Progressive Income Taxation; Marjorie E. Kornhauser,

The Origins of Capital Gains Taxation: What's Law Got To Do With It?, 39 Sw. L.J. 869 (1985).

8. See David Bradford, Untangling the Income Tax 18 (1986); Richard Goode, The Individual Income Tax (rev. ed. 1976); Stanley Koppelman, Personal Deductions Under an Ideal Income Tax, 43 Tax L. Rev. 679, 685 (1988).

centrally, the SHS definition rejects the transactional method of measuring income—the heart of the accounting methods that enshrine realization as a requirement for inclusion of an item in income. The ideal income tax proposed by Henry Simons would apply to all accrued gains, whether converted into disposable property or not. "Accretion" or change (positive or negative) in net worth lies at the heart of the measurement of gain, and hence of income, on his proposed definition. Thus, for example, a person who consumes out of accumulated wealth should not be liable for tax because the positive consumption component of the equation is offset by a negative change in accumulation. This does seem to capture a basic feature of the income tax base that makes it intuitively attractive to the populace at large. By contrast, realization was and remains a touchstone for the income tax with which we are familiar, and there is no room for this "exception" to income for accrued gains under the SHS definition.

It is against this backdrop that the supposedly "normative" status of the SHS definition must be seen. Indeed, when Surrey and other proponents of tax expenditure analysis refer to that definition as normative, they mean only that the definition has won out in a limited sphere of debate over rival equations of "income" with consumption or cash flow or any of several alternatives that are now simply called by these other names.[9] Simons's quite limited discussion of the practical application of an income tax altogether ignored the classification of government transfer payments, personal damages, scholarships, medical expenses, casualty losses, and charitable contributions. Can it be said nevertheless that the SHS definition identifies the ideal or the pure tax base that people have in mind or ought to have mind when they think of income taxation?

Theorists disagree. There are good reasons for preferring the SHS definition to other sweeping definitions of income. Some of these reasons have to do with what the word "income" already means to most people, and to that extent the SHS definition is merely an elucidation of received wisdom. But to the extent that this or any other formal definition represents positive arguments for *choosing* to tax income rather than something else, it may of course establish a standard against which the actual implementation of an income tax might be judged. So, for example, if we are persuaded that the reasons behind the SHS definition can be extended to favor a certain treatment of gifts (their inclusion in income, say, or the denial of a deduction from income for the donor), the definition sets a standard and, indeed, a norm with implications that we should unpack. Some defenses of the SHS definition do just that: they do not merely insist on its widespread acceptance as a good reason for accepting it but probe its unstated attractions. The most important of these elaborations on the pull of the SHS

9. See Stanley S. Surrey & Paul McDaniel, Tax Expenditures 186–88 (1985); Richard Goode, *The Economic Definition of* *Income*, in Comprehensive Income Taxation 1 (ed. Joseph Pechman 1977).

definition focus our attention on the equity of treating all market-oriented forms of economic power as income, regardless of source.[10]

On the other hand, the implicit assumption of much discussion of income definitions and tax expenditure theory is that *some* broad definition of income must be better than others *and* must control our thought about the details of any real-world income tax. This, unfortunately, is not true, or if true, no argument for it has been articulated by any of its defenders. It is tempting to consider slavish allegiance to any unmitigated standard in this connection a kind of cultural or political mistake. Why should a definition that solves general conceptual puzzles, especially those of almost exclusive concern to economists, be *assumed* to hold lessons for the luxuriant reality of real tax policy decisions?

Seen in this light, the dilemma between the normative approach of tax expenditure theory and the pragmatism of messier alternatives is really a clash of arguments, perhaps at different levels of generality, all concerned to the same extent with the purpose and consequences of taxing income. And since the very definition of income is thought to be at issue, we must of course have in mind here a more primitive concept of which the SHS definition would be one possible refinement.

7.4 CONSUMPTION AND THE PRECLUSIVE USE OF ECONOMIC RESOURCES (WITH PRIMARY REFERENCE TO CHARITABLE CONTRIBUTIONS)

Now that the stage is set, or seen to be in initial disarray, consider once more the implications of equating income with the sum of consumption and net accumulation (possibly negative). Obviously, as Simons stressed, the point of the definition is to zero in on gain—gain to the individual, which also a proper part of aggregate social gain. It can be true by definition that any gain an individual enjoys must either be kept or lost, saved or consumed. In other words, we can *make* this true by using the notions of accumulation and consumption as both mutually exclusive and exhaustive of the possibilities. But there is a not-so-obvious twist to such a stipulated definition: it seems to alter the sense in which we use both terms, at least in some special circumstances.

The accumulation of capital by society as a whole is a traditional point of reference for those (usually called macroeconomists) who would theorize about the behavior of the economy as a whole. Accumulation is of interest to macroeconomists primarily as material for economic growth. (In this respect a preoccupation with the effect of taxes on macroeconomic phenomena unites early nineteenth century "holistic" tax policy with late twentieth century op-ed tax policy; see Chapter 1.) But does accumulation by individuals, as it figures in the SHS equation, add up to social accumulation? This question should recall the ques-

10. See Mark Kelman, *Personal Deductions Revisited: Why They Fit Poorly in an "Ideal" Income Tax and Why They Fit Worse in a Far from Ideal World*, 31 Stan. L. Rev. 831 (1979)[hereinafter *Personal Deductions Revisited*].

tion viewed from various angles in the previous chapter: does national income equal the sum of individual incomes, using the SHS definition of income? If national accumulation equals the sum of individual accumulation, we may not want to allow individual accumulation to include "psychic" gains such as the satisfaction an individual derives from living in a politically stable environment or endowing a hospital. That is because we do not usually consider psychic additions to personal wealth, which would presumably be a sort of human capital, as a potential source of economic growth. Are all psychic gains then "consumed" as soon as they are harvested?

Consider the gain an anonymous donor experiences when she gives money to a museum. What gain? Certainly, no market gain. Nothing of value is transferred for something of even greater value. But we may consider it axiomatic that no one willingly does anything without a prospect of net benefit. And if this is true, even if only contingently in our case, the benefit is a gain for the donor. This putative gain poses two problems for the SHS definition of income. Is the benefit consumed (by the donor or anyone else)? And whose benefit is it? From the statement of facts, it may appear that the benefit is clearly the donor's and is consumed by her. But note that if the donation had been withheld, the capital available to fuel further economic growth would have been the same in quantity as it is after the donation is made— although the donation takes place, capital is conserved—and when the gift is made, nothing else is used up, at least if labor and capital are the only factors of production, because labor is certainly not involved. If the donation is a nonproductive event, how can it produce any gain at all, much less a gain that is promptly consumed?

It is this conundrum that leads some writers to speak of "psychic gain" in this context. What they mean is precisely a nonmarket, nonproductive gain. But are there such, and if so, why should they be taken into account in the design of the income tax base? Indeed, it is common for tax theorists to assume with a flourish that no attention need be given to resources on which no market value can be placed. This was even a fairly common theme in early judicial decisions interpreting the income tax laws in this country.[11]

But even if there is a psychic gain worth considering, whose is "the gain" on the transfer? Surely, the beneficiary or beneficiaries of the donation are primarily people other than the donor, and the psychic benefit to the donor is both slight and ephemeral. Observations along these lines prompted William D. Andrews to argue that the charitable contribution deduction is justified, not as a tax incentive for private charity, but as equitable treatment for the consumption that is involved. He granted that there was consumption, and that the donor and beneficiaries alike consumed things of value. But he offered this principle to account for what differentiates charitable contributions from other forms of consumption: "The personal consumption at which

---

11. See, e.g., Burnet v. Logan, 283 U.S. 404 (1931).

progressive personal taxation with high graduated rates should aim may well be thought to encompass only the private consumption of divisible goods and services whose consumption by one household precludes their direct enjoyment by others." [12]

Thus, Professor Andrews thinks making a gift to charity is consumption but not the sort that garners the benefits of consumption exclusively for the person who is responsible for bringing the episode of consumption about. In his view, the peculiarity of nonpreclusive consumption should be taken into account in the very definition of the tax base, not merely in providing well deserved relief from the otherwise harsh consequences of too rigid adherence to the ideal. The analysis dovetails with a broader critique of the advantages and shortcomings of the SHS definition of income. Professor Andrews thinks it vital to delineate the notion of consumption that is used in the definition in order "to try to move toward a more refined concept [of income] defined ultimately in terms of real goods and services." [13]

This sounds like an aspect of the general project of making the SHS definition agree with the concept of individual product. (Professor Andrews' point was apparently not that some of the benefit of consumption is lost or is of such generalized sort that it cannot be assigned to anyone.) Is there any merit to the thought that preclusive consumption alone, and not consumption that spills over from the initiator of consumption to others, should be counted towards income *or* product? The answer is yes, if we understand the point here to be that the donor does not use up "real goods and services" that others consume, and that the donor's income therefore should not include those goods and services. But, this simply begs the question. It disregards the benefit to the donor, the psychic income, on the grounds that this benefit or income is not real goods and services. By the same reasoning, gambling and personal losses also deserve exclusion from the tax base. But that apparently was not Professor Andrews' contention. (More on gambling and personal losses below.)

7.5 INCOME AS ECONOMIC POWER

If Professor Andrews' position is rejected, and it has not attracted much of a following, how should one formulate the alternative view? Should we always impute to the donor, gambler, noncasualty loser some benefit in the expectation of which the gift or gamble or loss was elected? And should we regard that benefit as having been plucked

---

12. William D. Andrews, *Personal Deductions in an Ideal Income Tax*, 86 Harv. L. Rev. 309, 346 (1972). As the quoted implies, Professor Andrews had in mind the comparison of charitable contributions with private giving, which is usually if not always confined to the members of one's family. There is no deduction for the donor of a private gift, which means that the value of the gift is taxed when it is acquired by the donor and that tax is never forgiven. Receipt of the gift is excluded from income, however, which suggests that the idea is to impose tax at the donor's marginal tax rate, because the donor and the donee are likely members of the same family and their household income is properly taxed at the donor's rates. Id. at 348–51.

13. Id. at 313.

from what otherwise seems a net loss? No one has gone for this either.[14]

Instead, the common thread of alternatives to Professor Andrews' position is to equate income with economic power acquired during a given accounting period.[15] Money received in compensation for services or as a return on an investment enables the recipient to command all the economic resources that money can buy. Whether the recipient of earnings or investment returns spends them or saves them should not matter, on this view. It is the incidence of economic power to which the income tax is and should be sensitive.[16]

If we accept this principle, the gaps in the SHS definition are fairly easily supplied, with the exception of shared benefit situations like that of the employer and the night watchman, who both get something out of it, though perhaps unapportionably, when the employer supplies the watchman with a bed on the employer's premises. But if we accept the equation of income with economic power, the equation of aggregate income with social product fails. The example of the night watchman apparently shows that economic power over the same economic resources, the same real goods and services, can be shared in ways that defy division into private preclusive bundles. The contribution to the employer's productive activity and the benefit to the night watchman may overlap because they are identical or because they are inextricable, but in either case no separation in principle is possible.

Interestingly, the definition of income in terms of economic power (first proposed by Haig) was the starting point that Simons thought he had refined in proposing the equation of income with accumulation and consumption. He argued that the further division of economic power into accumulation and consumption was necessary to ensure that income includes only gain. The point was well taken. A person's, or a whole society's, economic power can survive from one accounting period into the next, or it can be used to produce more economic power, or it can be used up unproductively. The important objective of saying what it is for a person's or a society's economic power to increase with time requires conscious discrimination between growth (or accumulation) and dissipation of economic power previously acquired.

Simons had another reason for revising Haig's original formulation. It had had the awkward consequence of including in a person's income all manner of private consumption that does not draw on riches

14. A possible exception is Professor Mark Kelman, who stresses that earnings potential is what the income tax is intended to reach, and that this potential correlates best with economic power acquired. Kelman, *Personal Deductions Revisited*, supra note 10, at 835.

15. Haig, of the SHS trio, had originally defined income in exactly this way. It was Simons's contribution to suggest handling puzzles about non-market transactions by dividing income into resources retained and resourses consumed. Robert M. Haig, *The Concept of Income*, in The Federal Income Tax 7 (R. Haig ed. 1921), reprinted in American Economics Ass'n, Readings in the Economics of Taxation 54, 55 (Richard A. Musgrave & Carl S. Shoup eds. 1959); see Turnier, supra note 2, at 270.

16. See, e.g., Surrey & McDaniel, supra note 9; Kelman, supra note 10; Koppelman, supra note 8.

otherwise at the disposal of production. For example, it would include services we provide for ourselves and must provide if we are to be productive in ways that affect society more generally. It also posed the problem of relativizing income to the preferences and tastes of the individual, since the measurement of economic power would have to be in subjective terms. Thus, the amount of "income" a society produced during a given period of time could vary with the changing psychology of individual members of the society, regardless of production in the ordinary sense. Simons needed, he thought, to tie all income measurement to the marketplace, where values were intersubjective and were more likely to correspond to nonpsychological events.

When Professor Andrews' critics retreat to a definition of income in terms of economic power, and no longer attempt to define consumption precisely, they take on the task of classifying what is commonly called "psychic income." Some such income, everyone agrees, cannot practically be brought within the scope of an administrable and politically acceptable tax base. Yet people can derive satisfaction in ways that mimick or replace market transactions without having recourse to a market, e.g., by making charitable contributions. Compare the physician who earns money in practice and donates it to charity, with the physician who donates his or her services in kind. Equity and public confidence in the administration of the tax system require that both be counted as income to the same extent. Hence, there should either be a deduction for amounts contributed to charity or inclusion of the value of the contributed services.

If the latter is the preferred alternative, then surely the physician's services to family members, as services given in kind to others, might also be included in the household income for tax purposes. Indeed, fairness would seem to require a presumption of inclusion for all nonmarket income, including imputed income from the use of a personal residence, from education, perhaps even from differences in talent and from unused earning potential. These inclusions would of course make a tax drastically intrusive, and probably politically unacceptable, but in any case an administrative nightmare, if feasible at all. All the same, if we want to achieve clarity about the basic features of fair and rational income taxation, we should certainly not let politics and administrative convenience shape the very statement of the definitional problem.[17] Most experts, however, have devoted their attention primarily to capturing what they believe to be our basic intuitive judgments about income and tax fairness, without considering such basic matters as how welfare is to be analyzed.

Instead, it has seemed to some theorists that the tax base must forthrightly respect the distinction between activities in which a person

---

17. See Thomas D. Griffith, *Theories of Personal Deductions in the Income Tax*, 40 Hastings L.J. 343 (1989) (disputing Surrey's, Andrews's, and Kelman's conclusions on the grounds that none relates the concept of income consistently with a broad concept of human welfare or considers alternative versions of the principle of fairness in distributional decisionmaking).

voluntarily resorts to a market and other activities. Some have indeed argued that although the focus of an income tax should ideally be on earnings capacity, because tax avoidance through refusal to earn should not be countenanced, market transactions are the appropriate measure of earnings capacity because the alternative is "to force people into the market" in order to pay their taxes.[18] Certainly, the general public would agree, if not on "libertarian" grounds [19] then from a robust sense that the broad imputation of income on economic principles would raise the spector of other forms of unfairness—over-valuing of imputed income by tax officials, greater tax avoidance by passive income recipients, and selective enforcement.

Despite the shoals of more complex tax administration, restriction of the tax base to items of income or loss that have been realized in market transactions clearly goes too far. Members of communes could escape tax altogether, since they would be entitled to tax exemption on income as well as contributions, so long as no clear quid pro quo could be identified in the communards' sharing arrangements.[20] More importantly, the tax could not be administered fairly or effectively if opportunities to avoid its application are so plentiful as to permit economically similar events to have different tax consequences. One of the reasons for limiting the tax base to market-oriented income therefore fails; ignoring income in other forms would encourage tax avoidance just as surely as would the attempt to tax such income. This brings us back to the core of the definition of income as economic power. The reason for so sweeping a definition was in part to accord equal tax treatment of those similarly situated. It is often possible to achieve the same increase in one's economic power by means of activities not involving a market as by market transactions. So, one stone will not kill two birds in this case: we cannot achieve fairness and respect individual choice whether to exercise earning capacity, simply by adjusting the definition of income. This important conclusion means that there is less magic in the choice of income as a tax base than many income tax proponents have thought.[21]

7.6 MEDICAL EXPENSES AND PERSONAL LOSSES

Charitable contributions are voluntary and involve the transfer of wealth to others. In a narrow sense, medical expenses and personal

18. Kelman, *Personal Deductions Revisited*, supra note 10, at 841–42 and passim.

19. Koppelman, *Personal Deductions Under an Ideal Income Tax*, supra note 8 (characterizing Kelman).

20. Under the right circumstances, such tax exempt status can contribute to massive cultural change. Wealthy subjects of the Roman state, for example, apparently strongly attracted to the tax exemption they could obtain by becoming Christians. Oddly enough, the church was exempt even though it promised its members "charity" amounting to retirement plans that could begin to pay benefits at any age. The Roman Empire struggled in vain to limit the tax dodge implicit in religious poverty, and pagan resentment of Christians was quickened by the spectacle of tax avoidance. Paul Johnson, A History of Christianity 78–79 (1976).

21. The faithful today are primarily the defenders of the definition of income as economic power, mainly followers of Simons and Surrey.

losses are involuntary. If we consider the wider context in which they are incurred, the motives that lead individuals to suffer economic losses outside the business context or to purchase medical treatment are personal, private and preclusive of benefit to others. As has been noted, the problem posed by deductions for personal expenses or items of loss arises in part because the important category of consumption is only sketchily defined: these items may be thought to represent consumption or not. Because personal losses and medical expenses are to some extent linked with personal endeavors and result in personal benefit, there is an argument for calling them consumption; but to the extent that they are involuntary and do not raise the individual's standard of living, a contrary argument can be advanced.

The problem may seem swiftly resolved by retreat to the definition of income as increase in economic power, whether that power is exercised or retained. When one pays household doctor's bills, economic power is certainly exercised, and under this definition of income that clinches it: the medical expenses do not affect the income computation. Similarly, economic power is used up for no productive purpose when a personal loss destroys it, and the loss does not reduce income.

On the other hand, medical expenses incurred to restore health do not make a person better off in a sense that should affect the comparison of his or her situation with that of others for most purposes, and perhaps for tax purposes as well. In this and the previous chapter we have seen that various objectives guide the attempt to define income. Perhaps the overriding objective—to ensure that existing wealth is not taxed as if it were new income—leads to the analysis of the notions of economic resources and economic power. But it almost goes without saying that, since income is to be taxed to individuals, the definition of personal income should also assist in the equitable distribution of tax burdens, with equity governed at least in part by the comparison of the economic situations of different individuals; the definition of income cannot attribute more income to one person than to another, if the two deserve to be treated similarly in all ways with respect to the item of supposed income that is at stake. Hence, if it is generally agreed to be unfair to assign disadvantages to people because they are ill (whatever the practice of society may actually be), then we should not tax amounts spent on account of ill health; consumption should not include medical outlays.[22]

There is some support for this approach to medical expenses in the existing treatment under U.S. tax law of damages received on account of personal injuries. If a tortfeasor provides medical services in kind, the value of the services is not taxed as income to the recipient. (Just why we think this natural, if we do, may not be entirely clear; we may be influenced by the familiar exclusion of gifts from income.) A specific statutory provision excludes money damages for personal physical

---

22. Andrews, *Personal Deductions in an Ideal Income Tax*, supra note 12, at 335–37.

injuries.[23] The reason for the exclusion is clearly not to lower the costs of the tortfeasor but to preserve the full value of the benefit to the victim. The same concern for victims might lead us to conclude that *all* nonelective medical expenses should be excluded from income, or so it has been argued.[24]

Actually, similar reasoning would somewhat support the exclusion of any restoration of losses, whether they are due to ill health or to ill fortune of another sort. And if the restoration should be excluded, then the unrestored loss should be deductible. But then what about gambling losses and the unexhausted value of durable assets (houses, cars, furniture) that a person loses at death? Should these losses not also be allowed to offset income declared and taxed in the year of death or earlier years? If we balk at the most sweeping implications of loss restoration under the tax system, it is presumably because the consequences would pretty clearly reinforce rather than limit wealth differences among individuals. That is *not* the case with medical expenses. Ill health falls to rich and poor alike, and there would be no facial preference for the more wealthy in allowing medical expenses to be deducted.

We should, however, consider further where the fairness argument leads. As Boris Bittker has observed, the refined application of the SHS definition of income can be viewed as requiring the inclusion in each person's tax base of the public services he or she consumes.[25] While the value for consumption of some public goods cannot be apportioned among the individuals who benefit from these goods without impossibly difficult assessments of idiosyncratic psychological characteristics of particular individuals, many governmental benefits are doled out in discrete packages (health service benefits, low-cost student loans, and so forth), and these could easily be taken into account in measuring income.

If no strong case for treating governmental and other benefits as components of personal income has been part of the broader debate concerning the personal deductions, perhaps the reason is that we implicitly take the purpose of the SHS definition to be that of providing a first approximation of individual incomes, with the proviso that equitable tax treatment will be achieved by further adjustments to income that do *not* merely refine the categories of accumulation and consumption but go well beyond them. If we consider the practice of Congress over the years since the enactment of the first personal income tax, this seems an apt characterization of the shared assumption that guides much tax legislative innovation.

It is fair to conclude that the attempt to squeeze a clearer understanding of income from the broad suggestions implicit in Henry Simons's categories of accumulation and consumption has borne fruit

23. I.R.C. § 104(b)(2).

24. Id. at 334.

25. Boris I. Bittker, A "Comprehensive Tax Base" as a Goal of Income Tax Reform, 80 Harv. L. Rev. 925 (1967).

primarily by exposing the variety of ways in which the SHS definition can be accepted. Some perhaps think it "normative" in the sense that it precludes further discussion of tax equity concerns; others, who are broadly content to use it as a starting point, regard it as no more than that.

7.7 STATE TAXES

State taxes, other than sales taxes, are now allowed as an itemized deduction. If the personal deductions are thought to refine the SHS definition in a fundamental way, and if government benefits could be ignored in the measurement of income, the personal deduction for these taxes is among the most defensible. Taxes reduce the income of the individual and reallocate the revenue among other individuals by providing governmental benefits or at any rate the benefits of government. It is not necessary to allow a deduction from federal taxable income for federal taxes paid, because allowance for the reallocation implicit in taxation can be accomplished by adjusting the federal marginal tax rates to take account of differences in tax liability. But state tax burdens differ, because state legislative goals differ, without regard to the economic similarity of citizens of different states. Federal gross income of $50,000 may not be subject to income tax in Texas, though it is reduced by a $1,175 income tax in Connecticut. It has been argued that in order to eliminate the resulting differences, the personal deduction for state taxes is appropriate.

If governmental benefits are *included* in income, on the other hand, state taxes may not call for any adjustment. The states notably differ in the benefits they provide residents. They are free in many cases not to offer certain benefits, and even of those benefits all states provide with federal funding, the states usually have some degree of freedom to delineate peculiar terms of eligibility, so that residents of different states receive somewhat different Medicaid benefits, for instance. Taxes account for some of these differences. A state with a lower tax rate structure cannot cater to the perceived needs of its populace as comprehensively as can another state with higher revenues per person. It would seem only fair, therefore, to recognize differences in total income that result from these benefit differences, and net state taxes paid against benefits received.

The netting of taxes against benefits, however, can only be approximate. Not only is there no guarantee that for every dollar in state taxes we pay we will receive a dollar's worth of benefits, but state taxes are often raised in order to allow states to redistribute income even more markedly than the federal government does through its taxing and spending programs. Most states, in particular, rely heavily on property taxes to finance schools and other benefits that flow to just some residents and not at all to others. It now happens more frequently than perhaps it did in the past, that senior residents pay higher property taxes (because they own more of the net value of taxable real estate than their juniors) while younger residents reap a greater share of the benefit of these taxes in the form of free public schooling for their children. Similar patterns may develop and disappear from time to time. The point here is that benefits and state taxes are not likely to offset each other for the individual.

This leaves us with the problem that states impose different levels of tax on people who receive identical treatment under the federal income tax. But surely the way to cure this if it needs curing, is not to tamper with the *definition* of income. After all, most states also impose income taxes. Equity certainly demands that whatever counts as income at the federal level should also count as income at the state level, for income taxes at both levels. The need for adjustment of total tax burdens is a problem of harmonization that cannot be solved by such an elementary strategy as merely providing a personal deduction for selected state income taxes. Indeed, this strategy does not even appear neutral, as the definition of income should be. We will consider the harmonization of state and federal taxes in greater depth in Chapter 13.

7.8 GAMBLING AND PERSONAL LOSSES

Conspicuous by their absence among the allowable personal deductions are gambling and personal losses other than casualty losses. The literature on the topic of personal deductions has yet to address this phenomenon at any length. One can only assume that the defenders and critics of personal deductions see nothing odd in it. Nevertheless, the defenders should find it discomfiting that these reductions of net worth are just as real, and that the beneficiaries of any amounts transferred, may succeed to the entire value taken away from the losers. The social product is not changed when a gamble takes money out of one pocket and puts it into another. A wallet lost on the street becomes at best a windfall to the finder. Given the conservation of social product that is associated with these items of net worth reduction, they too are candidates for deduction or exclusion from income.

Personal casualty losses have always been deductible under the U.S. income tax (not under other countries'). A casualty loss is essentially one that is sudden and unforeseeable. The size of the loss is not crucial. Thus, an enormous loss resulting from the decay of a building that could have been maintained so as to avoid the loss is not a casualty, but a small theft loss is. As these examples suggest, the casualty loss deduction can seem sensitive to the fault or innocence of those who suffer losses. But the deduction is just as sensitive to the foreseeability of losses; those of which the sufferer had some warning are not deductible, while losses that compromise the sufferer's finances in a particular accounting period, and for which no provision could have been made, are deductible.

The casualty loss deduction thus has something in common with the medical expense deduction. Both seem to allow taxpayers a deduction when their losses exceed foreseeable levels (represented in the U.S. tax computation by the standard deduction and by the thresholds for deducting medical expenses and the costs of prescription drugs). Thus, the deductions have the effect of spreading certain personal costs over periods longer than the tax accounting year. But if income averaging were the goal of the deduction, other income and loss items should receive similar treatment, and it would have to be admitted that there is no reason to distinguish casualty losses from medical expenses or to impose threshold limitations on the latter.

In brief, the personal deduction regime is crude tax policy with regard to losses and involuntary expenses. But Congress has long since concluded that this is so. The 1986 Tax Reform Act was considered by many legislators to represent a step in the direction of the repeal of personal deductions apart from that for charitable contributions. As originally proposed, the bills that most influenced the shape of the final legislation eliminated all personal deductions. One by one, the home mortgage interest deduction, the state tax deduction, and the medical expense deductions were reinstated. Each was considered too sacred to some broad political constituency to be done away with merely for normative purity.

Given the strong flavor of political reality that surrounds the surviving personal deductions, it is no wonder that tax policy writers have lately had little to say about them.[26] Fewer writers today forthrightly regard the SHS definition as an ideal guide to the design of the income tax, and all of those few recognize that difficult political and moral issues lurk beneath the surface of the case for the SHS definition. Delving into the foundations of the personal deductions has had a salutary theoretical effect. It has not quieted debate about the ultimate merits of these deductions.

7.9 A SHIFTING FOCUS

How unstable are the foundations of the definition of income? It has been argued that value judgments are implicit in every decision concerning whether a tax provision is intrinsic or extrinsic to the underlying purposes of taxation. If this is so, then "tax expenditures" can only be diagnosed by broad-ranging and broadly participatory moral debate of the merits of particular inclusions in and exclusions from income, tax credits, tax deductions, and so forth.

> Experts can help to clarify the implications of one tax policy choice over another. They can show how one choice favors one particular set of moral, political, or economic commitments over another. They can argue for greater consistency in the way tensions among such commitments are resolved. They can estimate the differences in the amount and distribution of revenues that would be collected under different regimes. But, the ultimate choice must rest with the citizen and not the oracle.[27]

26. William J. Turnier, *Personal Deductions and Tax Reform: The High Road and the Low Road, 31 Villanova L. Rev. 1703 (1986).*

27. Douglas A. Kahn & Jeffrey S. Lehman, *Tax Expenditure Budgets: A Critical View,* 54 Tax Notes 1661, 1662 (March 30, 1992).

In brief, all is politics, and theoretical perspectives are worthless apart from the light they shed by characterizing the implications or effects of particular tax measures.

To this it may be responded that all the experts and technicians could have hoped to accomplish is to show how one narrow tax provision favors a particular set of moral, political and economic objectives over another. That is the point of discussing definitions of income and refinements thereof. If the point of the critics of tax expenditure theory is other than this, it may be to skewer the seeming neutrality of definitions like the SHS definition. That goal has certainly been achieved in a variety of ways by the multifarious positions advocated, and discussed in this chapter, on the merits of the personal deductions.

It seems worthwhile, however, to recall that one of the problems with highly general definitions of income, like the SHS definition, and consequently with tax expenditure theory, is that by generalizing the definitional problem, the theorist may quietly enshrine some values at a higher level in commitment to the continuing tax system than has been fully grasped by the public and the legislature. Henry Simons's great prestige and magisterial touch may have misled a generation of tax law writers in this regard. Although it must be hoped that the illusion of finality associated with the SHS definition has been dispelled once and for all, much that one may read in the tax policy literature preserves the illusion to some extent.

Chapter 8

DEPRECIATION AND AMORTIZATION OF BUSINESS ASSETS

8.1 INTRODUCTION

Just as people are the ultimate taxpayers, so too are they the ultimate owners and operators of businesses. Taxes on businesses are therefore taxes on individual investors, managers, lenders, and employees. A longstanding feature of this country's tax laws is its respect for the legal distinction among these categories of participation in business. Only investors are entitled to take deductions associated with business enterprises even though other individuals may be interested in the outcome and share in the gross or net profits.

A principal type of business deduction allows owners to recover their capital investment to the extent that it is considered to be used up in the process of conducting a business. The need for this sort of deduction is peculiar to income taxation. Indeed, the principles that govern cost recovery play a part in the very definition of income. This is because the measurement of gain or loss on the use or sale of property depends largely on whatever allowance is made for previously taxed investment in that property. Thus, for example, we measure gain or loss on the sale of nonbusiness property by permitting the cost of the property sold to be "recovered" first out of the sale proceeds, and by regarding only the excess of the amount realized over this "basis" as gain to be included in income, while any shortfall is classified as a loss and may be deducted from other income absent a statutory limit on the deductibility of the particular kind of loss involved. The tax system requires that we keep track of the basis of property, whatever the purpose for holding it, in order to permit gain or loss to be measured. The basis of property may have to be adjusted more than once during the period it is held in the light of transactions or events affecting the value of the property or its deemed value for tax purposes. Thus, while a cost basis is usually the starting point for gain or loss measurement, the adjusted basis of property may differ markedly from initial cost.

Although cost recovery problems come in a variety of forms—involving instances of partial dispositions of property, dispositions of divided interests in property, events affecting the value of so-called human capital, and specially devised accounting rules—some types of business operation constantly raise a distinctive sort of difficulty concerning the loss in value of property that has not been sold or exchanged for other property but that contributes to the production of new value as part of the business enterprise. The foregoing circumlocution is intended to describe what is usually called "depreciation" where tangible business assets are concerned. Accounting custom requires a business to subtract annual reserves for the replacement of productive assets, in order to ensure that the business does not *overstate* its profits. Income tax laws took over the idea, which was after all a conventional feature of the measurement of business profits for nontax purposes, but regulated the deduction of depreciation reserves in order to ensure that business did not *understate* profits. The accounting rules that were mimicked by income tax rules, however, did not extend to all manner of assets whose value might gradually be used up in the production of profits. Hence, the notion of cost-recovery schedules for productive assets is necessarily broader than the conventions of depreciation for financial accounting purposes.

Not only tangible business assets but intangible assets as well, and both financial and nonfinancial assets may be used in producing new wealth. To the extent that such assets will serve the productive enterprise for a foreseeable period of time, and are thus said to have an ascertainable *useful life* or *service life*, their cost arguably should be recoverable as a deduction from profits for income tax purposes.

But *methods* of cost recovery can be generous, allowing more of the cost to be recovered sooner, or stingy, requiring more of the cost to be recovered later. If income is to be unambiguously defined by reference to gain that augments previously accumulated economic resources, the choice among these alternative methods cannot be left to the whim of the business owner or tax authority. There must be a baseline method of depreciation and amortization that properly allocates the cost of long-lived business assets among the years of productive use. In view of the traditional accounting preference for the straight-line method of depreciation, which allocates $1/n$ of the cost of an asset to each of the n years of its service life, it has sometimes been thought, perhaps by tax legislators and tax policy theorists alike, that the baseline should be straight-line depreciation of tangible assets and straight-line amortization of intangibles.[1]

Cost recovery of business assets for tax purposes has evolved significantly over the years. For the first two decades of the income tax in this country, taxpayers were allowed to claim depreciation

1. Current U.S. tax law mandates straight-line amortization of intangibles and structures on real estate and permits straight-line depreciation of other tangible property, though it prefers to allow a more accelerated depreciation, with greater tax benefit, of most tangible business assets. I.R.C. §§ 167, 168.

deductions, using any of several allowed methods, but applying these methods to useful lives the taxpayers themselves had chosen, and the tax authorities made little effort to audit the results. Then began a long period of administrative oversight under an evolving series of depreciation regulatory schemes. In the 1930's, the Bureau of Internal Revenue began to audit depreciation deductions. In 1942, the renamed Internal Revenue Service published Bulletin F, in which depreciation lives for each of thousands of asset classifications were prescribed. In 1962, a new regime called Guideline Lives replaced the Bulletin F. It established 75 broad industrial and general asset categories and permitted service lives shorter than those in Bulletin F. Then in 1971, the Service switched to the Asset Depreciation Ranges (ADR) scheme, a revision of the Guidelines with an additional element of permissiveness: taxpayers could add or subtract up to 20 percent from the service lives previously prescribed for similar assets. The effect was to allow higher depreciation deductions across the board for tangible assets. And so, this innovation amounted to an accelerated depreciation system. The trend throughout these administrative experiments with depreciation, however, was to limit the discretion of business operators to choose their own useful lives, and to pay for the administrative confiscation of that discretion by allowing more generous depreciation.

Finally, in 1981 Congress itself got into the act, by adopting the Accelerated Cost Recovery System (ACRS).[2] The Code now prescribes what is a reasonable allowance for each of only five classes of assets and in every instance permits quicker cost recovery than traditional straight-line depreciation using conventional or ADR service lives. Alternative depreciation, permitting slower cost recovery, can be elected. In either case, ACRS ignores salvage value, the portion of the value of an asset that remains when the asset is taken out of business use. The result is to permit the entire basis of business property to be recovered at accelerated rates over the short periods prescribed. At the same time, Congress introduced *expensing* (immediate deduction of the entire cost basis) for the first several thousand dollars worth of depreciable property placed in service by a business taxpayer in a given year.

The evolution of cost recovery for tangible assets has obviously been influenced by considerations other than a simple concern for accurate income measurement. Administrative convenience and the need to wrest information from taxpayers have played a key role. In 1981 the additional purpose of stimulating the slumping economy was an avowed purpose behind the acceleration of cost recovery. There were then and still are trading partners that permit expensing across the board for most business assets.[3]

It is noteworthy that, where individual asset cost recovery is concerned, our tax laws still treat intangibles much less generously

---

2. I.R.C. § 168; see U.S. Treas. Dept., Adoption of the Asset Depreciation Range (ADR) System (June 21, 1971).

3. The Taxation of Income From Capital 42 (United Kingdom), 96 (Sweden), 160 (West Germany) (eds. Mervyn A. King & Don Fullerton 1984).

than tangible property. For example, the purchase of a patent entitles the purchaser only to straight-line depreciation of the cost of the patent, less salvage value, over the period during which the property is expected to be economically useful to the taxpayer.[4] For this purpose, property is depreciable or amortizable only if its useful life is definite and predictable (there is furious litigation over the amortizability of customer lists), unless the statute assigns an arbitrary useful life, as it does for the organization costs associated with partnerships and corporations, for instance.[5] On the other hand, intangible value is sometimes preferred very considerably over tangible value, for instance, in connection with permitted amortization of purchased goodwill and in the preferential treatment of going concerns.[6] The cost of buying a business can be "subsidized" in large part by the amortization deductions the purchaser will be allowed to take with respect to any defensible allocation of the purchase price to good will as opposed to accounts receivable or inventory.

8.2 A THEORETICAL DEBATE

Against this pragmatic background a debate has nevertheless unfolded concerning the propriety of various depreciation methods. The starting point is the view that the taxation of business or investment income would treat different ventures with the least inherent discrimination if productive assets could only be depreciated on a *sinking fund* basis. The sinking fund approach is founded on the premise that "the annual allowance [for depreciation] should be no more or less than ... the taxpayer's economic loss from the year's [exploitation of the asset] ... measured by the decline in the present value of anticipated receipts [from the asset] which takes place between the beginning and the end of the taxable year."[7] Thus, the proper depreciation deduction is the difference between the present value of the remaining *income stream* from the business use of the asset, determined at the beginning of the year, and the present value of the remaining income stream, determined at the end of the year. The sinking-fund analysis is sometimes referred to as *economic depreciation*. More precisely, economic depreciation is the actual decline in value of a productive asset over a period of time. Since the value of a productive asset is generally thought to be best defined as the present value of the remaining income stream from that asset, economic depreciation becomes equivalent to sinking-fund depreciation.[8]

An illustration of sinking-fund depreciation that has figured in several discussions of depreciation methods is given in Professor Marvin Chirelstein's wonderful treatise. Consider a machine purchased for

4. I.R.C. § 167(a).

5. Id. §§ 248, 709.

6. Martin J. Gregorcich, *Amortization of Intangibles: A Reassessment of the Tax Treatment of Purchased Goodwill*, 28 Tax Law. 251, 254–71 (1975); George Mundstock, *Taxation of Business Intangible Capi-*

tal, 135 U. Penn. L. Rev. 1179, 1192–99 (1987).

7. Marvin Chirelstein, Federal Income Taxation 143 (6th ed. 1991).

8. William D. Andrews, Basic Federal Income Taxation 807–10 (4th ed. 1991).

$4,000 at the start of year one. The purchaser, who owns a business, estimates that the machine will produce $1,200 in business proceeds in a lump sum at year's end for each of five years. She anticipates that the machine will not require repair or maintenance and that its value will be completely exhausted after five years. It turns out that the owner's expected rate of return on the machine is just more than 15%. Fifteen percent is the discount rate that yields the present value of the expected $1,200 per year income stream, given the $4,000 purchase price. What this means is that the present values (purchase prices) as of the beginning of the first year of the expected returns for each of the five years, add up to $4,000, if we divide $4,000 into parts that yield these expected returns at 15% interest compounded annually. Thus, for example, the purchase price of the first year's expected return of $1,200 is $1,045, because one year's interest on this amount at 15% is roughly $155, and the sum of $1,045 and $155 is $1,200. Similarly, the purchase price of the second year's expected return of $1,200 is $905, because two years' interest on this amount at 15%, compounded at the end of the first year, is roughly $295, and the sum of $905 and $295 is $1,200. And so on.

To illustrate how sinking-fund depreciation is computed in this case, Professor Chirelstein offers the following schedule: [9]

	Present Value of Investment	Present Value of Remaining Payments					Annual Loss in Present Value
		1	2	3	4	5	
Start of Year 1	$4,000	1,045	905	790	687	573	
End of Year 1	3,427		1,045	905	790	687	$573
End of Year 2	2,780			1,045	905	790	687
End of Year 3	1,950				1,045	905	790
End of Year 4	1,045					1,045	905
End of Year 5	–0–						1,045
						Total	$4,000.

Now what may not at first be apparent about the sinking-fund depreciation of an asset is that if the same revenue is anticipated from each year's use of the asset, and the discount rate is assumed not to vary, the loss in value of the asset is much smaller in the first year and larger thereafter. In other words, depreciation deductions start small and increase with time. This can be seen from Professor Chirelstein's schedule of the present value of remaining payments. After the first year's use of the asset—and receipt of $1,200 in revenue—the present values of the remaining payments for the next four years are $1,045, $905, $790 and $687, for a total of $3,427. Thus, the asset loses only $573 in value during the first year, and this is the amount that should be treated as its depreciation or economic decline in value. Obviously, the sinking-fund approach represents less rapid cost recovery than even

9. Marvin Chirelstein, Federal Income Taxation 143 (6th ed. 1991)

the straight-line method, which allocates an equal part of the total value of the depreciable asset to each year of its use.[10]

Sinking-fund depreciation is the mirror image of the way in which a bank amortizes the principal amount of a level-payment mortgage loan. Each payment is divided into a principal component and an interest component. The principal portion of early payments is smaller (in a thirty-year conventional mortgage, *much* smaller) than the interest portion. The principal portion is the bank's recovery of its loaned capital. Similarly, the relatively small economic depreciation amount assigned to early years on the sinking-fund approach is the taxpayer's recovery of her tax investment or basis.

There are numerous administrative and nontax policy reasons for deviating from an equation of tax depreciation with economic depreciation. As has been noted, the government may find that it is wise to give up accuracy in the measurement of economic depreciation for a cooperative taxpaying public. Tax depreciation may also be skewed in favor of investment in order to promote economic growth. But it has been held (indeed, a majority of tax experts probably hold) that, apart from these considerations, sinking-fund depreciation is "true" depreciation and should be at least the baseline for tax depreciation schedules. Funny, that it never has been, and that straight-line depreciation seems to hold that beloved place in the hearts of tax collectors.

In a famous analysis of the pros and cons of accelerated depreciation, Professor Douglas Kahn argued that the foregoing account of the normative status of sinking-fund depreciation is all wrong.[11] His argument is both a challenge to the equation of sinking-fund depreciation with economic depreciation and a challenge to all idealization of the concept of income. Professor Kahn is one of the foremost critics of the idea that tax expenditures can be distinguished in an objective fashion. He believes that all definitions of income reflect decisions on a variety of social and political as well as economic topics. What we may consider the best definition of depreciation for tax purposes, in his view, is just another of these loaded, value-judgment-laden decisions.

Briefly, Professor Kahn's position is that proper depreciation of an asset should allocate that part of the asset's purchase price to each year that corresponds to the present value of the income stream expected in that year. This exactly reverses the sinking-fund approach. In Profes-

---

10. For those versed in tax depreciation accounting, it is necessary to add that throughout this discussion straight-line depreciation is assumed to allow equal deductions in each year beginning with that in which the asset is placed in service, just as if assets were always placed in service on the first day of a tax year. Since assets are not really always placed in service on the first day of a tax year, tax rules provide various "conventions" limiting the owner of a depreciable asset to only a portion of the full depreciation deduction for

the first year of service. One such convention, the "half-year convention," allows half the usual annual allowance, giving the hypothetical treatment of full depreciation for an asset placed in service at the middle of the tax year.

11. Douglas A. Kahn, *Accelerated Depreciation—Tax Expenditure or Proper Allowance for Measuring Net Income?*, 78 Mich. L. Rev. 1 (1979); *Accelerated Depreciation Revisited—A Reply to Professor Blum*, 78 Mich. L. Rev. 1185 (1980).

sor Chirelstein's example, the amount attributable to the purchase of the first year's $1,200 revenue is $1,045. That, according to the argument, is the cost of exploiting the asset for the first year and accordingly should be regarded as what is spent or exhausted by the first year's exploitation of the asset. Following it, $1045 is the depreciation not for the first year's use but for the fifth (or last) year's.

What is going on? We see first that the reverse-sinking-fund approach does not satisfy the principle that depreciation should be equated with the annual decline in value of the asset. Professor Kahn does not maintain that at the end of the first year's exploitation of the asset in the example, the value of the asset has fallen by $1,045. Under current tax law, the sale of the asset at the beginning of the second year for its expected fair market value, equal to the unrecovered cost on the sinking-fund approach, would always yield a gain if the reverse-sinking-fund approach governed tax depreciation allowances; on the sinking-fund approach to tax depreciation, such a sale would yield neither a gain nor a loss.

Second, we should recognize that on the sinking-fund approach the expected *appreciation* of the asset during its useful life is taken into account in determining how its cost should be recovered. At the end of the first year, the present value of the second year's exploitation of the asset has gone up from $905, where it was at the beginning of the first year, to $1045, for the simple reason that the second year's revenue of $1,200 is that much nearer in time. Hence, this temporal slice of the asset has appreciated, and the appreciation is taken into account in the valuation based on the present value of the remaining income stream. This may be important to the analysis because our tax laws (and other countries' income tax laws) do not tax unrealized appreciation of this sort. Although basing depreciation on values that reflect unrealized appreciation is not the same thing as taxing unrealized appreciation—a taxpayer may have to borrow to pay tax on unrealized appreciation but will not as obviously be inconvenienced in this way by slower depreciation of business assets—the two are closely related. If a taxpayer can rent the business asset for a series of rent payments whose discounted value at the beginning of the first year do not exceed $4000 (the purchase price in the original hypothetical), since the rental payments would not normally increase as the asset is exploited, the deductions for rent would yield greater tax advantage than sinking-fund tax depreciation.

But, third, there is every reason to suspect that the purchase price of the asset in the hypothetical is lower than the sum of the discounted present values of annual market rent of the asset for five years, because the outright purchase of the asset gives the purchaser the benefit of implicit untaxed interest income on the investment. The purchaser of the machine loses income (at an assumed 15% rate) that she would have earned if she had elected to invest in another comparable opportunity. It is to be presumed that the value of the machine to her business compensates her for this lost income, and the appreciation of the machine, gauged by the present value of the remaining income stream at the beginning of each successive year, indicates the receipt of this income. Even though unrealized amounts are not usually taxed, the imputed interest income enjoyed by the asset owner may well be thought deserving of early taxation.[12] That, however, is only a reason for regarding economic depreciation as appropriate. To have to descend to offering reasons already shows that economic depreciation is not in any sense above debate. The sinking-fund approach cannot simply be called "true" depreciation.

One clear outcome of this debate is that the original attraction of equating tax depreciation with economic depreciation as such is lost. Economic depreciation, we should recall, is just the annual decline in value of a wasting productive asset. At first glance, this seems a natural candidate for the measurement of the cost attributable to the exploitation of the asset for tax purposes. But if decline in value is measured by considering the prospective value of the asset at the beginning of each new interval in its useful life—by looking forward from the beginning of the second year and taking the value of the asset to be the present value *at that time* of the remaining income stream— then economic depreciation is biased in favor of early taxation of unrealized appreciation. A justification for this bias must be offered if sinking fund depreciation is to be considered normal or even defensible. The enjoyment of implicit interest by the asset purchaser may well provide that justification. But, as one defender of the sinking-fund approach has put it: "Misunderstanding ... can arise if the equation of [tax depreciation with economic or sinking-fund depreciation] is allowed to overwhelm the point that the sinking-fund notion ultimately rests on the imputation of interest."[13]

It is worthwhile to review the role of the doctrine of realization in some of the foregoing arguments. If imputed interest is the foundation of sinking-fund depreciation, that foundation may seem to beg the question whether taxpayers should be taxed on accrued as opposed to actually received gains. Under our tax laws, some taxpayers are authorized to use the *cash receipts and disbursements method of accounting* (usually referred to as the "cash method" for brevity). The cash method does not require that amounts to which a taxpayer is entitled be included in income until the year of their actual or constructive receipt. It does require that amounts received be included in income even though the taxpayer's legal right to these amounts may still be unsettled in certain ways. In other words, whether income is properly booked in a certain taxable year depends primarily on whether the taxpayer has control of the income during that year and not on the time when rights to the income vest or become fixed. Taxpayers may also elect the *accrual method*, which requires that an item of

---

12. Walter Blum, *Accelerated Depreciation: A Proper Allowance for Measuring Net Income?!!*, 78 Mich. L. Rev. 1172 (1980).

13. *Id.* at 1183.

income be taken into account when the right to it becomes fixed and the amount can be determined with reasonable accuracy. Many businesses are required to use the accrual method. Other accounting methods may also be devised with the approval of the tax authorities. Given this variety, it may be wondered how the bias of sinking-fund depreciation in favor of early accrual of implicit income can be considered normal.[14] Are there not in fact several available norms, some of them paradoxically elective, for the treatment of accrued but uncaptured gains?

14.   Kahn, supra note 11, at 9–10, 40–43.

Chapter 9

THE CASE FOR A CONSUMPTION TAX

9.1 BASIC IDEAS AND ARGUMENTS

The conviction that people should be taxed in accordance with what they take away from society rather than with what they bring to it has had a long career. Although usage varies, for the moment we may refer to the relevant subtractions from the common pool[1] as "consumption," and to additions as "income." If consumption is roughly what one spends, income is the sum of one's spending and saving. A very distinguished band of tax theorists—Thomas Hobbes, John Stuart Mill, Alfred Marshall, Alexandre Pigou, Irving Fisher, Nicholas Kaldor, and the United States Treasury among other authorities—have strenuously advocated a consumption tax. With the exception of Hobbes, all were prompted to do so by the contrast between a tax on consumption and a tax on income, whether consumed or not. It is still chiefly as an income tax alternative that a consumption tax seems attractive to its admirers.

If "income" is defined in the modern way, an income tax by definition falls on the sum of one's spending and saving. Saving is putting off until tomorrow the option of consuming what is now at one's disposal, and so, it is sometimes argued, a tax on both spending and saving is normally a double tax on the consumption that saving makes possible. There is an immediate tax on the amount saved and later the yield of the savings is taxed as it is earned. On one way of looking at it, the effect is a greater rate of tax on spending that has been postponed than on current spending. Thus, a tax on income, whether saved or spent, seems to discriminate against saving. In contrast, if consumption alone were taxed, and saving were exempted, saving would apparently be treated fairly. Economic standard of living, rath-

---

1. The metaphor of the common pool is of course part of the argument for a consumption tax. See Alvin Warren, *Would a Consumption Tax Be Fairer Than an Income Tax?*, 89 Yale L.J. 1081, 1094–95 & n. 39 (commenting on the use of this metaphor by Thomas Hobbes, Nicholas Kaldor, and Charles Fried and disputing its implications).

er than the individual's contribution to the common pool, would be the index of a taxpayer's debt to society.[2] This "equity" argument, for which Mill usually gets the credit and the blame, no longer seems cogent to many commentators,[3] though it has had some prominent recent defenders.[4]

Today, consumption tax advocates are more often concerned that, regardless of the equities, income taxes may discourage saving and hence distort the decision whether to save or consume. Taxes that favor consumption, as against other uses of wealth that would be equally attractive in the absence of taxes, create a bias in the economy against these other uses. If one is convinced that people acting from self-interest make the best economic decisions for society as a whole, then a tax that distorts these decisions causes economic inefficiency. To protect the efficient, undisturbed operation of the economy, some argue that a tax on consumption alone is optimal. This is the "tax neutrality" argument. Note that for it to go through one must accept some version of the invisible hand hypothesis—that individual economic decisions in a pre-tax world would be to the collective benefit.

A similar, but importantly different, third argument condemns any tax on saving, whether distortion results or not, on the grounds that such taxes discourage capital accumulation, which is claimed to be good for society at all times because it permits the economy to grow. This is the "pro-growth" argument. Note that it presupposes less than the "tax neutrality" argument: it simply takes for granted that we want growth, whether we can know this to be in everyone's interest or not. The pro-growth argument makes macroeconomic assumptions that may or may not be well founded. Studies by economists of the effect of taxes on capital accumulation are proliferating on the bare assumption that the availability of capital is crucial (necessary? sufficient?) for beneficial economic growth. The pro-growth argument for consumption taxation is often linked with these studies.

A fourth important argument for taxing consumption alone came to light only a few decades ago. If an income tax is to treat different income-producing activities fairly and efficiently, it must be applied equally to equal amounts of *net* income. If instead gross receipts were taxed, then an activity that uses a more valuable raw material than another would pay higher taxes, even if the two activities were of equal benefit to society. Equalizing the burden on productive activities that use economic resources in different proportions poses an administrative problem. Taxes are always assessed periodically; they *have* to be

2. William D. Andrews, *A Consumption–Type or Cash Flow Personal Income Tax*, 87 Harv. L. Rev. 1113, 1166 (1974); Alvin Warren, *Would a Consumption Tax Be Fairer Than an Income Tax?*, 89 Yale L.J. 1081, 1093 (1980).

3. Nicholas Kaldor, An Expenditure Tax 80–84 (1955) (explaining that Mill's

"double tax" on consumption was really a confusion based on Mill's and Fisher's tautologous definition of income); see also Mark Kelman, *Tax Equity and Time Preference*, 35 Stan. L.J. 649 (1983).

4. Kaldor, supra note 3, at 84–87.

because of the nature of human endeavors and the problem of collecting revenue when the taxpayer still has it to surrender to the collector. Unfortunately, income-producing investments pay off or enhance production over different periods. A dollar invested today in equipment or in another person's business may repay itself in earnings in one year or over many years. Accordingly, an income tax must allow for "capital recovery" (as it is sometimes called). To be fair, the allowances must differentiate among capital investments that are expected to aid productive activities gradually over different useful lives or holding periods. If there is inflation or deflation, the cost of capital has to be adjusted constantly to reflect this, because capital recovery allowances are otherwise over- or understated. The administrative difficulty of making these adjustments is very great indeed. So far, no country that has an income tax—even the United States, whose tax laws hold the record for complexity—has been willing to face the practical task of indexing cost recovery allowances for inflation. There are related and equally annoying problems concerning allowances for interest expense. But the problem exists only for a tax, like the income tax, that reaches investment *not* dedicated to a productive activity.

A consumption tax does not have to deal with any of this. All investment, since it is not consumption, is tax exempt. Moreover, the exemption does not have to differentiate between long- and short-term investment, because doing so would favor consumption from some income sources over income from other income sources, and that is at odds with the goal of only taxing consumption. Hence, the fourth argument for a consumption tax is in a sense the marriage of the first two. It is the "growth neutrality" argument.

Finally, a closely related argument that nevertheless hooks up with quite a different set of concerns is the "simplicity" argument. A consumption tax would almost certainly be simpler for the great majority of the public to live with. Some versions would be more burdensome to businesses. Others would not. Simplicity would be gained largely by dispensing with the whole apparatus for netting gross receipts against costs and allowances for capital investment, though there would be other sources as well. This advantage is closely related to that highlighted in the fourth argument for consumption taxation, the growth neutrality argument: we could dispense with the complex and compromised cost recovery systems of the modern income tax if we were to retreat from taxing investment altogether.

On the other hand, some of the most notorious conceptual and administrative problems that income taxes face are just as troubling for some consumption taxes. Distinguishing between personal and business use of property is a central example, one that afflicts all consumption tax schemes and would perhaps be even more vexing for them than for real-world "income" tax systems like our own, which give consumption tax treatment to some items of income but not others. A consumption tax must distinguish between personal and business property for the obvious reason that the purchase of personal items is taxable consumption but the purchase of property to be used in a business is tax-exempt investment.

Not surprisingly, consumption tax alternatives also have their own special disadvantages, some of them theoretical, some political, and some administrative. Perhaps the greatest is the separation, inherent in the design of a consumption tax, of the two wings of public finance, taxing and spending. It is essential to the simplicity and growth neutrality of a consumption tax that the tax system should not be used as a vehicle for income redistribution or any other implicit governmental goal. A consumption tax must remain free of extraneous objectives if it is to remain faithful to the equity, neutrality, simplicity and other arguments for its adoption.

Before turning to a closer inspection of the pros and cons, we must first consider the choice of terms a little more carefully. What is "consumption" in practical legal terms? We must also look briefly at different ways of taxing consumption, because there are significant alternatives.

9.2 DEFINING TERMS

Economists of course use the term consumption with great frequency, and they do so in what seem to be technical ways. But let's build up to them. Basically, consumption is using up something of value in a way that returns nothing to the common store. Someone, for example, destroys a valuable object through carelessness. This loss of value diminishes the available wealth, at least to the extent that it exceeds what it would have cost our clumsy actor to be careful instead. Wealth is thus consumed.

But not all conduct that uses up something of value is consumption. That is to say, we do not mean by consumption every kind of wealth sacrifice. Some add to the pie, and these productive sacrifices escape the consumption category. Even though you might say that valuable raw materials are "consumed" in the manufacture of a new product, that is contrary to the common usage of the area. So the purpose for which something is used up can matter when we classify that sacrificial act as consumption or not.

If this definition were to be strictly applied, classifying particular human acts (or events that people allow to happen) as consumption or not would require a scrupulous before-and-after comparison of society's wealth. It would also require a causal inquiry into any change in that wealth, to determine what role the acts or events in question played. If I gleefully destroy the crops I produce on my farm, this may be consumption but it also may not be. The destruction may be part of a carefully calculated, governmentally required scheme of price maintenance, which requires that some crops be destroyed in order to prevent a glut that would drive some farmers out of business and lead to shortages in future years. Or, there is no price maintenance scheme, but a television audience derives great pleasure from the destruction as part of a dramatic narrative.

It could be thought that, even if I am the only audience of the destruction, in gauging whether the result is consumption my enjoyment of the experience should be balanced against the loss. If the amusement of the television audience counts as an increase in social wealth, why shouldn't whatever pleasure I experience in isolation also count? Does it matter whether a market transaction is involved, a transaction that gives us an easy standard for assigning value to the pleasure derived?

At first this may seem a trivial point about whether to regard certain types of satisfaction (utility, welfare increments) as wealth, and hence as consumable. If we regard the peculiar pleasures Mr. Hyde relishes as wealth, then the race between Hyde's bad works and Dr. Jeckyll's good works is closer. We may also have to recognize as consumption what appears to be saving. When Scrooge scrimps on his own meals, it may look as if no wealth is used up, but by enjoying his miserliness Scrooge may have added to the total satisfaction experienced by society and, as a matter of fact, may have withdrawn that quantity of satisfaction from circulation without replacing it. It may even be that Scrooge has consumed more than he has saved. How could that be? His act of frugality has indirect consequences throughout the economy. We are now all familiar with the thought that consumer restraint can contribute to the causes of a recession or delay recovery from one. Scrooge may therefore cause indirect harms. If we could measure them, we might find that they cost society more than his saving, which presumably counteracts the indirect social consequences of his nonfeasance as a consumer, contributes. But this theoretical difficulty about unscrambling consumption from saving is not the only problem raised by the question whether we should regard non-economic satisfactions as part of the common pie.

The pleasure of keeping up with the Joneses, sometimes referred to as "emulative" satisfaction, and the pleasure of wielding the power that goes with wealth are as palpable as any satisfactions our society has to offer. They accrue to some of those who "save," at least in the generic sense of "invest," large amounts of wealth. They do not accrue at all to anyone if the same amount is saved by many individuals in smaller amounts. The aggregate social wealth is less if there is less conspicuous wealth. But if there is conspicuous wealth, only the wealthy benefit disproportionately from it (philanthropy may spread this benefit but can, by definition, only within tight limits).

This point figures in one famous episode in the debate over the fairness of a consumption tax. Responding to William Andrews' claims that consumption taxation is more equitable than traditional income taxation, Alvin Warren argued that a consumption tax is essentially a tax on "wages," in the sense that the tax base excludes earnings from property and includes only earnings from other sources which are dominated by the rendering of services. As such, consumption taxation cannot redistribute wealth. Warren presented this observation as if it were independent of whether consumption or traditional income taxation affects social wealth by affecting the distribution of ostensible wealth (money and what money will buy). But of course a tax on consumption that leaves out the consumption of implicit income from the sheer possession of wealth favors a certain distribution of the wealth society has.

More accurately, by favoring the accumulation of wealth in the hands of comparatively few individuals, it has a variety of effects: (1) there is some tendency for more money to end up in the hands of relatively few people, causing a (politically unpopular) net gain in the personal satisfactions of the rich; (2) the failure of the tax system to lessen the gap between rich and poor would cause some loss of social wealth, in the form of political disgruntlement; (3) business cycles would probably be more extreme in the absence of the dampening effect of taxes on profits, and this would reward success and punish failure more markedly, perhaps causing a net loss in overall utility; (4) payments by the government to individuals that can no longer be packaged as income tax rebates would probably cost more to distribute by other means; (5) the loss in political stability that would result from greater disparity between the wealthy and the poor (if that greater disparity indeed materialized) would reduce aggregate wealth; and so forth. Obviously, some of these gains and losses are among the most difficult changes in social welfare to measure. There is all the more reason to define consumption with care enough to remind us of their possible effect.

The foregoing relates to the indirect causal effects of wealth sacrifices and their bearing on whether a use of resources should be counted as consumption. On the other hand, my purpose in using up valuable goods may be decisive in the classification of this act as consumption or not. If I intend to make something even more valuable but do not succeed—because it is impossible to make what I intended to make or because I made a mistake in the productive process or because competition in the market renders what I succeed in producing worthless—we will not want to classify my exhaustion of the value of what was involved as consumption, at least if negative tax consequences are going to follow from treating this as consumption. We will give the benefit of the doubt to well-intentioned acts that strive to add to the pie but fail.

This shows that the application of the term "consumption" can rest on both causal and intentional analysis of events in which something of value is used up. Unintended results matter, apparently, if they flow from intended results or negligently produced results. But good intentions can prevent a sacrifice of wealth from falling into the category of consumption. Presumably, the relevant good intentions must be at least reasonable under the circumstances. We have also seen that the application of the term consumption may be affected by whether we consider the effect of economic acts on total social wealth or only the effect of those acts on that part of social wealth that passes through the market.

Where the analysis of harms and benefits becomes somewhat technical, tax policy analysts usually lose interest. In the economic tradition it is simply assumed that the distinction between consumption and other economic behavior can be drawn and applied with the requisite degree of precision. Problematic cases are ignored. But this approach may not be satisfactory in the context of tax theory.

Some expenditures that have come to be closely identified with a particular segment of society, the middle class, are particularly hard to classify. Business expenses that may benefit the spender in his non-business capacity, education expenses (perhaps a subclass of the expenses first mentioned), and payments for insurance that protect one's productive capacity are all examples of this. As a consequence, the writing of the tax laws is burdened by the subtler aspects of the task of drawing these distinctions.

How should they be drawn? Obviously, the purpose for which we draw them matters, and this purpose may differ significantly depending on whether a consumption tax or a tax on consumption *and* saving is to be served by the definition. Take education costs, for example. Under our tax law, a student and his or her parents are not allowed a deduction for tuition and related expenses in most cases. This is in part because education appeals to both the ant and the cricket in us; it can involve simultaneous consumption and investment. If both are taxable under the version of income tax in force, then there is not much to be gained by distinguishing the consumption and investment features carefully. At best, some part of the expense should be deductible from the receipts one eventually earns by reason of educational advantages. But it is hard to trace what education contributes to income-producing capacity, and in any event, education almost always includes some elements of current enjoyment (skipping class?). While current enjoyment is not necessarily consumption (one can enjoy working too), it certainly may look like it, and if the educational process does not make the student more productive, what are we to say about the purpose for which the educational expense was paid?

These questions have no solid answers, not because they are too theoretical or abstract, but because the purpose for which we draw the consumption/investment distinction in the first place is shaky, at least in the context of a tax on consumption-plus-saving.

Would it be different if we were going to apply a tax to consumption only and leave saving untaxed? Then to treat all (or almost all) education expense as consumption would bias the individual or the individual's parents against paying for education and would presumably cause society to pay for less education overall. This might be good, if it led to more effective self-education. Great thinkers, inventors, business people and so on once came largely from the ranks of the self-educated; arguably, they still do. On the other hand, the prime effect of education on society as a whole may be to turn out a more uniform supply of unthinking drones.[5]

9.3 THE MECHANICS OF CONSUMPTION TAXES

The main feature of a consumption tax is the exemption of saving from all tax liability, but there are various ways of building this into a tax scheme. Two broad types of consumption tax are those which measure and tax the cash flow of the taxpayer and those which apply to consumption expenditures (they look like sales taxes).[6] We will consider the latter, transaction-oriented consumption tax alternatives first.

The *value-added tax* (VAT), which is fashionable in Europe and has worked well there from a political point of view, is usually a kind of consumption tax.[7] Indeed, for all practical purposes, it might as well be the only kind of consumption tax, since it alone seems to have a chance of being instituted in this country and in many other countries that could only embrace a consumption tax by making the difficult transition from a traditional income tax or from no comprehensive tax. The main features of a VAT are that it is collected like a sales tax and that it is designed to be borne by all ultimate sales to households but not by intermediate sales, such as sales between firms in the chain of production. In these two respects, it closely resembles a retail sales tax. The big differences are that it is collected differently, that it applies more broadly, not only to goods but to services as well, and that it often provides rebates to consumers who do not reside in the taxing country.

The phrase "value-added tax" is probably meant to be descriptive but the implied description is somewhat inaccurate. The tax is one paid by designated sellers of goods and services. (All goods and services might be subject to the tax, but usually some of each are exempt.) The amount of the tax is usually a flat percentage of receipts for goods or services sold, with a credit for VAT paid by the producers of goods or services used in the production process. Each firm in the chain of production files a tax return. A firm that purchases parts in order to

---

5. One of the changes which most infallibly attend the progress of modern society, is an improvement in the business capacities of the general mass of mankind. I do not mean that the practical sagacity of an individual human being is greater than formerly. I am inclined to believe that economical progress has hitherto had even a contrary effect....In proportion as they put off the qualities of the savage, they become amenable to discipline; capable of adhering to plans concerted beforehand, and about which they may not have been consulted; of subordinating their individual caprice to a preconceived determination, and performing severally the parts allotted to them in a combined undertaking.

John Stuart Mill, Principles of Political Economy, Bk. IV, Ch. I, § 2, at 698 (ed. William Ashley 1909).

6. David Bradford provides a more elaborate account of consumption tax design alternatives. David Bradford, *Untangling the Income Tax* 59–99 (1986).

7. The VAT can also be designed to serve the same purpose as an accretion-income tax on the income of firms. Instead of requiring firms to pay a tax on the difference between outlays for production and receipts from sales, the VAT on firm income would be levied on the difference between receipts from sales and costs allocable to the period of production (such as the depreciation of property used in producing the goods or services sold). *See* Bradford, *supra* note 6, at 60–64.

manufacture a final product must obtain certificates of taxes paid by the parts supplier, if it is to escape paying a full VAT on the price its customers pay for the final product when sold. In principle, the accuracy of these returns is guaranteed by the returns of subsequent firms in the chain, because the latter have an interest in not understating the price they paid for whatever the previous firm in the chain sold. The return of the last seller in the chain goes unchecked by this method, but retail sellers are vulnerable to spot checks for the accuracy of the receipts they give customers and the correspondence between these receipts and amounts shown on their returns.

Note that when a firm buys a piece of equipment that will serve its production process for many years, it is entitled to an immediate credit for the VAT already paid on that equipment by its producers. In subsequent years the equipment user is allowed no reduction in VAT to compensate it for the loss in value of the equipment during those productive periods. Thus, as a measure of earnings, the VAT will grossly overstate or understate the economic activity of firms in different periods. This is intended and crucial, in order to prevent the VAT from serving as a tax on earnings, i.e., an income tax.

It must be noted right away that VAT schemes have worked well only when supplementing other taxes. Some developing countries have tried them as the main tax and have found them inadequate, in large part because tax compliance by merchants in unsettled, haphazard economies is hard to establish. In Europe the VAT answered the need for a politically palatable tax increase. So the political underpinnings of VAT tax policy should not be forgotten. What makes the whole idea attractive to its current principal proponents is a clutch of negative features: the relative painlessness of the tax, the neutrality of the tax among competing goods and services, and of course the VAT preference for saving (which in more apt political terms amounts to the fact that the final burden of the tax falls on consumers rather than businesses).

Another reason for the popularity of VAT schemes in Europe is the relative ease with which exports can be exempted. The central idea is that the seller notifies the government when a sale is made to someone outside the country. These notifications can of course be audited. Some countries also allow nonresidents to claim a refund of the VAT on departing the jurisdiction. Trade groups sometimes consider the favorable treatment of exports vital to their competitiveness with foreign trade. They may even be persuaded that it gives them a competitive advantage over businesses in other countries that pay a tax on profits in lieu of a VAT tax.[8]

Bearing these main features of a VAT in mind, we can easily spot some theoretical and practical problems. The model for the VAT is the retail sales tax. Sales taxes are notoriously difficult to enforce in some ways. If an income tax has been in effect for some time, black markets

---

8. Whether this competitive advantage really exists has been sharply debated. See Martin Feldstein, *Introduction* in Taxation in the Global Economy (1990).

may exist even before a VAT is introduced, and it will of course be difficult if not impossible to collect the tax from sellers in these markets who already have defenses in place against the other tax collection and regulatory efforts. Even respectable markets make it difficult to distinguish consumption sales from business sales to people who are in a position to use business property for personal purposes. Many VAT regimes simply do not try to distinguish. They impose the tax on all meals, whether eaten for business reasons or for idle pleasure. They often exempt business automobiles, on the other hand, even if a sole entrepreneur buys them and uses them for all purposes. The simpler form of reporting by taxpayers that is one of the selling points of the VAT does not permit as searching an inquiry into the personal versus business use of property as does income tax reporting.

It is often said that a VAT is easier and less expensive to administer than income taxes. This is largely a function of the number and complexity of returns that must be filed. Nevertheless, the administrative costs of a VAT are much higher than those of a retail sales tax. Every firm that sells anything must file, and certificates of VAT paid must in principle be matched. The transition in Britain from a one-level wholesale sales tax to the VAT increased the number of taxpayers eighteen fold and required six times the administrative personnel.[9]

So why not just go with a retail sales tax? That is the next alternative. Sales taxes are well entrenched in the United States. Most state governments derive a very substantial part of their revenues from them, while the federal government itself collects significant sales taxes (called excise taxes) on specified classes of goods, such as heavy trucks. The proposal of a general federal sales tax keeps coming up.

How does a retail sales tax zero in on consumption and leave saving and everything else unaffected? It is just presumed that sales to certain types of buyers, namely, those that aren't businesses, are sales to households and hence the last market transactions before consumption occurs. Who collects the tax? Retail sellers do, a fraction of the firms who would be involved in collecting VAT. This signals a gain in efficiency of a sort over the VAT, but it should also be noted that the burden of keeping track of the amounts collected and of remitting them to the government thus falls exclusively on a small and possibly resentful and certainly politically active part of society. How much is the tax? A flat percentage of the price paid by the buyer, which is the same net effect as the VAT. Like the VAT, a retail sales tax can be made more or less progressive by varying the rate of tax on goods presumptively bought in greater quantities by those with the lifestyles of the rich and famous.

Two political features of VAT and retail sales taxes deserve special mention in this discussion. First, as has been noted in passing, a federal version of either, for the United States, may not be politically viable, because most states already have heavy sales taxes. The exis-

9. John A. Kay & Mervyn A. King, The British Tax System 129 (5th ed. 1990).

tence of state sales taxes poses a twofold problem: since the states that have them cannot be expected to reduce or repeal these taxes, the combination of federal and state taxes on the same ultimate sales to consumers could face severe resistance from the public, and discrepancy among tax burdens on these transactions in different states would perhaps encourage large-scale tax avoidance at the tax-collecting states' expense. Of course, neither of these disadvantages would plague a transaction-oriented consumption tax that *replaces* and is not merely in addition to existing taxes. But the political means of achieving this are not available in federal states like our own.

The consumers who are intended to bear the ultimate burden of a consumption tax would pay the tax directly under some proposed schemes. All of these are levied on the cash flow of consumers. (If firms were also made to pay a cash-flow consumption tax, the goal would presumably be to catch personal expenditures of owners, managers or employees that would otherwise escape, or for political reasons be excluded from, the net of the consumer-paid tax.) The measurement of cash flow would be based on traditional cash-method bookkeeping, with a few important differences.

Basically, all receipts in cash or its equivalent would be included in the tax base for the time period in which they are received. All cash or equivalent outlays for saving would be subtracted from the base, as measured for the period in which the outlay occurs. The tax collection could follow the pattern established by our "self-assessed" income tax, i.e., taxpayers could file returns showing the cash flow calculation with appropriate deductions for saving. The administrative task of auditing these returns and of overseeing secondary "information" reporting by employers or others who make payments to taxpayers would be comparable to, though technically a great deal simpler than, the current administration of the income tax.[10] Unlike the VAT and retail sales taxes, this direct cash flow tax can easily accommodate different rates of tax for different amounts of consumption. (Recall that the only way to accomplish this with the former types of tax is by setting different tax rates for sales of goods associated with wealthy purchasers.)

A simple variation on this scheme, the Hall–Rabuschka Flat Tax, which made the headlines a few years before the 1986 Tax Reform Act and again as part of Jerry Brown's campaign for the presidency in 1992, would divide the obligation of paying the tax on consumption between firms and consumers. Firms would file tax returns similar to those required under a VAT, except that they would deduct wages paid. Employees (but not, for example, people living on accumulated wealth) would file a cash flow return with a standard deduction and allowances for dependents. The amount declared as taxable income on a firm

---

10. See David Bradford & U.S. Treasury Tax Policy Staff, Blueprints for Basic Tax Reform (2d ed. 1984); Bradford, Untangling the Income Tax, supra note 6, at 82–94; Kaldor, An Expenditure Tax, supra note 3, at 191–242; Institute for Fiscal Studies, The Structure and Reform of Direct Taxation: The Report of a Committee Chaired by Professor J.E. Meade (1978) (the "Meade Report").

return would broadly correspond to the amount left off employees' returns by reason of the standard deduction and allowances. A person who lived off accumulated wealth would of course be exempted from tax entirely, which seems boldly inconsistent with the goal of taxing consumption. Obviously, special transition rules would be needed to ensure that consumption out of existing fortunes would be taxed equitably, if any taxation would be required. Though not essential to this proposal, its proponents in fact came out in favor of a flat rate of tax on both the firm and the consumer portions of the tax base. This feature gains a certain simplicity in tax calculation that has been attractive to the public; the much-vaunted advantage is that tax returns could be a simple as postcards.

Other variations of the cash flow tax arise from different treatment of problematic types of consumption. As important as any is the treatment of consumption that is paid for long before it occurs, especially by purchase of assets that provide consumption benefits over a number of years (consumer durables). Conspicuous among these is owner-occupied housing. Home ownership poses a problem because the purchase price of a house is large in relation to current rental value, the value of current consumption, but a house can last a lifetime and an owner can live rent-free for the duration. Not having to pay rent in each year of occupancy of the house is what economists consider true consumption. Therefore, accurate taxation of the consumption involved would be achieved by allowing the owner-occupier to deduct the cost of the house when purchased but to pay tax each year on the imputed rental value.

Imputed rent computations, however, would be an administrative nightmare. There is certainly no fair way to estimate the rental value of dwellings in terms of widely shared characteristics of the real estate in question. Individualized estimates would obviously depend largely on information over which the taxpayer would have significant control. (The problem is something like that of devising an accurate but fraud-resistant method of calculating depreciation allowances under our current income tax; the Treasury has thrown in the towel in view of the recalcitrance of the administrative detail required by realistic estimate techniques.)

The obvious alternative is to tax the purchase of houses and other consumer durables as if they were consumed in the year of purchase, and then not impute or tax consumption in subsequent years. This "tax pre-payment" approach could approximate the ideal treatment of deduction of the purchase price followed by taxation of the imputed consumption in after years, but only if the price paid for the durable accurately reflects the value of the in-kind income stream.[11]

11. The analysis sketched in the text refers to the possibility that house prices may correspond to the value of future imputed rent. Each year the occupant enjoys a benefit equal to that for which rent would have to be paid, but does not in fact pay rent. The enjoyment of these deemed rental payments on one's behalf is like an

A cash flow consumption tax may therefore adopt either the more accurate but cumbersome approach, allowing the cost of a house (or other long-lasting consumer item) to be deducted from taxable consumption in the year of purchase but requiring tax to be paid on the rental value of the dwelling in each year of occupancy, or it may tax the purchase of a house as if the whole present value was consumed when the transaction is closed. A hybrid approach would follow the ideal treatment of the most expensive consumer durable purchases and require tax pre-payment for all others.

A more elaborate, and perhaps more attractive, alternative is to estimate the taxpayer's lifetime consumption and impose a progressive tax on that amount. Only the present value of the cost of future consumption would be included in the lifetime consumption total. Taxes would be assessed on the basis of that current value, and they too would be adjusted in amount according to time of payment, again by reference to the present value of the original tax obligation. As the principal author of this proposal says, "[t]he particular path of earnings or expenditure experienced by the taxpayer will not affect his tax burden." [12] While it sounds wildly difficult to provide this tailor-made tax assessment for the unknown future income and consumption of millions of individuals, the Treasury proposal includes a clever means for doing just that.

Finally, consumption tax advocates have devised ways to phase in full cash-flow consumption taxation with as little disturbance to current tax law as possible. These phase-in proposals can seem surprisingly moderate to tax lawyers steeped in the lore and detail of the current tax code. Most of the effect of a full consumption tax could be achieved within the framework of the current income tax by:

1. Phasing in full deductibility for all contributions to IRAs, Keogh plans, and qualified retirement savings vehicles generally, but removing all restrictions on withdrawals.

2. Phasing in full exclusion of interest, dividends, and capital gains, except withdrawals from retirement savings vehicles.

3. Gradually accelerating depreciation of business property until full expensing (i.e., full deductibility) is achieved.

4. Phasing out the deduction for interest paid.

annuity. We normally value annuities by reference to the *present value* of the deferred income they provide. The present value of future income is the amount that would have to be invested at a stated interest rate so that principal and interest together would equal the expected income when it is received; the present value of an income stream is the sum of the present values of each installment. Hence, the prices of houses on average may be expect-

ed to reflect the present value of the corresponding deemed rental income streams, absent all sorts of changed circumstances. Bradford illustrates this without noting the artificiality of assuming that house prices do accurately reflect the imputed rental value for long periods of occupancy. Bradford, Untangling the Income Tax, supra note 6, at 67–69.

12. Id. at 90.

5.   Phasing in complete taxability of borrowing from retirement savings vehicles, along with deductibility for repayment of borrowed amounts.

Of course, home owners, banks, and the residential construction industry might not like 4 very much.

9.4 TREATMENT OF VARIOUS TRANSACTIONS

Consumer durables and the line between personal and business expenses have already been singled out as trouble spots for consumption taxation. A few others deserve brief mention as well—gifts, bequests, charitable contributions; employee fringe benefits; and the barter income and consumption implicit in bank checking and some savings accounts.

Gifts, bequests, and charitable contributions are troublesome because they present aspects of consumption and saving simultaneously. The donative intent required for these transfers does not imply, much less guarantee, that they do not reward the donor in a manner comparable to the spending of the value in question. On the other hand, the material value of what is given remains to be used by someone else and is thus not consumed. The problem here, such as it is, really only goes to an aspect of the definition of consumption that we noticed in passing in section 9.2, above. If consumption includes any net withdrawal of wealth from the total available to society, other than with the intention of producing more wealth, then the preservation and transfer of the whole inherent value of what is given away should prevent most gifts, bequests, and charitable contributions from counting as consumption at all. Gifts and bequests to animals and perhaps to some socially disfavored recipients (a demolition derby museum?) would count as consumption, at least if society has not chosen to reclassify these as charitable contributions. In fact, the category of charitable contributions would have a special place in a consumption tax regime, as permitting legislative broadening of the definition of consumption in this way.

If the preliminary definition of consumption is so broad as to include any enjoyment of value, other than with the purpose of producing more, then certainly gifts, bequests and charitable contributions all technically involve consumption on the part of the donor—but often, and perhaps usually, without net subtraction from the total available to society. The wealthy parent who gives money to a child no doubt finds this rewarding, but the money given is worth at least as much to the child as if it had come from elsewhere. It can even be saved by the child, with the same benefit to society as if saved by the parent. Must we therefore tax the pleasure experienced without social cost by the parent? Bear in mind that this pleasure is only caused by the making of the gift; without the transaction, there is no utility or welfare gain for society to share anyway. It seems clear that we must tax this only if the resultant escape of pleasure would otherwise demoralize the public.

Some fringe benefits raise a similar problem directly; all do indirectly. Section 132 of the Internal Revenue Code now excludes from income what are there called "no-additional-cost" fringe benefits. These are benefits that can be provided to an employee without increasing the employer's costs of operation. Typically, they represent productive capacity that would otherwise go unused. It is of course doubtful that some of the supposed best examples of no-extra-cost fringes really cost the employer nothing—free flights for airline employees, for example, surely put more weight on airplanes that would otherwise fly with empty seats, and more fuel is surely burned for each pound added to the load. Assuming, however, that some employers can indeed provide benefits to employees without increasing operating costs, is it fair not to tax the employees on this benefit?

At first glance, the answer should surely be that there is no net benefit. If the definition of consumption is sensitive only to this fact, no consumption is involved. But what about the scandal to members of the public who are not eligible for these freebies? Will they not think, no matter how well you explain the definition of consumption, that exempting benefits to favored employees constitutes a flaw in the tax system? If the tax is an income tax, the answer need not depend alone on the significance we attach to public perceptions of abuse. Even if employees who receive no-additional-cost fringe benefits consume nothing that would otherwise be added to society's wealth, their wealth may be increased, because they can save money they might otherwise have spent on air travel or some substitute for that delight. We cannot reasonably assume that these employees fly just to sop up the pleasure that would otherwise go to waste, and that their wealth is unaffected by this diversion. Surely, eligibility for free flights is one of the attractions of their jobs, precisely because it adds to their wealth.

But under a consumption tax, the effect of this kind of fringe benefit on the recipient's wealth is of no significance, all else being equal. What about mistaken public perception of abuse? The resolution of this problem must hinge on the tax system's response to other perceptions of abuse, and on the comparative intensity of public reaction to this perceived abuse. It is tempting to say that "in theory" there is no abuse. But is even that quite right? We saw in section 9.2. that the definition of consumption is far from straightforward in several respects. We might count crop failures as consumption. Although the farmer planted the crop in order to produce more wealth, that purpose was not fulfilled, and the result was a net sacrifice of whatever went into the effort. If the definition of consumption excludes sacrifices like this, the reason can only be that we do not wish to discourage efforts that may be productive. Similarly, it may be argued, the very definition of consumption must *include* transactions that involve no net sacrifice, if taxpayers might be discouraged by any other definition.

Other fringe benefits raise related problems. For example, employees whose employers are not in a position to give them no-additional-cost fringe benefits, simply because of the nature of the employers' operations, may feel cheated if they cannot receive what seem to them to be comparable benefits without taxation. A sales clerk in a department store must regard free or discounted clothing as the nearest approximation to the airline employee's free flights, even if the department store's profits are narrowed by providing the fringe benefit.[13] More generally, though, once the line between personal and business expenses has been declared not to coincide with the distinction between consumption and saving, taxpayers not able to receive personal benefits without tax will certainly begin to regard all rules about the inclusion of employment related benefits as arbitrary or political.[14]

Moreover, the definition of consumption leaves open a genuine difficulty about classifying some employer-provided benefits. As we saw, consumption does not encompass all instances of wealth sacrifice. Things of value must often be used up to produce new things of even greater value. Even net losses in value do not count as consumption if they result from well-intentioned attempts to increase wealth. Does this mean that a producer may choose one means of generating new wealth rather than another, because the first confers benefits on employees, owners, or friends of the producer, and still not indulge in "consumption"?

Consider the hotel owner who provides a lavish suite of rooms to the resident manager, so that the manager will be on hand to deal with the business of the hotel *and* so that the manager remains a contented employee.[15] Assume that the hotel owner's objective, apart from good relations with the manager, could be accomplished by providing a cot in the manager's office. Is the manager then a consumer of the extra value of the lavish suite? Does it matter whether achieving good relations with the manager is likely to increase the hotel's profits? These questions suggest that, in order to prevent abuse of the consumption tax, we should define consumption to include the exhaustion of valuable things that is directly due to the *inefficiency* of a firm's efforts to make a profit.

Note that this difficulty too is greater for a consumption tax than for one based, more generally, on accretion or increase in wealth. If a tax is intended to apply to any increase in wealth, whether consumed or not, there is reason to tax employee benefits that contribute to the production of new wealth, even if these benefits might escape some definitions of consumption. The same reason applies here that applied in connection with no-additional-cost fringe benefits: accumulation is enhanced by inefficient operating methods that confer inessential bene-

---

13. See I.R.C. § 132(a).

14. The obviously political truce that resulted in current § 132 and related provisions of the Internal Revenue Code is compelling evidence of this hunch.

15. Cf. Benaglia v. Comm'r, 36 B.T.A. 838 (1937).

fits on employees, because these employees do not have to spend other resources in order to get those benefits.[16]

We should also note that the difficulty about expenses that can count both as expenses for production and personal benefits to individuals involved in the productive process may be aggravated by the seemingly harmless stipulation, usually imposed on discussions without careful consideration, that tax policy need consider only the use or retention of "economic resources," and not the pleasures and pains, satisfactions and disappointments that are not "generally the subject of market transactions in our society." [17]   By choosing to ignore non-market benefits and burdens—what economists themselves sometimes refer to as "externalities"—tax policy writers complicate their task. Although a transaction involving employer and employee may encompass benefits both in cash and in kind, it is of course administratively impractical for the tax authorities to measure or attempt to tax the latter.   It does not follow from this impracticality, however, that questions of consumption and accumulation posed by these transactions must be analyzed, even in theory, as if no wealth were created or extinguished apart from the use of cash.   Of course, a convincing theoretical treatment of problems like those we are considering may not be what is called for.   The problems may be regarded as essentially administrative after all.

Thus, the effects of fringe benefit arrangements on parties other than the employer and employee may be a significant social cost. Taxing benefits closely related to an employee's work may provoke an irrational sense of injustice, a social cost on the other side of the balance.   Policing the area is costly for the employer, employee bargaining representatives, and the tax authorities.

9.5   THE EQUITY ARGUMENT

In recent years the argument that a consumption tax is fairer than an income tax has generated more heat than any other argument on the matter, although several commentators have suspected that behind this lie concerns that relate to arguments not based on equity at all. For the moment, we consider the equity argument in strict isolation from other arguments.

In a world without tax, an investment of $100 of wages at 9% compounded annually would be worth $800 after 25 years.   The ratio of total yield to invested principal is 8 to 1, assuming that the dollar itself has not changed in value.   If there has been inflation or deflation, the total yield must be adjusted to take account of that fact.   Interest rates,

16. This is actually a major asymmetry between the income tax base and the consumption tax base.   For consumption tax purposes, it makes sense (though it is not necessary) to insist that society's total consumption should equal that of the individuals who make up the society.   For income tax purposes, it is difficult to see how we

can avoid taxing accumulation by individuals that really amounts only to a transfer of property from other individuals, without net gain to society.

17. Warren, *Would a Consumption Tax Be Fairer Than an Income Tax?*, supra note 1, 89 Yale L.J. at 1084.

like the 9% assumed in this example, may be affected by inflation as well as by tax rates (or the absence of all tax).

Now consider what would happen to the investment if a flat income tax of 33% applied throughout the period. The $100 investment would be reduced to $67 at the outset. Part of the annual yield at 9%, assuming that this was not affected by the general imposition of the tax, would also go to pay taxes. After 25 years, the investment would only be worth $267, and the ratio of total yield to initial investment would accordingly be only 2.67 to 1, again assuming no change in the dollar's value.

To consume $267 worth of anything in the twenty-fifth year, one would only have had to earn $398.50 that year, and not $800 or even $800 minus a 33% tax, or $536.

Suppose that in year 1, when the $100 was first invested, the investor had been able to buy a special sort of consumer durable that would be consumed only in the twenty-fifth year, and suppose that the item had the peculiar characteristic that it appreciated at 9% compounded annually. Suppose further that, as would be the case under current United States income tax law, the appreciation of property were taxable under this income tax regime only at the time of "realization," i.e., when the property is disposed of in a sale or exchange. Then the early purchase of the consumer durable would permit the investor to enjoy consumption that would in year 25 be worth eight times the purchase price in year 1—the 8 to 1 ratio of yield to investment that prevailed in the no-tax world could still be achieved.

On the basis of this example, it has been argued both that an income tax therefore discourages saving and that an income tax is unfair to saving.[18] Certainly, given the assumptions mentioned, you get less for your money if you save for future consumption than if you consume right away. Perhaps this shows the first of the propositions to be true. We are concerned here with the second proposition, which is the core of the equity argument for consumption taxation.

The following objections are worth considering:

(1) If there is an income tax, investors will demand a higher pre-tax rate of return to compensate for the tax to be paid on the yield, with the result that something closer to the 8 to 1 ratio of the pre-tax example may be maintained.[19]

(2) The right treatment of deferred consumption is *not* that of the consumer durable that bestows a delayed benefit without subjecting its

18. Andrews, *A Consumption–Type or Cash Flow Personal Income Tax*, supra note 2, 87 Harv. L. Rev. at 1125, 1167–69; see also Irving Fisher & H. Fisher, Constructive Income Taxation 56–57 (1942) (slightly different example cited by Andrews).

19. Warren, *Fairness and a Consumption–Type or Cash Flow Personal Income Tax*, supra note 2, 88 Harv. L. Rev. at 937–38.

owner to renewed taxation; conversely, it is not appropriate to discount the value of future consumption for comparison with present values.[20]

(3) Taxing saving plus consumption is fairer than taxing consumption alone because under the latter sort of regime the benefit of possessing wealth would be preferentially treated.[21]

To take these in turn: The influence of taxes on interest rates is still not at all clearly understood. What little empirical research there is has been inconclusive, and a priori surmise is really worthless. At any rate, the objection works only if it is understood as implying that interest rates generally or almost always counteract the effect of an income tax on deferred consumption, and there is no reason to think this is so. The objection therefore merely points out that an income tax does not necessarily disturb the pre-tax difference in value between immediate and postponed consumption.

The argument that we cannot reasonably expect to improve our consumption opportunities by deferring them can be very complicated. In one version the issue is whether interest is the standard psychological "price" to be paid *to* a person who agrees to put off his or her consumption in order to save. If interest is instead a function of other forces within the economy, such as the demand for capital, then "the interest rate will be positive even if no significant psychological time preference exists." [22] The trouble with this argument is that it confuses descriptive and normative issues. It may well be that interest rates are in fact set by market forces other than lenders' time preferences. It does not follow that lenders should not receive compensation if they agree to resist a bias in favor of current consumption.

Another version of the argument simply asserts that the satisfaction given by a particular type of consumption, say, eating a good meal, does not (or should not) depend on timing. The enjoyment of a good meal today is equal to the enjoyment of the same meal tomorrow, and no allowance need or should be made, in comparing these enjoyments, for how soon or late they occur. Hence, the argument goes, it is nonsense to expect *a priori* that I must be offered something to compensate me for postponing eating a good meal, more than the assurance that I can indeed enjoy it tomorrow—something more, in other words, than the maintenance of the economic power to command the meal tomorrow.

There can obviously be two views of the merits of this claim. The law has traditionally ignored the time value of consumption deferred in calculating tort damages, and there is no doubt something to be said for the traditional approach. On the other hand, commentators regularly deride the traditional approach, with little more than a nod towards the

20. Kelman, *Time Preference and Tax Equity*, supra note 3, 35 Stan. L. Rev. at 649, 655–57 & *passim*.

21. Kaldor, An Expenditure Tax, supra note 3; Nicholas Kaldor, *Comments on* Andrews, *A Supplemental Personal Expendi-* ture Tax, in J. Pechman, ed., What Should be Taxed: Income or Expenditure?, at 151 (1980).

22. Kelman, supra note 3, at 672.

widespread view that all value is time-sensitive: a dollar taken away today and returned tomorrow without interest is a diminished asset, even if there has been no inflation.

Does it matter what people actually feel or think about the postponement of consumption? Some discussions of the matter are framed as if this is the only real issue. Thus, for example, it is argued that rational people value deferred consumption less than immediate consumption of the same kind and intensity because deferral makes the outcome less certain, and so forth. These observations, if true, are relevant to the present discussion only if they imply a relationship between the timing of consumption and the welfare of the individual consumer. More particularly, they only matter if the subjectively felt gratification one derives from consumption is always an unqualified addition to one's well being. On a moment's reflection, this of course seems an absurd presumption. Instant gratification of some, even most, varieties has at best a weak correlation with a flourishing existence. What must lie behind references to people's actual preferences for current or delayed consumption is either a mistaken assumption that such preferences directly determine the individual's welfare or a more complicated assumption about what does determine the individual's welfare. Unfortunately, no proponent of consumption taxation has spelled out what that more complicated assumption would be.

In brief, although the fairness of a consumption tax does ultimately depend on how the timing of consumption affects individual welfare, the debate over the matter has not brought forth any very definite account of this. We must consider this a weakness of the traditional arguments.

We next consider whether taxing saving plus consumption is fairer than taxing consumption alone because, under the latter sort of regime, the benefit of possessing wealth is preferentially treated. Professor Warren presents a popular form of this argument by characterizing the consumption tax as a tax on wages.[23] His idea depends on the theorem that under an income tax a deduction for the cost of property is equivalent to exempting the income from that property from the tax. Hence, since all invested amounts are excluded from a consumption tax base, the tax has the same effect as permitting a deduction, and so excluding these invested amounts from an income tax base. Thus, in his caricature of the consumption tax, it emerges as a tax on wages alone.

This is a peculiarly culture-bound objection to the consumption tax ideal. In this country, certainly, the effect of an income tax would be conspicuously to tax wages (understanding that term idiosyncratically to include the "wages" business owners pay themselves for their services) but not to tax the build-up of wealth. Of course, if a wage-earner invested some of his or her wages, no consumption tax would be paid on

23. Warren, *Fairness and a Consumption-Type or Cash Flow Personal Income Tax*, supra note 3, 88 Harv. L. Rev. at 938–41.

the invested amount. The point is that if we think of people as spending out of current earnings, whether from services or investment, a tax on consumption turns out to be Warren's tax on wages.

But a consumption tax also applies to spending from the one source that is not "wages," namely, accumulated wealth. If the very wealthy matter much to us, either because of the ratio of their wealth to all the wealth of society, or because their status in society is politically and culturally important, we will notice that the consumption tax must also apply to what they consume, even if they toil not, and do not even realize gains. The wealthy are in a position to "dis-save", to spend without getting more. One consumption tax advocate, Nicholas Kaldor, made this point his central argument for a consumption tax,[24] and it is of course a good one, if the role of the rich in society and in the politics of taxation matters enough to us. Perhaps they did to the British public in the years after the last world war. Perhaps they do not matter so much to the American public, or any other nation of taxpayers, today. Certainly, in dollars spent, the most conspicuous consumers among us are neither the wealthiest nor the most powerful members of society. The enormous growth of consumer debt allows the penniless to consume heavily. We still believe that a majority of the wealthy among us are nouveau riche and so likely to be spending what they have just earned. So, for us, there is something to Warren's comment.

What there is to it consists largely in the recognition that if we expect the tax system to level the distribution of wealth, taxing consumption alone probably will not satisfy us. And if other taxes are imposed to confiscate excessive wealth, those taxes will be at odds with taxing consumption alone and will defeat the goals that justify limiting the primary cash flow tax base to consumption.

The point can be generalized: if the goals of taxation are not exclusively those served by a consumption tax, the goals of the consumption tax may have to be compromised. This may sound rather obvious, once it is stated, but the beguiling feature of the debate over whether to tax consumption or income has been the ability of consumption tax advocates to blind their opponents to this glaring truth. There are several other ways in which a consumption tax is incompatible with goals that are likely to be just as central to the voting public as those of treating saving fairly, promoting growth, making the tax system more efficient, and so forth. These other goals include, as just mentioned, the goal of redistributing wealth so as to make society fairer to all (this could of course take lots of different forms, and those who favor redistribution do not necessarily agree that all forms of redistribution are preferable to none); the goal of correcting market allocations of resources by providing tax incentives and disincentives for particular kinds of investment; the goal of making those who benefit from

24. Kaldor, An Expenditure Tax, supra note 3, at 14, 30–41; *Comments* on William Andrews' *A Supplemental Personal Income Tax*, supra note 21.

government pay a proportionate tax, whatever their income; and others.

What is the upshot? The objection that the goals of income taxation do not comprehend all the goals that taxation might serve does not tend to show that consumption itself is put at a disadvantage by income taxation, and that was the point on which the consumption theorist insists. But the consumption theorist wishes to turn this conclusion into a general one about the fairness of income taxation. Without some strong additional assumptions about what is fair and what isn't, this won't go through. To put consumption at a disadvantage may be necessary to other adjustments that fairness mandates. Whether this is so or not presumably cannot be shown by such abstract arguments as that offered by the consumption tax advocates.

9.6 THE "NEUTRALITY" AND "PRO–GROWTH" ARGUMENTS

The argument that a consumption tax is needed to remove the distorting influence of income taxation on people's decisions whether to spend or to invest is attractive for several reasons. Whatever may be the outcome of an empirical study of actual tax incentives, many people believe that a tax should be designed to disturb as little as possible such basic economic decisions as whether to save or spend. A variety of reasons can be given for this belief. Some accept on faith the economic efficiency of untrammeled market forces, which of course resolve themselves into these decisions by individuals.[25] A more limited ground for urgent concern about the disincentive to save under an income tax is the plausible view that saving is essential for economic growth and even for the health of a static economy, while oversaving by society in general is neither likely nor dangerous to the common good.[26]

To the first, "invisible hand" version of this argument, it may be replied that even if the market mechanism were known to be better than other mechanisms for directing the economy, the bias of a tax system for or against saving must be judged by reference to the entire effect of government taxing *and* spending on the psychology of the individual taxpayer. The "rational" person of some classical microeconomic analysis would of course take into account all the near and remote effects of taxes on the consequences of his or her economic behavior. Any advantage to be gained by consuming right away instead of saving for later consumption would be recognized and seized. The "equity" argument for a consumption tax attempts to isolate one such advantage, that resulting from "discrimination" against consump-

25. See, e.g., Paul Craig Roberts, *Taxation, Relative Prices, and Capital Formation*, in Dwight R. Lee, ed., Taxation and the Deficit Economy: Fiscal Policy and Capital Formation in the United States 87 (1986). More critical economists have always recognized the nonsequitur of presuming that perfect competition leads to a maximum of satisfaction. Paul A. Samuelson, Foundations of Economic Analysis 204–06 (2d ed. 1983) (noting that the leading economists Alfred Marshall and Knut Wicksell in their day already objected to this postulate, though Marie Esprit Leon Walras accepted it or a confused simulacrum thereof).

26. Kaldor, An Expenditure Tax, supra note 3, at 102–29.

tion under an income tax. So it may be thought that a consumption tax eliminates a distorting incentive to consume as soon as possible.

Even on the classical view of taxpayer rationality, however, there would be other effects to consider. Professor Warren has suggested that the imposition of an income tax may affect the yield on saving, because investors would demand higher returns from their investments.[27] More remote effects of taxing consumption alone include the possible de-stabilizing of investment markets because of the tax incentive to invest more, the potential political distortion that might ensue if wealth were concentrated in the hands of fewer citizens, the destruction of political incentives for voters to favor national health and retirement benefits, and possibly much else. If the potential saver considered all this, the resultant incentive or disincentive to save might be greater or less under an income tax than under a consumption tax; no a priori assessment is possible.

Human irrationality probably favors the "neutrality" and "pro-growth" arguments. If part of the immediate and most obvious rewards for saving disappear under an income tax, it does seem likely that people will save less. To complete the argument for a consumption tax, however, we must factor back in the remote effects of income taxation overlooked by the irrational taxpayer, since these may not only have an impact on his or her decision whether to save but may also influence the economic consequences of his or her behavior, including the consequences for overall economic growth. It has often been pointed out that an issue of this kind can only be resolved by reference to a kind of economic analysis that is still largely unavailable—one that takes into account all the consequences of economic behavior, both those which are primary and obvious and those that represent the adjustment of other behavior to compensate for or take advantage of the primary behavior—what economists call a "general equilibrium" analysis.[28] Such an argument cannot for the present be taken for granted.

It is perhaps for this reason that a broader brush is sometimes applied to the problem. Even if a consumption tax cannot be shown to be more "neutral" in its general equilibrium effects on decisions whether to save or consume, it may be thought that less saving is bound to occur if saving is taxed and that more saving is virtually always beneficial, at least to one goal that the policy-maker can justifiably prefer, namely, economic growth. If saving is taxed, the riskiness of saving is exaggerated, because at least without regard to general equilibrium consequences the rewards for saving are reduced. If there is indeed an overall increase in the risk associated with investment, the economy will not respond as quickly to the opportunity for growth. This together with whatever reduction in the overall saving rate of the

27. Warren, *Fairness and a Consumption-Type or Cash Flow Personal Income Tax*, supra note 1, 88 Harv. L. Rev. at 937.

28. Carl S. Shoup, Public Finance 21–47 (1969); Jeff Strnad, Taxation of Income from Capital: A Theoretical Reappraisal, 37 Stan. L. Rev. 1023 (1985); Periodicity and Accretion Taxation: Norms and Implementation, 99 Yale L. J. 1817 (1990).

society there is as a result of the tax on saving can be expected to hamper growth.

The principal objection to this argument, in the light of current research, is that the effect of taxes on the pool of capital that is available to prime the pump and assist economic growth is entirely in doubt.[29] Saving for investment is not always of the sort that permits the economy to respond to short-term opportunities for growth. Much of what is saved is "invested" in consumer durables—homes, cars, refrigerators. Another portion is invested in relatively illiquid things like land, which though part of the productive process cannot be made to serve potential growth investments without considerable transformation and delay. It has been concluded, in part on the strength of this observation, that no matter how saving is defined, "there simply is no strong evidence that loanable-funds saving can be manipulated by policy aimed at changing the after-tax rate of return to saving."[30]

9.7 THE "GROWTH NEUTRALITY" ARGUMENT

Numerous features of the current United States income tax regime are necessary to solve a pervasive accounting problem that exists for all income tax schemes. A tax on income must be a tax on *net* income. A tax on gross income would really fall not on income but on wealth measured in a peculiar way. To arrive at net income, one must subtract from receipts the cost of producing them. If tax liability is measured at regular intervals, as it really must be under any workable tax scheme, this means that if an outlay to produce income benefits the income-producing process in two or more intervals, some rule must tell us how that cost is to be divided among the intervals in order to be subtracted from the receipts assignable to each. Most tax systems offer two mechanisms for making this allocation of costs.

Capital cost recovery as a whole is dreadfully expensive and disturbing to economic motives. Administrators must either accept taxpayers' estimates of how much of the value of capital investments will be lost over a given period of productive use or prescribe arbitrary cost recovery schedules. In view of the danger of abuse, methods are prescribed for "allowing" the tax-free recovery of most capital costs. These capital recovery allowances are called depreciation or amortization deductions under the United States tax laws, capital cost "reliefs" under the British tax law, and so forth. Even-handed treatment of the different rates at which capital is used up in different kinds of productive activity requires that there be some tailoring of these capital cost recovery methods to particular types of enterprise. Otherwise, the income tax will direct investment towards the least capital-intensive industries, whether these are in net terms the most productive or not. Inevitably, the very need for capital cost recovery methods offers an

29. E. Philip Howrey & Saul H. Hymans, *The Measurement and Determination of Loanable–Funds Saving*, in J. Pech-

man, ed., What Should be Taxed: Income or Expenditure? at 1, 30 (1980).

30. Id.

opportunity for political and legal wrangling by competitors for tax-based advantages. For example, in response to a proposed reduction in the rate of tax on corporate income, the representatives of some industries lobbied *against* the rate reduction and *for* higher short-term capital recovery allowances.[31]

Comparatively passive long-term investment poses a related problem. If an investor reaps the gains or suffers the losses from an investment, not by engaging in productive activity directly, but by buying and selling interests in such activities, or by buying and selling commodities or land, the income tax ideal would be to tax any increase in the value of particular investments at the end of each tax accounting period. The market values of some such investments are readily ascertainable at all times because they are regularly and publicly traded. Other investments, of which land is the obvious and largest problematic type, cannot easily be valued. In response to this problem, tax systems usually postpone taxing the return on such investments until they are liquidated (in tax parlance, until gain or loss is "realized") and exempt part or all of the proceeds of these investments from taxation. The ideal is to tax only that part of the proceeds that constitutes a return on the initial investment, at a rate that takes into account the delay in taxing any appreciation that occurs in earlier tax accounting periods. For example, if a piece of land purchased for $5,000 in one year is sold five years later for $15,000, the purchase price of $5,000 (or its equivalent in current dollars) should be subtracted from the proceeds before they are taxed; and they should be taxed more heavily than earnings from other current sources, in order to take into account the taxpayer's enjoyment of untaxed appreciation during years 1 through 4. Since investment values in the currency of the country may become inflated or deflated, the initial cost should be adjusted accordingly. Matters become more complicated still if outlays are made to protect or increase the value of investments while they are held, if investments are divided up and sold in smaller units, and so forth. Some countries, including Great Britain, index capital gains from such investments; others, like the United States and Germany do not index but tax capital gains at a lower rate than other gains. Indexation is costly to compute; a capital gains preference encourages taxpayer efforts to disguise ordinary gains as capital gains. In brief, the whole matter of taxing investment returns only upon realization is complex and hard to administer.

Capital cost recovery and realization rules would have no role in a consumption tax regime. The whole point is to exempt the yield on investments from taxation unless it is consumed. Hence, it would suffice to measure consumption alone, and this can be done by permitting all investments costs to be deducted or otherwise excluded from the

---

31. Rick Wartzman, *Some Lobbyists Seek Investment Credit Instead of Cut in Corporate Tax Rate*, Wall St. J. p. A5, col. 1 (February 18, 1992) (citing opposition of American Council for Capital Formation to corporate rate cut).

tax base without adjustment for inflation or matching of costs with investment returns.

A related problem for income taxation also disappears under a consumption tax—the problem of tax arbitrage or tax shelters. As a general proposition, if an entrepreneur is able to deduct the costs of generating a profit at the beginning of the profitable enterprise, the yield will be tax-free. Similarly, if the entrepreneur is able to deduct the costs *before* the activity begins, the yield will be subject to a negative tax rate—it will yield a tax saving against other profitable activities, assuming that the deductions from one activity can be used against the profits of another. This, in a nutshell, is the basis for many tax shelters. When, in the early 1980's, it was possible for a real estate investor to depreciate a building for tax purposes at rates that far outpaced the actual expected life of the building, the investor who had other income to shelter could count on making money at the government's (or other taxpayers') expense so long as the value of the building declined no faster than was reasonably expected when the investment was made. The tax shelter provided represents a particular instance of the more general phenomenon of tax arbitrage—dealing in property for benefits due to the tax system and not to the market. The benefits of tax arbitrage under an income tax can sometimes be magnified by borrowing. Since borrowed amounts are not considered income, the investment of these funds is effectively deducted before they are really invested (i.e., before the borrowed principal is repaid), with the result that the tax rate on the investment is driven more negative still.

Both aspects of the familiar tax shelter are eliminated under a consumption tax. Investment triggers no tax consequences at all, and hence cannot trigger a tax saving. Given the urgency of the legislative campaign to end tax shelters in this country, this advantage of consumption taxation is perhaps the most important.

9.8 PARTIAL IMPLEMENTATION OF A CONSUMPTION TAX

The contrasts between consumption and income taxation with which the classical debate is concerned arise between pure forms of the two alternative tax schemes. To the extent that a tax system combines elements of consumption and income taxation, the net effect on saving would be blurred; the superimposition of a VAT on as massive an income tax as our present one would have only an obscure effect on saving, one so obscure as not to be empirically ascertainable. Nevertheless, consumption tax advocates often argue for partial implementation of a consumption tax, e.g., exemption of invested amounts from income taxation with no change elsewhere in the tax system,[32] or a tax on consumption alone to be levied in addition to existing taxes.[33]

32. See, e.g., Hans–Werner Sinn, Capital Income Taxation and International Resource Allocation (1989).

33. William D. Andrews, *A Supplemental Personal Expenditure Tax*, in J. Pech-man, ed., What Should Be Taxed: Income or Expenditure? 127 (1980).

Proposals of this sort are not usually premised on the full panoply of arguments for a consumption tax. Usually, they are designed only to provide one or another of the advantages discussed in the principal arguments surveyed in this chapter. Thus, when these proposals are taken into account, the debate about the merits of consumption taxation takes on kaleidoscopic complexity, because consumption tax advocates differ strenuously over the equity and practicality of hybrid consumption-and-income taxes.[34] The debate over the hybrids is not very rewarding, and so this summary will ignore its details.

9.9 CONCLUSION

The comparative success of the VAT in Europe along with the continuing interest of experts in the theoretical advantages of consumption taxation make it likely that consumption tax proposals will continue to surface in national debates about tax reform and simplification. Much of the argument has by now been reduced to short-hand terms by the experts. While the transition to a pure consumption tax would be highly visible to voters and create great uncertainty for government budgets, both pure consumption tax schemes and the introduction of further consumption-tax elements into the current hybrid tax will continue to provide a backdrop for the analysis of tax policy issues raised by current tax regimes.[35]

34. See, e.g., Kaldor, *Comments on Andrews*, supra note 21, at 151, and Klein, *Comments on Andrews*, in Joseph Pechman, ed., What Should Be Taxed: Income or Expenditure?, at 157 (1980).

35. Kay and King illustrate the sort of discussion to which the "binocular" vision of existing tax systems in terms of pure consumption and pure income tax alternatives leads. Kay and King, supra note 9, at 94–102.

Chapter 10

TAXES AND PUBLIC DEBT

10.1 DOES DEBT MATTER?

What to make of their abiding and growing national debts is one of the most pressing and difficult questions for tax policy both in poorer countries and in the prosperous nations of the "developed" world. Everywhere it is a platitude that the financial deficits of national governments amount to passing problems on to future generations and indeed undermine current prosperity, with incalculable effects on otherwise thriving economies (and otherwise reasonably constructed tax systems). But the frequency with which these apparent truths have to be repeated suggests that the majority of the population do not believe the obvious or that the obvious is suspect.

In order to see whether and, if so, why there is a tax policy problem about national debt, a few elementary propositions need to be examined. First, it is common for tax theory discussions to touch upon "Ricardo's theorem." This label is sometimes given to the observation that since the purpose of taxation is not literally to raise money for governmental use but to suppress private use of a part of the social wealth so that public use can be made of it, taxing and borrowing are, within some limits, equivalent means of doing the same job. Consider a community whose economy regularly produces at least a certain aggregate income, distributed among individuals by the free play of markets. The role of government is to provide things the markets happen not to provide. Those things cost something. Government may obtain the wherewithal by confiscating it (or the things to be provided, if the point is merely redistribution) or by borrowing it. If government finances its activities by borrowing, it may have to borrow more in order to pay interest on the debt. But the goal of taking economic resources out of private circulation and devoting them to public goals can as directly be achieved in this way as by transferring ownership of the resources to government outright. And any interest paid to members of the society whose government is doing the borrowing goes back into private hands to remain available for private productive use.

Common sense (see also sections 2.2 and 5.3 above) will caution that this theorem holds true only under very limited circumstances. Taxing and borrowing may be equivalent in a practical way only as long as government ultimately claims title to resources with which to retire any debt it may have taken on in the short run. Several considerations point to this.

First, if debt is allowed to build up, interest payments begin to raise the cost of further borrowing higher and higher, because would-be *private* borrowers have to bid up the price of loanable funds and government has to trump that by raising the interest rates *it* offers.

Second, a community that trades with other communities and whose members can borrow from people in other communities—whose economy is *open* rather than *closed*—can replace the economic resources their government borrows from them by borrowing from other economies. This can drive up interest rates elsewhere, but an equally important point is that the borrowing government ends up paying interest directly or indirectly to people outside its own community. The result is a persistent drag on the rate at which the debt-encumbered society can produce new wealth. That is part of the meaning of "debt burden" in the context of national borrowing.

Third, government borrowing (or for that matter, private borrowing) affects the trade balance between the borrowing economy and other economies. When the government borrows, there is less available in private markets for those with wealth to buy. If the economy is open, this may re-direct the demand for goods to markets elsewhere. As a result, the effect of government borrowing may be to increase the purchase of imports, instead of damping domestic consumption. And the result, if all this happens, is to worsen the balance of trade between the debt-laden economy and others.

Fourth, a government that issues notes and bonds into private hands increases the supply of financial tokens, the equivalent or near-equivalent of money. This effect is likely to be felt most decisively first within the community whose government is doing the borrowing, and later in other communities, if the borrowing has strong enough ripples. But to increase the supply of financial assets that are traded as easily or almost as easily as money is like printing money. So inflation is another by-product of certain levels of government borrowing.

Taking all these exceptions to Ricardo's theorem into account virtually crushes the theorem into practical insignificance. (Historical note: Ricardo himself realized that most of these strictures apply.) The list of exceptions is worth noting, however, because it is a partial index of the problems government debt can cause.

It is worth thinking through Ricardo's theorem for another reason, the overwhelming influence of the Keynesian revolution on tax policy in this and a few other countries. John Maynard Keynes is of course known for advocating the proposition that government spending can be the cure for the short-run poor performance of an economy. He thought this to be so, largely because he disbelieved what in his day was still an economic dogma linking economic equilibrium with full employment. Keynes, on the contrary, argued that an economy can be in equilibrium with persistent positive unemployment. Government spending spurs the economy, at least to the extent that the economy behaves as if it were closed. Increased economic activity, in turn, should on the whole reduce unemployment. And higher employment can replace the economic resources borrowed by government in order to reduce unemployment. This at least is the Keynesian prescription that initially reached government ears in the 1930's and had wide influence on fiscal policy for the next three decades or so.

As recently as the 1960's government advisors strongly urged fiscal planning along these lines, with the inevitable involvement of tax policy in the effort to "fine-tune" the economy. Government spending was considered the natural first choice of fine-tuning instruments, but selective tax incentives and disincentives are natural concomitants of broad short-run government intervention in the private economy, and these too abounded in the planning and sometimes in the implementation of the tax system here and in Great Britain.

It is now often said that the Keynesian revolution has petered out, and that "fiscal" tax policy—tax policy in harness with the effort to fine-tune the economy—is out of favor. The truth is more complicated than that. At the theoretical end, the Keynesian revolution ran into strong criticism early on. The criticism concerned the basic economic model Keynes offered both as proof of his theory and as a practical tool to be used in formulating concrete governmental action.

The slow loosening of the Keynesian grip on government planning seems to have had less to do with the virtues and vices of economic models than with the impracticality of attempts to fine-tune anything within the the cumbersome and recalcitrant processes of democracy. By the time government economists can diagnose a need for inflation or deflation, it is already too late for a legislature to begin its arduous progress towards the requisite fiscal response. Tax breaks for home construction begin to stimulate home building long after a demand for housing has been satisfied by other means or has receded due to a change in interest rates. And so forth. This sort of observation has become second-nature to legislators and their advisors. At the same time, widely received wisdom has spread similar thoughts among op-ed writers and leaders of political factions of all sorts. The ideal government computer, aware of all needs and ingenious in devising immediate solutions, has become a laughingstock in all quarters.

But fiscal planning through tax policy did not just go away. Monetary policy, in large part, replaced it. The monetarists of course believe that you *can* fine-tune the economy to avoid short-run extremes of recession and destructive "overheating," by controlling the money supply. This general idea is, in a sense, another offshoot of the increasingly sophisticated critique of Ricardo's theorem. We now recognize that the central banks of economically powerful countries like France, Germany, Great Britain, Japan, and the United States can dictate short-run lending practices by the simple means of making money (or its equivalent in instruments of various sorts) available to banks at a "discount" or interest rate that differs from the average market interest rate for similar loans. The original justification for having central banks in the first place was to shore up financial markets by influencing the availability of credit. This role already implies a broader influence, since highly developed economies respond so swiftly and dramatically to changes in the market for capital. The systematic pursuit of broader monetary influence has now become a common feature of economic planning in countries with sufficiently independent economic markets of other kinds. And this serves in part to replace fiscal planning, both because fiscal and monetary planning cannot be pursued independently of each other, and because monetary planning is regarded as less political, limited as it is by the realities of financial markets.

10.2 WHAT'S LEFT OF THE KEYNESIAN REVOLUTION IN TAX POLICY?

In the prevailing fashion of classical economics, the economic tradition as it had been transformed by Jevons, Menger and the marginalists, Keynes offered an equilibrium model in defense of his broad conclusions about how real world economic systems regulate themselves. His model was necessarily, however, a *macroeconomic* as opposed to a *microeconomic* model. That is to say, the determinants of economic outcomes according to his model were not exclusively variables or quantities that corresponded to descriptions of economic decisions taken by individuals. Models limited to such information are labelled microeconomic, not because they do not purport to tell us anything about the functioning of the entire economy, but because the fundamental terms in which the model describes economic goings-on are confined to the "micro" level at which people, rather than institutions or trends, act and react to their economic environment. A macroeconomic model may rely on terms that describe such micro events but, by definition, also relies on variables that cannot be reduced, at least on the theory embodied in the model, to aspects of economic decisions by individuals.

Prior to Keynes, the common assumption among those who cared about the issue had been that equilibrium for an economy could be characterized in a way that would hold good for a long period of time, such that throughout the period the economy would fluctuate within a narrow range of values close to that equilibrium. The crucial assumption, however, had been that long-term equilibrium was determined by supply and demand, without allowing any essential role to money, and hence without considering the effect of money and its value on other market values. In his *General Theory of Money, Labor and Employment*, Keynes argued, based on very general theoretical considerations, that a monetary economy might produce an equilibrium characterized by unemployment of indefinite duration. The Keynesian revolution as it was understood by Keynes's contemporaries ousted earlier views, especially in policy-making circles. Many of the wealthier nations' governments accepted that they had the ability and therefore ought to maintain full employment by managing demand within the economies they attempted to govern.

No single account can be given of why the Keynesian bubble burst. The Keynesian consensus among economists collapsed in the 1960's roughly, and it did so partly as a result of gnawing theoretical criticism of Keynes's macroeconomic model. Working in the now dominant neo-classical paradigm, economists had been working to restore the plausibility of the equilibrium theory that represented the whole economy, at least for broad purposes, as the intersection of two curves describing aggregate supply and aggregate demand. What was new was the thought that if money wages were "flexible," the aggregate supply curve became vertical, so that output and employment were determined entirely by supply conditions; any changes in demand could only affect the level of prices. (Only if money wages were inflexible, for reasons unrelated to what was going on in markets, e.g., for political or legal reasons, would the aggregate supply curve slope upwards, implying that an addition to demand would have some effect on real activity. This view explained Keynes's model as a special and unusual case of the broader neo-classical equilibrium model.)

The neo-classical model is, like all models, open to revision and refinement. It has for some time provided academic support for a monetarist approach to the very limited management of the economy. During the 1960's and 1970's that approach was taking hold within the Federal Reserve Board and among the parts of the public who care about its activities. It would be naive, however, to suggest that the conviction that monetary controls are the only proper controls depends entirely on economic theory and not to a great extent on political reality, which in turn depends on popular convictions about what causes what to happen. Nevertheless, the current consensus shows signs of weakening, if not of crumbling. One of the weaknesses lies in an assumption that has been common to all general equilibrium models—the assumption that there are prices that would simultaneously clear all markets (the "market clearing" assumption). If there were such prices, then as markets approached setting those prices, supply would correspond more and more closely with demand, including labor supply and demand, implying that there would be no involuntary unemployment. In basic neo-classical theory, the full-employment equilibrium for a monetary economy is defined by the prices of real product, labor (in the form of money wage), and money (the rate of interest). The oddity of the model lies in the accompanying assumptions. While it is assumed that there can be only one price per trading episode and that all transactions are carried out simultaneously, so that they do not require money, debt or a banking system, it is paradoxically also assumed that there is a given supply of money.

Monetarists essentially assume that this problematical model is the real world or that the real world should be made to resemble the model. Virtually all other macroeconomists study the gap between the model and the real world, as the source of the model's real explanatory power. They study such things as "rigidities" or time lags between an occurrence in one market, e.g., the market for real product, and another, e.g., the market for labor.

Increasingly, the more powerful theorists (e.g., John Hicks) and policy-makers have despaired of the improvement of the neoclassical model unless its market clearing assumption can be modified—unless something more like the real world with contracts as well as instantaneous transactions can be introduced into the model. This is a sore point largely because of the nature and functions of money. Transactions that are assumed to occur in general equilibrium models do not need money. They are "spot" transactions both in the sense that they involve immediate exchanges and in the sense that they could just as well be done by barter as by creating financial obligations, for which some means of evidencing long-term financial obligations—money—would be necessary.

An interesting question at the theoretical level is whether giving money a genuine function in macroeconomic models will vindicate Keynes after all. Even if it does, some of the reasons for the collapse of the Keynesian consensus among policy-makers are not likely to go away. One of them is the awkwardness of attempting to manage the economy through the cumbersome apparatus of a modern pluralistic democracy in which news travels instantaneously. Adjustments to legislation can happen too fast for the legislation to have its desired effect, while legislation, because of greatly overheated lobbying processes and one-issue voting by the public, grinds exceeding slow. The result is sometimes, perhaps always if current political wisdom is believed, that legislation provides needed correctives to market inefficiencies too late or too early for them to be effective. But rehabilitating Keynes's theoretical position could provide a different sort of contribution to the debate over the use of government debt. This touches on the reasons for thinking that debt is a burden to future generations, and in order to explore that subject it is worthwhile to return for a moment to Ricardo's theorem.[1]

10.3 THE "BURDEN" OF THE PUBLIC DEBT

It is now commonly said, virtually without dissent, both by academic economists and by political journalists that public debt is a detriment to our immediate future and to future generations. The

---

1. See Joseph Minarik, *Countercyclical Fiscal Policy: In Theory, and In Congress*, 44 Nat'l Tax J. 251 (1991).

immediate and longer term effects of public debt may seem to be part of a single malign phenomenon, but there are different reasons for worrying about the two. Much that is written today about the bad effects of public debt on the near future is about the danger of a shortage of capital for private economic expansion. No one is quite sure how capital flows from one part of the global community to another, and we live in strange times for such flows, given the recent reunification of Germany, and the absence of large sources for inbound investment (such as, in the not so recent past, South Africa and the OPEC countries). But theorists and ideologues sometimes have different things in mind when they characterize the public debt as an inevitable burden on future generations, *whatever* current capital needs may be.

Throughout the period in which Keynesian fiscal policy had widespread academic support, theoretical economists generally believed that public debt had *no* burdening effect on the future *per se*. What could they have had in mind? Isn't public debt an obvious burden on the later taxpayers who must pay the interest on that debt as well as their own share of current government expenditures?

Those academic economists who long believed that public debt, as an alternative to taxation, placed no burden on future generations reasoned as follows. They took for granted as a starting point, not the Keynesian view that economic equilibrium might be consistent with long-term unemployment, but the older equilibrium view according to which full employment was the normal state of affairs around which actual economic conditions would fluctuate. Given an absence of unemployment and a fixed program of government expenditure, they concentrated on the effects of financing that program with borrowing rather than with taxes. By definition, borrowing introduces a gross debt burden, and it is borne by those whose taxes must repay the debt. But the gross burden is offset by benefits that flow from the program of expenditure, and it is not obvious that these benefits will not exceed the burden. Employing a worker today may improve the lot of that worker's children in the future, and government expenditure that bolsters full employment could have this effect. So this was not where the issue of *inevitable* burdening of future generations was focused.

Instead, the reasoning that traditionally led economists to deny that the burden of public expenditure could be shifted forward in time by government's issuance of obligations rather than by taxation was that public debt had no effect on *current* uses of available resources. If a government program uses the resources available now to the economy, this reduces private use of resources. But future payments of interest or principal merely effect a transfer of money from taxpayers to government bondholders. At least for a closed economy—and it was in terms of the closed economy that proponents and opponents of public debt used to base their arguments—the worst that could result from the repayment of government debt was a redistribution of income. There could be no net effect on available resources during the period of debt repayment, because the money changing hands remained within the affected economy.[2]

This sort of conclusion is obviously of academic interest rather than practical import, because it does not account for the ill effects of replacing all tax with public debt: unpredictable redistribution of wealth and comparatively unpredictable additional deadweight losses on the economy that might result from the need for comparatively heavier taxation in one period of time than in another.

The view that debt-financing of government expenditure was generally benign did eventually elicit a more theoretical range of objections. Some still have vocal advocates. Most prominent is the view that all payment of taxes is a burden *per se* because taxes are unavoidable. On this view, government borrowing inevitably shifts *that* burden forward. Of course, not shifting the burden forward has the effect of burdening today's taxpayers. But the message implicit in this approach to the economic issue is that the burden of having to pay tax is a special sort of intrusion on one's natural rights as a human being, a violation of the limits on the social compact, and should therefore not be imposed by one group of people (one generation) on another group of people (another generation).[3] It should be noted that this argument has nothing to do with tax effects on incentives and on resource allocation. In other words, intergenerational shifting of tax burdens is morally or politically wrong, even if it improves resource allocation or heightens efficiency by reinforcing the right incentives.

The claimed significance of the contrast between government imposition of a tax and government interference with markets by less overtly compulsory means, such as issuing government bonds with above-market rates of interest, is a matter of moral or political theory. In effect, this is a corollary of a libertarian view of the moral limits of proper state action. See section 4.3(1), above. As a result, it seems fair to say that the argument makes no special contribution to the analysis of the shifting of economic burdens.

Another more sophisticated account proceeds from an acceptance of the traditional conclusion that public debt-financing of government expenditure does not alter the burden on current resources. It is argued, however, that current public debt primarily displaces private investment, while taxation primarily displaces private consumption. The difference gains significance if we posit that each generation will have approximately the same propensities to save and consume as any other. Then for government to borrow now is to decrease the national rate of capital formation, with the effect that a future generation will not inherit its natural allotment of previously accumulated wealth.[4]

2. James Tobin, *The Burden of the Public Debt: A Review Article*, 20 J. Fin. 679, 679–80 (1965).

3. James M. Buchanan & Gordon Tullock, The Calculus of Consent: Logical Foundations of Constitutional Democracy 48 (1962).

4. Franco Modigliani, *Long–Run Implications of Alternative Fiscal Policies and the Burden of the National Debt*, 71 Econ.

This may also sound like a moral argument, dependent on some assumptions about moral rights to a certain capital stock. Indeed, it does raise a problem about inter-generational tax equity. Why should taxes be the only means at society's disposal for influencing consumption and saving? The answer must lie in a welfare analysis more sophisticated than any yet proposed in detail.

Another account of why public debt burdens future generations directly contradicts the psychological assumptions of the account just described. Suppose that government borrowing disproportionately draws current resources away from consumption rather than from investment. Presumably, this might happen if high-yield Treasury obligations induced more people to save today with the prospect of bingeing in the future. When the savers of one generation grow older and feel it is time to consume heavily, the younger generation may have fewer current resources than they otherwise might because their parents will be selling off government securities, reducing the benefits government can provide to the younger generation. They in turn must either save or forgo investment because they have less in their pockets.[5]

Exploration of the effects of public debt obviously must take into account the difference between a closed and an open economy. If public expenditure is financed by the government's obligations to its own citizens, later repayment of the debt will, as the traditionalists argued, replace resources at the same time that it takes approximately equal additional amounts in taxes. But if foreigners hold government obligations, repayment of interest and principal removes resources from the debt-ridden economy long after the benefits financed by the debt have been felt. Still, the implications for rational planning and inter-generational equity are not clear. It has been demonstrated that internal and external debt both adversely affect the social welfare if the economy would otherwise be perfectly efficient, but that otherwise both kinds of debt may have either beneficial or detrimental effects.[6] In the second-best world we actually inhabit, then, there is no clear lesson. As usual.

10.4 SHORT–TERM ILL EFFECTS OF TOO MUCH DEBT

The foregoing summary of theoretical debate about the significance of public debt cannot be allowed to obscure the fact that this country's public debt may at times be too high for the good of the economy. This is of course to be distinguished from the view that public debt invari-

J. 730 (1961); but see James Barro, *Are Government Bonds Net Wealth?*, 82 J. Pol. Econ. 1095 (1974) (arguing that the effect of government debt on perceived household wealth depends on government efficiency in the credit market and the existence of uncertainty as to future tax liabilities, among other things).

5. Alan J. Auerbach, Jagadeesh, Gokhale, and Laurence J. Kotlikoff, *Generational Accounts: A Meaningful Alternative to Deficit Accounting*, 5 Tax Policy and the Economy 55 (1991).

6. Peter Diamond, *National Debt in a Neoclassical Growth Model*, 55 Am. Econ. Rev. 1126, 1147 (1965).

ably burdens future generations. The dangers of disproportionate current public debt are at least threefold: too large a share of government revenues must go to interest payments to permit reasonable planning in other respects; too great an intrusion into capital markets by the government as borrower drives up interest rates and may conflict with monetary controls that are designed to affect the money supply by influencing interest rates; and government may give in to a temptation to borrow just to cover the interest on the public debt, with a snowballing effect.

The recognition of these dangers is commonplace. The problem with the advice implicit in that recognition is that it calls for political restraint that may be beyond the leadership ability of any political party or individual politician. This is a major defect in the very idea of fiscal planning based on the judicious use of government borrowing. But it is also an inevitable hazard of government budgeting for any but the smallest and most autocratic of societies. Government cannot always avoid borrowing because of the necessity of covering the occasional shortfall of tax revenues, which are inherently not fully predictable. Balancing the public budget after debt exists is a goal whose urgency depends on the circumstances, both economic and political. If the politics of a given country create the danger of fiscal license, making it preferable to clear public debt as soon as possible under all circumstances, the forces that tend towards fiscal license are likely to undermine efforts toward restraint. Prosperity can solve the problem, but excessive public debt threatens to squelch prosperity.

Unexpected structural changes in the relationships among national economies have increasingly had a dramatic effect on the significance of public debt. Losing a war, for example, can decrease the significance of the public debt of the loser; the international need to restore it to political stability can cause other governments to take over the debt of the vanquished or make it difficult for private creditors to collect their due. International perceptions of the political strength of a nation whose public debt is already large can make its currency a desirable investment, thus lowering the rate of interest it must pay on additional borrowing to retire the erstwhile debt. And so forth.

Thus, the analogy between the private household and the public household, between private debt and public debt, is sometimes misleading. Private debt rarely goes away by itself. Public debt sometimes shrinks more or less without pain to the society that has spent the borrowed funds.

On the other hand, public debt sometimes has a more crushing effect that anyone could have anticipated. The Third World debt crisis of the 1970's and 1980's illustrates the point. The governments of less developed countries could not resist borrowing even on the unfavorable terms available in the mid 1970's, when inflation drove banks to take on more risky borrowers in order to earn higher loan yields. Arguably, these growing industrial nations could have outgrown their debt burdens by carrying out debt-financed government programs to encourage the growth of their private sectors. But in most instances, the growth programs would have required further borrowing. When lenders as a group felt insecure, the flow of new loans dried up, and the national debts became insupportable.

Expert predictions of how public debt will affect a country have been as unreliable as weather forecasts. They have perhaps also been as reliable as weather forecasts. Again, no clear lesson can be drawn.

10.5 THE INTERACTION OF CENTRAL BANK ACTIVITIES AND TAX POLICY

Central banks can affect interest rates within a country and abroad by expanding or contracting the supply of loanable funds. They do so by extending credit, or refusing to extend further credit, to private banks. Private banks thus borrow from central banks and in theory repay their borrowings out of what they earn by lending to private borrowers. The extent of a country's loanable funds, however, may be increased by the amount of outstanding government obligations that are in the hands of domestic lenders. This is so at the micro-economic level because government obligations can be traded and invested. Whether the "money supply" is in fact increased by public obligations depends on public perceptions of the effect of these public debt instruments on the economy. While they may be considered valuable in themselves if the government is at all stable, the recognition that government debt can hurt the economy as well may devalue not only government obligations but other financial assets as well. If there is a glut of government obligations, taxpayers may foresee higher income tax burdens in the future and invest less. The increased money supply may also herald future inflation, which would have the effect of devaluing the yield of current investment. So the possible effects of public debt on central bank activities range from helpful to counter-productive.

We should not overlook the plight of private banks, which are caught between the lending arm of the government, the central bank, and the borrowing arm. Government borrowing is designed to trump private borrowing, so the government must offer interest rates on its obligations higher than those on private obligations. This of course competes with private banks' ability to borrow from their depositors. If the capital market works very efficiently, those who would deposit their savings in private banks will prefer to lend to the government instead. So private banks have to offer other inducements to win deposits, such as higher interest rates or free services (which may be tax-free to the depositor).

But whatever they do, private banks find their profits squeezed by the government's borrowing. The profit squeeze encourages private banks to look for higher yield borrowers, like the government and high-risk ventures. Other private borrowers are unable to borrow from banks, because they will not take on the risk of the higher interest rates. If private credit becomes tight enough, the central bank more or less automatically lowers the rates at which it extends credit to the private banks, to induce them to lend at lower rates to their customers. The government, which is always in the unfortunate position of lending at low rates and borrowing at high rates, is programmed to increase the spread between these rates. This weakens the government's ability to function at the same time that it weakens private banking and shuts down the private capital market. (It makes matters worse for private banks when some of their best former credit customers begin to borrow directly from the public who were the banks' former depositors by issuing commercial paper, the short-term debt instruments of commercial borrowers.)

Other sources of capital can of course alleviate the problem. If both the government and private borrowers can obtain loans at reasonably low rates from foreign lenders (oil magnates, international criminals), the strain on the domestic capital market relaxes. By the same token, foreign competition for capital can worsen the strain on the domestic capital market, and exaggerate the difficulty of the government's dual role in the capital market as both borrower and lender.

These problems are of course relevant to tax policy. Government can in principle levy taxes instead of borrowing. The less government borrows, the lower the interest rates it must pay to borrow at all, and the smaller the spread between those interest rates and the discount rates it charges private banks for credit. Another way of lessening the spread is for the central bank to accept government obligations as payment from private banks for the credit the central bank extends to them.

This strategy turns government debt into money. To increase its debt holdings, the central bank may buy government obligations directly from the government. It would compromise the bidding for those government obligations, however, if the central bank did not pay for the government obligations with funds taken in from private banks—money essentially withdrawn from general circulation. But the central bank may also buy government securities on the open market, i.e., not directly from the government itself when the obligations are first issued but from others who purchased them directly. If the seller is a private bank, the central bank can "pay" by crediting the account of the selling bank with the amount of the purchase. This increases the money supply, shifting the ability to spend from the government sector back to the private sector, by the simple expedient of turning public debt into loanable funds in the hands of private banks. And that can be both good and bad: good primarily in the short-run benefit that an increased money supply may sometimes bring to the private sector by stimulating the economy, and bad because the long-run effect of a steadily increasing money supply may be to cause inflation if the economy does not expand at a comparable rate.

Economists label the process whereby government turns its obligations into money "debt monetization."[7] As a means of increasing the money supply, monetization is like other tactics available to a central bank, although not all central banks have the option of using this one because not all are authorized to hold substantial reserves of government obligations. In this country, the Federal Reserve Bank system does engage in monetization. The percentages of total public debt held by the Fed have never been higher than about 12% and are currently less than 3%. Nevertheless, long shifts towards monetization or demonetization (reversal of the Fed policy of accepting government obligations in repayment of credits to private banks) seem to correlate roughly with inflationary and deflationary effects. While changes in the Fed discount rate are well publicized, changes in the Fed's holdings of Treasury obligations are harder to recognize and their effects are felt more gradually.

10.6 ADJUSTING TAX POLICY TO PUBLIC DEBT AND CENTRAL BANK ACTIVITIES

The broad contours of fiscal planning are set by the balance of taxation and public debt. The balance alone, however, does not determine fiscal policy in any detail or even in broad direction. Whether domestic or foreign lenders hold national debt obligations, whether the central bank monetizes such obligations, whether the economy is growing, and whether markets are relatively efficient at the time all seem to contribute significantly to the brew. Moreover, the factors just enumerated by their nature affect outcomes more or less remotely, and consequently, more or less quickly. Public debt monetization, for example, seems to take years to affect the consumer price index by some accounts.[8]

The uncertainties that beset fiscal planning are formidable. As has been suggested, fiscal planning has indeed fallen into disrepute with a broad public, though its champions still influence opinion as well. It seems a fair assessment of the debate over public deficit spending to say that the empirical issues on which the ultimate policy decisions should depend will remain open to research long after those decisions have been made by default. If that is correct, then the conjectural status of public debt analysis simply masks a great unknown with which policy makers and the public have to deal. Most governments, ours included, have scarcely begun factoring that unknown into concrete tax legislation and administration of the existing tax system.

7. Alfred E. Malabre, Jr., *Fed Assumes Bigger Share of U.S. Debt: Many Economists Fear Shift Will Spark Higher Inflation*, Wall St. J., at A2, col. 4 (March 17, 1992).

8. Id.

Chapter 11

THE DOUBLE TAXATION OF CORPORATE INCOME

11.1 INTRODUCTION

Almost all advanced industrial countries levy a tax on the earnings of corporations that is distinct from other business taxes. Since incorporated businesses are the norm in these countries, the discrepancy between the corporate tax and the ideal of a universal business tax has sometimes been considered unimportant. That is no longer the case. There is a lively and politically influential debate about whether corporate taxes should be repealed or at least tamed by a system of credits, deductions, or other allowances to shareholders that would remove any extra burden on doing business in corporate form. One would have to be well insulated from popular political discussion not to be aware that part of the public is also highly suspicious of the peculiar economic power of large corporations. With this goes a willingness to tax corporations of all sorts more heavily than individuals, whether those individuals compete in business with corporations or not.

Before attempting to evaluate the debate over corporate tax alternatives, it is first worthwhile to consider in the abstract what purpose a corporate tax might serve. One view, perhaps the dominant view, of the principles of corporate tax policy is as follows.

11.2 THE NEOCLASSICAL RATIONALE OF CORPORATE TAXATION

Imagine a society blessed with an income tax, otherwise like our own, except that there are no corporations. Familiar tax and related legal principles apply, so that business owners pay tax on business earnings just as if these earnings were compensation for their personal services. Under this regime, it does not matter for tax purposes whether one works for oneself or for another. And entrepreneurial profits, however owners share them, receive the same tax treatment as other income (including rents or wages). They do, that is, unless the tax laws specify different rates of tax for income from different sources, as did the early British income tax laws.

One might then argue that the "pure profits" of a business, the return beyond a normal yield on invested capital, should be taxed more heavily than wages and salaries. Businesses can be regarded as producing two kinds of income. One is the return that is passed on to investors and lenders to compensate them for the use of the capital they place at the disposal of the venture. The other is the reward of the entrepreneur, who may still be in control of the business or may have sold the right to this income to another person. Because a normal yield on capital and above-normal profits play different roles in the economy, the reasons for which we might choose to tax them differ.

Capital of course attracts different nominal rates of return depending on how it is invested. More risky investments typically have to offer higher rates of return in order to lure investors away from less risky investments. Sometimes factors other than risk (e.g., the traditional preference of a given society for investment in insurance ventures) seem to influence the supply and demand for capital. But if the capital market were free of historical and accidental distortions, risk would be the only factor responsible for different rates of return. Assuming for the moment that we have such a capital market, the "fan" of different yields presented by the market can be understood as a function of some standard normal rate, variable as time passes of course, and the risk attendant on the particular investment. Determining what the underlying normal rate of return is would of course be a theoretically vexing problem. But people might agree that the average bank prime rate, or some other easily ascertainable figure, is a reasonable proxy.

The profits of inventors, brilliant managers, and successful monopolists often far exceed the cost of capital to their enterprises. If it were not so, there would almost certainly be fewer entrepreneurs. Of course, not all success in business therefore deserves the high reward blind economic forces might provide. Above-normal profits are sometimes the fruit of sheer luck. Tastes change, showering gold on a forgotten and poorly managed firm that happens to be the only producer of whatever the current taste is for. The success of monopolists and those who cater to the more reprehensible of childish and adult tastes is in the view of many not only not deserved but should perhaps be frustrated altogether. And the lucky should not necessarily be allowed the full measure of their good fortune, in view of the corresponding losses of the less fortunate; economic and welfare stabilization could motivate governmental intervention to compress the range of success and failure.

Hence, a tax on pure profits might be thought to advance reasonable social goals without undue burden on entrepreneurs. (This chapter assumes that a case has been made; chapter 9 discusses more exactingly the effect of taxation on capital investment.) But how would it work? One way is to tax all business profits at a higher rate than other income. Even this blanket approach would present administrative problems, because once the higher business tax was announced, a new industry of tax avoidance would spring into existence, bent on disguising business profits as something else. In addition, there would be a forceful argument against taxing that part of business profits that must be used to compensate the investors and lenders of the capital on which businesses depend. At least in the sort run, such a tax on business investment would tend to drive capital elsewhere. (Arguably, in the long run, the return on investments taxed at lower rates would fall and the return on business investments would rise, erasing the effect of the tax; but in the meanwhile, socially valuable business enterprises might be lost.[1] This whole line of speculation cannot be tested empirically.) It would obviously aggravate the administrative problem to confine the business tax to profits above a certain percentage of the net worth of the particular firm—with a view to exempting the return on invested capital from the higher business tax. But this would have the theoretical merit of focusing the tax exclusively on earnings that do not provide a normal return on capital.[2]

So far the concept of a tax on pure profits does not appear to be very workable. But administrative problems might be lessened if businesses, in exchange for valuable legal and economic advantages, were persuaded to make themselves more vulnerable to public oversight—if, for example, the owners of businesses were granted immunity from the debts and torts of their businesses on the condition that the books and financial affairs of the businesses be strictly separated from the owners'.

At this point, we let corporations back into the hypothetical world of the debate over business taxes. They complicate the picture in several ways. First, they raise the issue whether the shares of corporate earnings assignable to shareholders should be taxed in the year (or other relevant accounting period) the corporation accrues them, regardless of when it distributes them to the shareholders. Some commentators apply the label "tax integration" to the principle of taxing shareholders on all accrued corporate earnings; others reserve this term for schemes under which corporations pay a tax right away on their earnings, and shareholders get credit or other tax relief for the tax paid by the corporation when corporate earnings are distributed to the shareholders. We will return to terminology later. The concept at issue here is whether corporate earnings should be treated as earned directly by the owners of corporations, and taxed at corporate rates if these differ from individual income tax rates.

If taxing shareholders on what a corporation earns but does not distribute is thought to be unfair or too burdensome to administer, there arises a second problem of coordinating the tax on business profits with the owners' enjoyment of these profits. Except in unusual circumstances, corporate shareholders simply have to wait until the

1. Alvin Warren, *The Relation and Integration of Individual and Corporate Income Taxes*, 94 Harv. L. Rev. 717, 725 & n. 20 (1981).

2. Hans-Werner Sinn, *Taxation and the Cost of Capital: The "Old" View, the "New" View, and Another View*, 5 Tax Policy and the Economy 25 (1991).

corporation's directors decide to pay a dividend. If corporations pay tax on earnings as they accrue, and shareholders are not required to include distributed corporate earnings in their income for tax purposes, there is no problem. But if shareholders pay a tax on distributions when they are received, the timing of these distributions governs the effective tax rate on the corporate earnings. A shareholder who receives his or her share of a corporation's profits in the year they accrued will pay a higher tax than one who receives his or her share in a later year, because postponement of the tax effectively lowers its value.

Matters become more complex when we factor into the analysis the principle that only "realized" increases in the value of assets are to be included in income for tax purposes. The realization principle allows taxpayers in most cases to choose to postpone the recognition of any increase in the value of corporate stock, even if the reason for the stock's appreciation is that the corporation has chosen not to pay dividends out of its earnings. Thus, if a corporation has earnings and does not distribute them, the shareholder can by selling the stock elect to receive, if not the full value of those earnings, at least a price reflecting them. If corporations regularly retain most of their earnings, and the realization principle gives shareholders relatively complete control over the timing of their receipts against these accrued earnings, the tax on dividends will tend to lock in stock gains, i.e., will deter shareholders from selling appreciated stock.[3] Further complications may flow from the interplay of different tax marginal rates on corporate and personal income, but more of that in a moment.

Despite the hurdles that corporations throw in the way of a tax on business profits, they also make such a tax possible in an important respect. People choose to form corporations largely in order to separate their affairs from those of the incorporated enterprise. The business entity is legally and practically separate for many purposes. Since corporate books and records thus highlight the contrast between business matters and matters personal to the owners, corporate earnings are a conveniently ascertainable kind of business earnings. In countries that have corporations, therefore, whatever reasons there are for taxing business profits are also prima facie reasons for taxing that part of the income of corporations that exceeds a normal return on corporate capital.

The difficulty of designing a tax that distinguishes between the normal return on corporate capital and above-normal profits has yet to be tackled by any taxing jurisdiction. Instead, most corporate taxes fall on all corporate earnings alike, without allowance for earnings that

---

3. Delays in the distribution of corporate earnings are made possible in part by the United States tax law's generous postponement of most consequences of the restructuring of corporations. In effect, current law creates a sort of presumption in favor of the continued life of corporations that have gone out of existence for other legal purposes. The "reorganization provisions" of the Internal Revenue Code are accordingly candidates for reform. I.R.C. §§ 354, 356, 368, 381; see David J. Shakow, *Whither "C"?*, 45 Tax L. Rev. 177 (1990).

merely compensate investors for the use of the capital they have placed at the disposal of the venture. It may be thought, however, that the market for corporate stock takes care of the distinction between the two parts of the corporate tax base. Corporate stock will fetch lower prices under a regime that taxes corporate earnings without allowance for a normal return on capital. Assuming full knowledge of the facts and self-interested conduct on the part of the buyer of stock, the bid will be less than the stock would be worth if there were no corporate tax, by an amount that at least equals the present value of the future tax burden on the earnings attributable to the stock. In other words, the seller must bear the part of the tax that falls on the normal return on corporate capital. Although this may or may not be unfair to those who start corporate businesses, and at any rate treats them differently according to buyers' different expectations about the longevity of incorporated businesses, the indiscriminate corporate tax would not continue to burden the normal return on capital but would instead fall only on pure profits. The tax rate might reflect this double incidence resulting from its impact on the combination of expected and current pure profits.

Our imaginary tax regime now includes a tax paid by corporations on their earnings. The premise of the tax is not that the corporation has a separate economic personality from that of its owners, but that by taxing corporations separately we may fairly skim society's share from pure profits. What then should be the combined effect of the corporate tax and the income tax paid by individuals? Is it appropriate to stack these taxes, by requiring corporations to pay the corporate tax and then requiring individuals to pay a second tax on distributions from previously taxed corporate income? The answer to this question obviously depends on missing parts of the picture.

An important element is the relative sizes of the tax burden on corporate earnings and the personal income tax. If the corporate and personal tax rates, taken separately, are both substantial (say 10% or more of the respective tax bases), the combined effect of the tax on corporate earnings and the tax on corporate distributions may be disproportionate to the rationale of the corporate tax. Although we were not very specific about that rationale, it did at least include the idea that a tax on business profits might only be acceptable if it did not deter entrepreneurs from entering the field in the first place. A high double tax on corporate earnings might have this effect.

Assuming that both the corporate and the personal income tax rates are relatively high, the double tax does indeed seem flawed. Several proposals for curing this are to be considered. First, corporate distributions might be made deductible by the distributing corporation. Second, corporate distributions might be excluded from the income tax base for individuals. Third, individuals might be required to include corporate distributions in their income for tax purposes but given a credit for all or part of any corporate tax that has been paid with respect to a corporate distribution. Fourth, the corporate tax might be limited to earnings in excess of some normal return on invested capital—this would take the form of an exclusion from the corporate tax base of earnings equal to a certain percentage of the corporation's contributed capital.

The principal issues of corporate tax policy are now all on the board. It should already be obvious that the rationale of the corporate tax may have some bearing on the merits of the alternative ways of eliminating the "double tax" effect. It should also be obvious that whether there is a double tax or not depends significantly on a number of factors: how high the corporate and personal tax rates are; whether corporations have unique or privileged access to tax preferences that lower the nominal tax rate on corporate earnings; how high inflation is; whether tax-exempt shareholders account for a significant part of the securities market; and so on. One point that needs development before the issues are more fully addressed is the wisdom of singling out corporations, among other possible business vehicles, as a convenient bearer of what is presumably a tax all businesses should pay, and ignoring unincorporated businesses, if that is indeed the design of the combined corporate and income taxes. Let's consider this further.

11.3 UNINCORPORATED BUSINESS VEHICLES

In most countries a business operation can take any of several forms that have distinctive legal attributes. The corporation, the partnership and the trust are the most common forms in the United States, although a newcomer, the limited liability company, is popular in some states. The corporation and the partnership are by far the most common in the United Kingdom and former Commonwealth countries. France and Spain have forms that resemble them as well, and Germany has what American lawyers sometimes think of as a hybrid of the corporation and partnership, the GmbH, while possessing forms more like the corporation and the trust as well. What distinguishes the corporation from other forms is that it limits the liability of its owners, the shareholders. They cannot usually be held accountable for the contracts, torts or other legal obligations of the business entity, beyond losing whatever their shares are worth if it cannot pay its debts. Other forms can limit the liability of some but not all owners. Limited partners of a limited partnership, for example, can only lose a set contribution to the capital of a partnership, although general partners (and there must be at least one) are held liable without any such limitation.

It follows from the variety of alternative business vehicles that taxing corporate profits may affect the choice between more and less risky business forms. In the United States, the contrast between the corporation and other business forms extends to another difference. Until the 1980's, shares of unincorporated businesses were rarely traded on the public securities exchanges. This meant of course that selling an interest in a partnership or trust could take longer, was more subject to hazards of strategic bargaining, and generally increased the transaction costs associated with doing business. Even now partnership interests do not trade as freely as corporate shares. Thus, incorporation may lower the costs of some businesses. But corporate stock is no longer unique in its access to public securities markets. Some partnership interests, in particular, are now publicly traded.

Another distinguishing feature of the corporation, in contrast with other business vehicles, rests on the bias of corporation law in favor of concentrating the control of all aspects of the venture in the hands of fewer than all the shareholders. The statutes that permit forming a corporation usually let the incorporators choose who will make decisions. The general practice is to reserve most important decisions to a small group of directors; shareholders must usually have the right to vote on liquidation and certain rare changes in the structure of the corporation. Centralized management, though no doubt frustrating for shareholders in some settings, is a cost-saving feature of considerable value to business owners. It eliminates the uncertainty and expense of disputes among owners.

A disadvantage of the corporate form is its comparative rigidity. Partnerships and trusts have their legal and social origins in times that were intolerant of formality and unfamiliar with the role of the lawyer as business adviser. Hence, virtually everything about these forms is flexible. Partners can choose almost any division of labor and authority among themselves; they can also vary the division of partnership profit and loss from year to year without tedious and expensive revision of their organizing instruments. Trusts have, if anything, less inherent legal structure than partnerships.

Although corporations differ markedly from rival business vehicles in their advantages and disadvantages, the imposition of a layer of taxation on corporate earnings, with no similar tax on unincorporated businesses, is now less palatable, especially in the aftermath of the limited partnership debacle of the late 1980's. Rapid and poorly engineered changes in the tax law during the 1980's first virtually repealed the corporate tax and enormously boosted business tax preferences (accelerated depreciation deductions, investment tax credits, deductions for expected business debt losses, and so on), perhaps with the goal of ending an economic recession, but soon afterward drastically curtailed the tax advantages of corporations, while leaving the business preferences available to both corporations and partnerships largely unaffected. It appears in retrospect that the tax advantages of partnerships siphoned investment capital away from the corporate sector and into real estate, where the partnership enjoyed a peculiar additional tax advantage, the details of which are not relevant to the present discussion.[4]

4. See Stephen G. Utz, Partnership Taxation in Transition: Of Form, Substance, and Economic Risk, 43 Tax Law. 693, 705–08 (1990).

Despite the recently vexed history of the corporate tax, however, corporate managers and the securities industry are still mostly indifferent to the prospects for tax relief. This has been true for some time, although the lukewarm reaction of the corporate lobby to corporate tax reform proposals during the debate leading to the 1986 Tax Reform Act was especially striking. More recently, corporate managers and shareholders have not responded at all to corporate tax integration proposals with Treasury backing. Some corporate managers, to be sure, have expressed an interest in corporate tax integration. Typically, they have represented industries least benefited by asset-related tax preferences such as accelerated tax depreciation and investment tax credits.[5] The importance of tax preferences in assessing the impact of the corporate tax is taken up in section 11.4 below.

After the desultory airing of corporate tax reform issues in connection with the 1986 Tax Reform Act, Congress appears to have taken its cue from the perceived gap between large and small corporations by moving towards a stratification of the corporate tax regime. In essence Congress made it more attractive for small corporations to elect full integration, taxing accrued corporate earnings as if they were earned directly by shareholders, whether actually distributed to them or not; shareholders elect this treatment by choosing "S corporation" status. While the S corporation election denies corporate owners the benefit of postponing a part of the tax, repeal of the lower rate of tax on capital gains along with an increase in the corporate level tax and in the taxability of gains upon liquidation of a corporation robbed deferral of its allure: corporate income would be taxed at a rate at least as high under the revised corporate tax as it would be if taxed directly to the shareholder. It should be kept in mind too that the shareholders of small, closely held corporations were always in a position to avoid the corporate level tax and include net corporate earnings in their income by designating themselves as employees and paying out as salaries whatever profits the corporations had. The 1986 changes simply made the equivalent S corporation election inevitable for corporate owners who would not otherwise have treated net corporate earnings as salary income to themselves.

Simultaneously, Congress reclassified publicly traded partnerships as corporations for tax purposes. So-called "master limited partnerships" (a term without technical significance under the tax laws) had become a common vehicle for the promotion and sale of limited partnerships that were marketed as tax shelters to large numbers of

5. See Alan J. Auerbach, *Taxation, Corporate Financial Policy and the Cost of Capital*, 21 J. Econ. Lit. 905 (1983) (overview of economic analysis of corporate investment incentives); Lee Sheppard, *Corporate Integration, the Proper Way to Eliminate the Corporate Tax*, 27 Tax Notes 637 (May 6, 1985) (discussing various pressures that may influence corporate managers'

and shareholders' views of the merits of integration); Krister Andersson, *Implications of Integrating Corporate and Shareholder Taxes*, 52 Tax Notes 1523, 1525 (April 1, 1991) (discussing the recently increased use of corporate debt in the United States, unmatched by other countries' corporate sectors, to provide working capital).

investors. The combination of the tax shelter advantages of partnership form with access to public securities exchanges was crucial to the marketing strategy. The change in the law made the combination impossible at one stroke, because large partnerships, once reclassified as corporations, were ineligible for S corporation status because they had too many partner/shareholders.

Thus, the only corporations that should still be paying the corporate tax are those large, mainly publicly traded entities that cannot make the S corporation election but consider it necessary that their stock should be publicly traded—most of the Fortune 500 and similar companies. The corporate tax probably was not a general business tax before these changes in the law, because the virtually unlimited deductibility of salaries and the availability of alternative business forms allowed a large percentage of would-be corporations to achieve the advantages of corporate form and yet escape the corporate tax. Since 1986, however, this de facto disparate treatment of large and small corporations has been reinforced by enhanced incentives for smaller corporations to choose S corporation status and by the classification of large, freely traded partnerships and trusts as corporations.

This brings up the possibility that the corporate tax is no longer grounded in broad considerations concerning pure profits or any other feature of business income generally. Rather, it may be thought that tax differentiation between the profits of large, publicly traded corporations (including the profits of partnerships reclassified as corporations) is proper because these profits are artificially high and made so at public expense. The legal and quasi-legal institutions that create and preserve securities markets make holding traded securities more lucrative, by underwriting the ease with which these securities can be bought and sold. The elimination of transaction costs adds to the value of corporate interests and enables corporate owners to claim for themselves a larger share of corporate earnings than would be possible if they were forced to obtain capital through the more cumbersome methods of small borrowers and promoters.[6]

A similar rationale for taxing large corporations and similar entities, such as publicly traded partnerships, is that of exacting payment for the more nebulous political and economic power such private concerns enjoy at public expense. On nonwelfarist grounds, John Rawls suggested that a principal purpose of taxation should be to break up the political power that accumulates with wealth, quite apart from the benefits the wealthy derive from society or the fairness of leveling

6. J.S. Flemming, *A Reappraisal of the Corporation Income Tax*, 6 J. Pub. Econ. 163 (1976); Rebecca S. Rudnick, *Who Should Pay the Corporate Tax in a Flat Tax World?*, 39 Case W. Res. L. Rev. 965 (1988–89); see also The Taxation of Income From Capital 265–67 (eds. Mervyn A. King & Don Fullerton 1984) (discussing capital investment incentives of certain institutional investors, such as insurance companies and tax-exempt pension funds, that

differences in endowments.[7] Some Swiss cantons explicitly make their corporate tax a tax on corporate wealth.

Certainly, these approaches to the task of justifying the corporate tax are as well grounded as the neo-classical focus on pure profits. They imply considerably less about the issue whether to eliminate the double tax on corporate income. Indeed, since both aim to harvest a portion of ill-defined benefits—free transferability of interests or economic and political power—they offer little guidance on the extent to which the harvest is proper. What is access to a securities exchange worth to the particular corporation? What tax burden is necessary or sufficient to deter the formation of economically based political power blocs? That the answers to these questions depend on imponderables does not mean that they are not indeed answers. But if the foundations of corporate tax are of this nature, corporate integration or dividend relief must also be left to the tastes of the beholder, and there is little to discuss about the merits of alternative ways of ameliorating the double tax.

11.4 CORPORATE TAX PREFERENCES

Another factor that pervasively alters the role and effect of the corporate tax, both before and since 1986, is corporate tax preferences, deductions and other ways of saving taxes that corporations are well placed to employ. Only one of these preferences is now exclusively available to corporations, though several were until very recently.[8] Two problems with respect to tax preferences and the double taxation of corporate income are: first, preferences may turn apparent double taxation into a scheme, positively desirable for some corporate owners, of partial tax shelter; second, if the double tax is to be removed, the means chosen should not eliminate for corporations, or "wash out," the benefit of tax preferences available to all businesses.

Under the first heading, consider the effect of corporate tax rates on investment incentives, given the deductibility of interest and the existence of inflation. It is reasonably well known to economists and experts on corporate finance that the higher the corporate tax rate, the higher the interest rate at which a corporation can borrow to invest in depreciable equipment, and that in general corporations can profit from debt-financed investment at higher interest rates than can individuals. The variables that determine the break-even interest rate for debt-financed corporate investment are: the rate of inflation, the rate at which the purchased asset actually loses value (the economic depreciation rate), the tax depreciation schedule together with other tax investment incentives, the corporate tax rate, the rate of return on the asset, and the risk to which that return is subject.

increase effective tax rates on corporate earnings).

7. John Rawls, A Theory of Justice 277–80 (1971).

8. The investment tax credit and safe harbor leasing were for a time limited to corporations that were not closely held.

At today's U.S. corporate tax rate of 34%, if a piece of equipment has a 10% rate of return and actually depreciates at a rate of 13% per annum,[9] a corporation can afford to borrow at rates as high as 16% compounded annually, assuming no inflation, or 30% compounded annually if inflation runs at 10% per annum. Absent taxes, the maximum interest rate at which such an investment would be profitable is only 10%.[10] Because interest paid to purchase business equipment is deductible, and because the cost of paying interest to purchase business equipment is thus subsidized by a reduction in corporate taxes otherwise payable, the higher the corporate tax rate, the higher the interest rate at which a corporation can profitably borrow to buy productive equipment. As David Bradford summarizes the situation, "the corporate tax system, coupled with income-measurement rules that are poorly related to one another and to the existence of inflation, creates strong pressures on the composition of corporate investment, pressures that are quite sensitive to the rate of inflation."[11] Reality bears out the numbers. When the House Ways and Means Committee recently proposed, in an apparent effort to win election year favor from industry leaders, to lower the corporate tax rate to 33% from 34%, *some* industry leaders rejected the idea as depriving them of any incentive to invest; in labor intensive industries, the response might have been otherwise.[12] A similar split within the business community occurred in 1986, when Congress repealed the investment tax credit and decreased the corporate tax rate from 46% to 34%.[13]

The anomaly of corporate support for higher corporate tax rates is one of the reasons cited by tax reformers for elimination of the double tax on corporate income.[14] Something is wrong with a world in which the nominal bearers of tax burdens embrace them, not out of idealism, but in order to make money at the expense of the system. On the other hand, there is no cause, at least in what has been said here, to disfavor corporate enterprises by washing out tax preferences in the process of eliminating the double tax burden. If corporations must pay a tax in order to avoid indefinite tax deferral, and shareholders enjoy some dividend relief, that relief must be designed not to re-impose the full tax burden on corporate income that has otherwise been ameliorated by

9. On average rates of economic depreciation in various industries, see Hulten & Wykoff, *The Measurement of Economic Depreciation*, in C.R. Hulten, ed., Depreciation, Inflation, and the Taxation of Income From Capital (1981). An economic depreciation rate of 13.31% was the average for manufacturing equipment as of 1981. The Taxation of Income From Capital, supra note 5, at 215.

10. This example assumes that the equipment is 5–year property for purposes of Code § 168, which provides for accelerated depreciation of tangible business property.

11. See David Bradford, Untangling the Income Tax 109–13 (1986).

12. Id. at 230–35; Rick Wartzman, *Some Lobbyists Seek Investment Credit Instead of Cut in Corporate Tax Rate*, Wall Street Journal, p. A5, col. 1 (February 18, 1992).

13. Cathie Martin, Shifting the Burden: The Struggle Over Growth and Corporate Taxation 170–71 (1991).

14. See Bradford, Untangling the Income Tax, supra note 8, at 107–13; John A. Kay & Mervyn A. King, The British Tax System 160–62 (5th ed. 1990).

depreciation or other deductions, when unincorporated businesses are eligible for these same deductions.

The one remaining preference (or family of related preferences) exclusively available to corporations is pertinent here. They concern investments by a corporation in another corporation. The corporate shareholder may realize income or gain from its investment in corporate stock just as any other investor does, but to tax such a gain would result in earnings being subject to corporate income tax both when they were received by the corporation that originally earned them and again when they were received by the corporate shareholder. To avoid this result, the Code contains several relief provisions. The broadest is the 100% deduction for intercorporate dividends from a subsidiary of which the shareholder is at least an 80% owner.[15] The Code has recently been amended, perhaps in response to comments from contributors to the corporate tax integration debate, to differentiate between two classes of less than 80% owners, permitting those with less than a 20% stake in another corporation to deduct only 70% of dividends received, but permitting those with between 20% and 80% to deduct 85%. The resulting three-tiered schedule of relief for intercorporate dividends arguably counteracts what would have been a bias in favor of corporate investors in corporate stock as compared with noncorporate investors.[16]

11.5 DIVIDEND RELIEF

Our partial overview of the reasons for corporate taxation has uncovered several reasons for supposing that the separate corporate level and shareholder level taxes on corporate earnings should be somehow ameliorated or at least coordinated to avoid arbitrary discrimination among shareholders and investment incentive distortions. Not everyone, of course, accepts this conclusion, but it does have a wide support. Recently, the evils of the double tax have been a fairly common theme among some businessmen, economists and politicians.[17] Given that trends come and go in tax theory as they do elsewhere, it is interesting to note that in this country there was little interest in integration before the 1970s.[18]

The goal of eliminating or reducing the double tax can be achieved essentially in one of three ways: (1) by repealing the corporate tax and attributing corporate income directly to shareholders, as the income of a partnership is attributed directly to partners (*true integration*), (2) by treating all or part of the corporate-level tax as a mere withholding tax to the extent that it applies to distributed income of the corporation

---

15. I.R.C. § 243.

16. See ALI, Federal Income Tax Project: Subchapter C: Proposals on Corporate Acquisitions and Dispositions 343 (1982) (Reporter William Andrews' separate report and recommendations concerning intercorporate dividend preferences).

17. See Statement of William E. Simon, in Tax Reform (Administration and Public

Witnesses), Hearings Before the House Committee on Ways and Means, 94 Cong. 1st Sess., pt. 5, pp. 3846–61 (1975); Jones, *The Need For Capital*, 28 Nat'l Tax J. 265 (1975).

18. Charles M. McLure, Must Corporate Income Be Taxed Twice? ix, 7–9 (1979).

(the *imputation* method),[19] and (3) by allowing the corporation a deduction for all or part of the dividends it pays (the *dividend-paid deduction* method) or by applying different rates of tax to distributed and undistributed corporate income (the *split-rate* method). The second and third methods can also be combined. The terminology of the area is unfortunately not as simple as this. Some writers call true integration "total integration" and the dividend-paid deduction form of relief "partial integration," but others apply the latter phrase to the pass-through treatment of corporate dividends and retained earnings. For our purposes the important contrasts are those among true integration, imputation and dividend relief.

True integration, by whatever means it is accomplished, would have the same effect as treating the corporation as a pass-through entity and attributing to each shareholder a proportionate part of each item of corporate income, deductions, credit and loss. Suppose, for example, that the corporation has taxable income, computed by netting gross income against deductions for business expenses and so forth, but the deductions for the year include a large charitable contribution. An individual taxpayer, under the current Code, may deduct certain charitable contributions up to 20% or 50% of his or her adjusted gross income, depending on the nature of the recipient charity. Partnerships are not taxable entities and so do not take charitable contribution deductions. But the charitable contributions of a partnership are separately reported to partners so that they may compute the allowable deduction, in the light of the 20% and 50% limitations based on each partner's AGI. In principle, corporate tax integration could take this path, but the practical difficulties would be enormous. It is already virtually beyond the ability of the Internal Revenue Service to audit partners, even with procedural rules that simplify the auditing process by requiring partners to take unanimous positions on controversial tax items. Tracking down the far more numerous shareholders of corporations, especially publicly traded corporations, seems to be out of the question. (Computer matching of information returns could of course alter that judgment, but judging by the Treasury's own proposals for integration, the government does not have the stomach for this task.)[20]

It has occasionally been thought that a close approximation to pass-through treatment is simply to "gross-up" the shareholder's income by his or her share of corporate income, i.e., to add the corporate income share to the shareholder's income, and then allow the shareholder a pro

---

19. The exclusion of dividends from the income of dividend recipients may be regarded as a form of imputing the corporate level tax to shareholders. Characteristically, however, dividend exclusion does not permit shareholders to claim a refund for *over* payment by the corporation of their tax liabilities on the distributed amount.

20. Interestingly, the Treasury has taken both sides on the question whether true integration is feasible. Compare U.S. Treasury, Blueprints for Basic Tax Reform (1977) (recommending partnership or S corporation treatment of all corporate income as the best plan for an income, as opposed to a consumption, tax), *with* U.S. Treasury, Integration of the Individual and Corporate Tax Systems: Taxing Business Income Once (1992) (discussing this alternative at length but rejecting it as not administratively feasible).

rata credit for the corporate tax actually paid. To illustrate: If a corporation with two equal shareholders pays a 34% tax of $34 on $100 of taxable income, we would divide the remaining $66 between the two equally, $33 each, then gross this up, dividing $33 by .66 (= 1—.34), so that we attribute $50 (= $33/.66) to each. Each shareholder would also be allocated half of the corporate tax paid, $17 = $34/2, as a credit against his or her separate tax liability with the grossed-up corporate share now included in his or her income. If the shareholders have marginal tax rates of 15% and 28% respectively, both will be entitled to credits for overpayment of taxes; the 15% shareholder has a tax liability of only $7.50 on the $50 share of corporate income, and should get back $9.50, while the 28% shareholder has a tax liability of $14 on the grossed-up corporate share and should get back $3.

In order to prevent the refund of all corporate taxes on distributed earnings, only a fraction of the corporate taxes actually paid might be credited to the shareholders. Suppose that shareholders got a credit for only half of their pro rata shares of corporate taxes paid. Then in the illustration, the 17% shareholder, with a tax liability still of only $7.50, would have a credit of $8.50 and would therefore be entitled to a refund of $1.00. The 28% shareholder would owe $5.50 = $14−8.50.

The gross-up and credit method, however, does not work well if corporations enjoy different levels of tax preferences, say, by benefiting differently from accelerated depreciation provisions. A corporation that buys much equipment may reduce its taxable income disproportionately by comparison with a corporation that buys none, since by definition accelerated depreciation outpaces the actual cost of the capital consumed in operations. If the tax preference is justified, the disproportionate allowance for capital costs is a good thing, and should be preserved in the tax relief to shareholders for corporate tax paid. We saw that, in the absence of such tax preferences, it works to gross up the shareholder's portion of corporate income by the corporate tax rate (i.e., to divide the pro rata share of post-tax corporate earnings by 100%—the corporate tax rate).

Grossing up by the corporate tax rate, however, does not preserve but instead "washes out" preferences. Thus, for example, if the corporation's after-tax income of $86 reflects economic income of $100 with a tax preference credit of $20 for accelerated depreciation, the depreciation preference will be washed out if it is added back to the corporate income attributed to shareholders. Hence, a sole shareholder should not be treated as if $130 of corporate income flowed through to him or her, but as if only $100 did. In order to arrive at this result, the gross-up of corporate income cannot follow the simple formula of dividing after-tax corporate income by the complement of the corporate tax rate (i.e., by 1—.34, in our example, using the current corporate tax rate). The structure of available business tax preferences will determine just how complex the gross-up must be. For example, a combination of preferential deductions and credits would require more complex treatment than mere deductible preferences.

The problem of tax preferences is effectively a problem about how corporate income and corporate tax payments should be imputed to shareholders. In other words, to describe corporate tax integration as requiring conscious allowance for tax preferences is to presume that integration will follow the imputation pattern. But there are other patterns.

Dividend relief can also take the form of a dividend-paid deduction for the corporation paying the dividend, or exclusion of the dividend from the income of the recipient shareholder. If the corporate payor of a dividend is allowed to deduct the amount paid to its shareholders, and the dividend is paid in the year the corporation earned it, the earnings distributed will have been taxed only once, at the shareholder's tax rate. Deduction of the dividend by the paying corporation exempts the amount distributed from the corporate tax. Distribution of earnings in a year later than that in which the corporation earned them increases the effective tax rate, by delaying the benefit of the deduction. The increase is a function of the corporate tax rate and the length of time between the year the corporation gets the income and the year it pays the dividend. In either case, however, shareholders lose the benefit of any corporate tax preference that might otherwise have sheltered the amount of the dividend—income that is exempt from tax, as deductible dividends are, cannot benefit from tax preferences. Corporate tax preferences are thus washed out of dividends.

An attractive feature of dividend deductibility is that this restores equal treatment of the two principal forms of corporate finance—equity investment and corporate borrowing. Interest in corporate integration may owe much to economists' observations concerning the interchangeability, in a world without tax, of these two sources of capital.[21] In contrast, the corporate tax makes debt financing superficially more attractive than the issuance of stock, because interest is usually allowed to offset income in computing the corporate tax, but dividends are not. To make dividends deductible, therefore, would, again superficially, restore the balance. On the other hand, perceptions of the equal attractiveness of debt and equity depend rather heavily on the stylized view that shareholders and lenders take similarly lenient views of the business judgment of managers. Although the owners of publicly traded companies can vote by selling their stock, lenders of course cannot usually sell their "interests" in debtor corporations. Corporate managers may have this and other reasons for resisting the siren call of debt. In any event, economic forces that have yet to be diagnosed seem to be at work in the real world. Despite the classical corporate tax, corporations routinely do issue stock, and not all the purchasers are

21. Roger H. Gordon & Burton G. Malkiel, *Corporation Finance*, in Henry Aaron & Joseph Pechman, eds., How Taxes Affect Economic Behavior 131 (1981); Franco Modigliani & Merton Miller, *The Cost of Capital, Corporation Finance, and the Theory of Investment*, 48 Am. Econ. Rev. 261 (1958); *Dividend Policy, Growth, and the Valuation of Shares*, 34 J. Bus. 411 (1961).

tax-exempt investors. The parity of debt and equity that would be achieved by dividend deductibility may even disturb an otherwise healthy equilibrium.

If instead dividends are excluded from the income of recipient shareholders, tax preferences are invariably passed through as if the recipient shareholder were taxed at the same rate as the corporation. This is so because the amount distributed *is* taxed at the corporate level (unless sheltered by a tax preference, in which case the preference is felt as a reduction in the corporate tax burden), and the effect of the distribution on the shareholders is the same, no matter what their tax bracket. For example, if a corporation earns $100, it will normally pay a tax of $34 on that amount. Without dividend relief of any sort, a 15% shareholder would pay a tax of $9.90 on receiving the remaining $66 in a dividend. If the dividend is excluded, the net tax burden on the distributed earnings is only $34, the amount of the corporate-level tax. Without dividend relief, a 31% bracket shareholder would pay an additional tax of $20.46, so that the net tax burden on the corporate earnings would be $54.46. With dividend exclusion, the net burden on either distribution would be only $34. This matters little under the current tax rate schedule. Most individual shareholders have marginal tax brackets of between 28% and 31%. There are probably not many 15% bracket shareholders. Thus, the dividend-paid deduction at the corporate level and the dividend-received exclusion at the shareholder level would be only subtly distinguishable.

France and Great Britain achieve similar results, under tax systems that ignore the variable effect of tax preferences, by imposing an addition to the corporate tax for dividends paid. France's *precompte* and Great Britain's Advanced Corporate Tax (ACT) require the corporate taxpayer to anticipate and, in effect, to withhold for the government an estimated tax to be paid by shareholders on dividends received. The result is an imputation system that allows shareholders to use a uniform gross-up approach.[22] Germany applies a combined imputation and dividend relief method designed instead to preserve the variable effect of preferences.

The effect of alternative tax systems on tax preferences remains a significant design problem for efforts to integrate the United States corporate tax. But what were until recently the largest and most widely available tax preferences—the investment tax credit, greatly accelerated depreciation, and percentage depletion deductions for mineral interests—were drastically curtailed or eliminated during the 1980's. The practical result is that it would not matter greatly whether dividend relief washed out tax preferences or not. The dividend-paid exclusion has become the Treasury's favorite among the alternative methods of dividend relief, in part because it washes out tax prefer-

22. Charles M. McLure, Must Corporate Income Be Taxed Twice?, supra note 18, at 97.

ences.[23] If Congress once again bows to demands to provide fiscal stimulus through the tax system, tax preferences would presumably re-emerge to trouble the choice of integration technique. High effective corporate tax rates, however, or the perception that these rates are high, may stimulate greater concern about integration, regardless of the effect of integration on tax preferences.

11.6 TAX–EXEMPT SHAREHOLDERS

Shareholders who enjoy an exemption from tax on all income can receive distributions of corporate earnings, even under a classical corporate tax regime, without suffering the burden of the double tax. For example, a tax-exempt pension fund that owns stock in IBM may receive dividends without any separate tax liability on receipt of the distribution. While the earnings out of which the dividend comes have been taxed once at the corporate level, the residue that trickles out to *this* shareholder faces no additional tax. From one point of view, then, tax-exempt shareholders are already a breach in the fortress of the classical corporate tax.

They are also a problem for dividend relief in the form of dividend exclusion. The tax-exempt shareholder who receives an excludable dividend of course pays no tax on it, but neither does the taxable shareholder. The distributions both receive are burdened to the extent of the corporate level tax, and this places the tax-exempt entity on a footing just as unfavorable as that of the person subject to tax. If the corporate tax is regarded as a surrogate for taxation at the shareholder level, the corporation should be allowed a refund of the tax it has paid on dividends to public charities and similar investors, at least if dividends to taxable shareholders are excluded from their income.

It may be objected that the rationale of dividend relief is that corporate profits as such, and not the income corporate dividends provide to shareholders, should be taxed. But if it counts against dividend exclusion that it distorts tax advantages shareholders could enjoy if they conducted corporate businesses directly rather than through a corporate intermediary, it also counts against dividend exclusion that it ignores the complete tax exemption of some potential business owners. Entities described in section 501 of the Code, though exempt from income tax on activities that serve their "exempt" purposes (the purposes that qualify them for exemption), are sometimes taxable at approximately the usual corporate rates (under the "unrelated business income tax" or UBIT) on profitable business activities.[24] Tax-exempts therefore present a dilemma for dividend relief. The exemption they usually enjoy cannot easily be preserved without special provision within any general scheme of dividend relief—the refund, perhaps, of an imputed corporate level tax on the tax-exempt share-

---

23. Dept. of Treasury, Integration of the Individual and Corporate Tax Systems: Taxing Business Income Once 19–20 (January 1992).

24. I.R.C. § 512.

holder's portion of distributed or even retained corporate earnings—but such relief should arguably be conditioned on a case-by-case analysis of the purposes of the tax-exempt recipient.

Matters are complicated by the overwhelming presence of tax-exempt shareholders in the public securities markets. Estimates vary but Treasury and Federal Reserve Board figures indicate that at the end of 1990 the tax-exempt sector owned 43% of all corporate equity and held 58% of corporate debt.[25] As a result, the amounts of revenue that might be involved in a scheme of dividend relief are considerably less than they might be if all shareholders were, like the typical individual, taxable on distributions from corporations. But by the same token, the problem of harmonizing integration with the range of policy decisions that mandate tax exemption in the first place is that much more acute. One approach is to presume that any corporate business in which tax-exempt organizations buy stock would be subject to UBIT if directly operated by the organization.[26] This of course is not necessarily so. A tax-exempt civil rights organization might, without being liable for UBIT, invest in minority businesses to which it could have made loans that would have served its tax-exempt purposes.[27] One can surmise the extent of this problem from the recent campaign by non-exempt business groups to curtail business activities by exempts.[28]

11.7   FOREIGN INVESTORS

Foreign investors who do not reside in the United States are typically not taxpayers in this country, but domestic corporations are required to withhold 30% of dividends paid to such shareholders.[29] Citizens of some treaty partners are relieved of this de facto tax and are thus on a footing with domestic tax-exempt shareholders.

11.8   RELIEF FOR NEW EQUITY ONLY

The distinction between pure profits and a normal return on capital suggests another approach to the goal of integration. Instead of allowing shareholders credit for corporate taxes paid or providing broad dividend relief, the tax law might narrowly unburden those distributions that compensate net newly contributed capital, while partially denying the corporate deduction for interest paid to creditors. The object would of course be to balance the attractiveness of debt and

25. Dept. of Treasury, Integration of the Individual and Corporate Tax Systems: Taxing Business Income Once, supra note 20, at 68.

26. See id. at 24, 36, 49.

27. See Rev. Rul. 74–587, 1974–2 C.B. 162 (low-cost and long-term loans and equity investments in business enterprises in economically depressed areas held to be within exempt purposes of entity formed to relieve poverty, eliminate prejudice, reduce neighborhood tensions, and combat community deterioration); Laura Kalick, *Reorganizing for the UBIT*, 41 Tax Notes 771 (November 14, 1988) (proposals to extend UBIT could be avoided by reshuffling of tax-exempt investment and business structures).

28. See James T. Bennett, *Unfair Competition and the UBIT*, 41 Tax Notes 759 (November 14, 1988).

29. I.R.C. §§ 871(a), 881.

equity as means of corporate finance, and yet to recognize that corporations and other investments compete for capital, so that corporate earnings should be allowed the advantage of deductibility that other investment pay-outs enjoy.[30]

11.9 A COMPREHENSIVE BUSINESS INCOME TAX

The difficulties of integration by imputation or dividend relief, though far from devastating, invite one to reconsider the approximate character of the corporate tax as a surrogate for a general business profits tax. The Treasury, in a recent report, seems to have found the idea of a broader tax, applicable not only to corporations but to unincorporated businesses as well, the most attractive solution to the integration puzzle.[31] The Comprehensive Business Income Tax (CBIT) would be imposed at a flat rate on all business income, measured without deduction for dividends, interest paid to creditors, or profit or interest withdrawals by proprietors or partners. It would, therefore, completely replace the current American approach to partnership taxation, which treats partnerships as pass-through entities and attributes shares of partnership income, deduction, credit and loss to partners as if they earned these items as sole proprietors. Distributions and withdrawals would, on the other hand, be uniformly excluded from all shareholders' income. The CBIT would not be refundable to tax-exempt shareholders, and there would be no provision for special treatment of fresh contributions to the capital of a business. It would indeed draw no distinction at all between pure profits and normal return on capital. In effect, then, the proposal abandons much of the neoclassical rationale for the corporate tax.

The Treasury's interest in the CBIT may be conditioned by the current state of the tax law that imposes the corporate tax with few tax preferences and by the sense that tax compliance and tax simplification should be prized above the niceties of further tinkering with the classical corporate tax. The present-mindedness of the recommendations comes through in the priority given to economic and administrative considerations at the expense of equity and distributive consequences. The flat rate tax washes out tax preferences, does not differentiate among shareholders with different marginal tax rates, and denies tax-exempt shareholders any benefit from integration. Nevertheless, it exposes at full stature what may be implicit in the very goal of a corporate tax, the political convenience of a tax that falls on a nonhomogeneous minority of the taxpaying public. With that in mind, we may be tempted to evaluate the CBIT by reference to other goals of corporate taxation that do not point in the direction of a broad and indiscriminate business levy. Those other goals that have so far been identified, however, are peculiarly controversial, at least from the

30. ALI, supra note 13, at 356–486.

31. Dept. of Treasury, Integration of Individual and Corporate Tax Systems: Taxing Business Income Once 39–60 & passim (1992); Richard Goode, Integration of Corporate and Individual Taxes: A Treasury Report, 56 Tax Notes 1667 (March 30, 1992) (the CBIT "appears to be the first choice of the [Report's] authors").

standpoint of traditional tax economics: they are goals that stress the "personality" of the corporation, the nebulous political impact of corporate wealth concentration, the immeasurable benefit of the relative liquidity of investment in corporations, and so forth.

It is fitting that we conclude our survey of corporate tax principles with the recognition that the variety of goals corporate taxation may serve has never been fully and finally debated in the public forum, and that the comparatively technical discussions to be found in government and think-tank publications on the subject lay bear the weakness of taking the clarity of the goals of corporate taxation for granted. The political reality is that the most prosperous nations are inured to the taxation of corporate income and, perhaps because of the obscurity of the motive for this practice, face a persistent and growing demand for its abatement.

Chapter 12

INTERNATIONAL TAX POLICY

12.1 TAX POLICY IN THE GLOBAL CONTEXT

Countries impose and collect taxes from citizens and others, largely on the basis of traditional legal assumptions about relations among sovereigns and relations between sovereigns and their subjects. Treaties sometimes refine or replace these assumptions. But neither the traditional bedrock nor the treaty superstructure is well suited to the needs of taxing authorities in the international context. Now that the national economies of what were previously highly independent prosperous industrial countries have begun to melt into each other, received notions of international jurisdiction and of the radical independence of sovereign states clash ever more noticeably with the needs of tax policy. In this chapter, we will consider the problem in broad terms first, next examine a particular episode in recent United States tax diplomacy, and then survey proposals for solving the problems by international harmonization of tax systems.

Most states claim full taxing authority over people, property and transactions "within" their territory. There would be no need to take thought specifically about the international context of tax policy if the people, property, and economic transactions of different countries could be kept separate—if economies and jurisdictions were closed to each other in relevant respects. But while it is usually easy to determine whether a person is in or out of a country, it is not always easy to determine where property is for this purpose, and not at all easy to determine where transactions occur. Most economies, if not borders, are fairly open, and not only to the relatively free movement of people and things, but open too in the sense that some things and events have no clear place within or beyond any territorial boundary.

The two main areas into which discussion of international tax policy falls are roughly issues of line-drawing, primarily in response to the difficulties just mentioned. and issues concerning the effect of taxes on the mobility of capital from one national economy to another. Like other tax problems, these have obvious equity and efficiency dimensions. Indeed, all line-drawing of this sort is essentially directed

195

towards achieving equity, usually equity among residents of the taxing country and its treaty partners. And efficiency, in the form of various conceptions of what is good for domestic and supra-national capital markets, seems to prompt tax laws designed to control out-bound or in-bound investment. Until fairly recently economists had little to say about the interaction of national economies, and so even simplistic views about what tax incentives for investment would favor a domestic economy can raise novel, and by their nature complex, economic issues.

Something else complicates the task of designing tax measures that will take the international context into account. People do not generally agree on principles that might define good or even acceptable behavior from an international perspective. What consensus about international morality and good politics there is can scarcely support discussion of the fair play and affirmative desirability of tax measures that affect many countries at once. There is no broad normative standard for assessing, say, how Switzerland taxes the business activities of multinational corporations (MNCs). It is as if we had to discuss domestic tax rules without even the shared presumption of equal treatment of individuals.

One reason for this dearth of principles is that we are not very good at making moral judgments about the behavior of groups, as distinguished from individuals; another is that international law has traditionally taken a minimalist or agnostic attitude towards most questions of transnational right and wrong. And the setting in which international tax policy must be implemented does not tend to supply answers to these questions. Differences in national standards of living, cultural differences that affect how law is regarded, and so on are just too great. Social and political variety in a moral and political vacuum accounts for the rudderless quality of much thought about international tax policy.

Those few familiar moral or political standards that arguably apply to domestic and international relations alike, being all we have, take on what is arguably too much significance. These include rudimentary notions of economic efficiency and justice. Because more sensitive appraisal of how many countries are faring at once seems impossible, economic efficiency is often, even usually, identified with capital accumulation measured in the crudest terms. Any sort of equal treatment of equals seems a decent enough approximation of justice in this setting that is both luxuriant with relevant factual differences and barren of shared moral standards.

Lest it all seem too easy, the legal implementation of national tax regimes, when they reach beyond national boundaries, becomes in part a matter of diplomacy. While the domestic politics of a taxing authority often dictates somewhat more harsh treatment for foreigners than for its own residents, foreigners can sometimes mobilize tax retaliation by their own (or even other) countries. Tax treaties, often called "double tax" treaties because they are designed in large part to prevent double taxation of the same income, grow out of or anticipate the problems of tax evasion and inter-governmental retaliation. They are deliberately more favorable to the citizens and resident corporations of the treaty partners than to others, in order to secure cooperation against tax opportunism. They usually require a great deal of rather technical negotiation because of differences between the party states' tax systems. They are perhaps for that reason hard to amend. They also require standing arbitral arrangements, access to which, by international legal custom, is limited to citizens represented by state sponsors. In view of the difficulty of negotiation and the cumbersomeness of arbitration, it is not surprising that a country's tax treaties are often out of sync with its international tax policy for long periods of time.

12.2 ANTI–DISCRIMINATION CLAUSES

The core of a tax treaty is its anti-discrimination clause, a mutual promise by the treaty partners to treat each other's citizens and corporations no differently than their own for tax purposes.[1] The United States has negotiated anti-discrimination clauses of an almost standard form in its tax treaties since 1980.[2] Under this clause, if the United States imposes a 10% excise tax on domestically produced heavy trucks, it may not impose a higher excise tax on heavy trucks produced in this country by an individual citizen of a treaty partner. It may not allow a state to collect higher death taxes from the estate of a treaty partner's deceased citizen than would be due from the estate of a U.S. citizen.

Anti-discrimination clauses make separate provision for the similar treatment of corporations. International law has its own standard for determining whether a natural person is a "national" of a state, but corporations and similar juridical entities are not usually thought capable of being nationals of a state. In the past, anti-discrimination clauses have typically left it to the law of each treaty partner to decide which non-natural persons and associations including non-citizens should be accorded the treaty privilege of nondiscrimination. The reason for this may be have been the lack of consensus as to grounds for recognizing the "nationality" of corporations or its equivalent.[3]

"Treaty-shopping" has begun to weigh heavily on this generous approach to the geographical situs of corporations. The term is used to refer to a "premeditated effort to take advantage of the international tax network and careful selection of the most advantageous treaty for a specific purpose."[4] Striking evidence that treaty-shopping poses a threat to international relations is to be found both in the United States' recent threat to break faith with its tax treaty partners over

1. See Cornelis Van Raad, Nondiscrimination in International Tax Law (1986).

2. United States Dept. of Treasury Model Income Tax Treaty, June 16, 1981, CCH Tax Treaties ¶ 1022 [hereinafter 1981 Model Treaty].

3. American Law Institute, Restatement of the Foreign Relations Law of the United States § 213, Comment e. (1965).

4. See H. David Rosenbloom, *Tax Treaty Abuse: Policies and Issues*, 15 Law & Pol'y Int'l Bus. 763, 766–68 (1983).

this form of corporate tax evasion and in the indulgent response of its treaty partners to that threat.

In 1986 Congress imposed a tax for the first time on the repatriated income of foreign corporations' "branch" operations in the United States. There is no express statutory exception from this tax for corporations of states parties to double tax treaties with the United States. Yet almost all treaties contain nondiscrimination clauses that forbid either contracting party to tax the other party's nationals or enterprises less favorably than its own citizens or than enterprises of the taxing state carrying on the same activities. Under U.S. law, later domestic legislation overrides a conflicting treaty. The branch tax legislation therefore seems to abrogate all U.S. tax treaties that include nondiscrimination clauses.

There were two important qualifying statements, however, in the legislative history. The first appears designed to recast the treaty-override provisions of the branch tax as an *interpretative declaration* for international law purposes:

> Congress believed that a branch profits tax does not unfairly discriminate against foreign corporations because it treats foreign corporations and their shareholders *together* no worse than U.S. corporations and their shareholders.[5]

Though not unambiguous, this may be taken as a claim by Congress that the branch tax is compatible with U.S. tax treaties in force, and with nondiscrimination clauses in particular. Can a tax that falls only on foreign corporations' branches really be thought not to discriminate against them?

Before 1987, a foreign corporation doing business in the U.S. was taxed at the usual U.S. corporate tax rates on any income effectively connected with a trade or business there. Foreign investment through a domestic corporation was subject to the same tax. If the foreign corporation transferred earnings to its owners who were not U.S. citizens, this distribution was not automatically subject to tax, as a distribution from a domestic corporation to foreign shareholders, or a distribution from a domestic corporation to U.S. citizens, would have been. Moreover, many U.S. tax treaties altogether exempted the shareholders of corporations of the treaty partner from tax on distributed earnings.

From the narrow perspective of taxes collected by the U.S. on enterprises within its borders, the branch tax makes tax burdens more equal. It is designed to resemble the tax on dividends to which U.S. corporations' distributions to domestic *or* foreign shareholders are subject. The branch tax *rate* equals the normal rate at which such dividends are taxed today.

5. Staff of Joint Comm. on Taxation, General Explanation of the Tax Reform Act of 1986 at 1038.

The branch tax, however, though arguably fair from the standpoint of the U.S. economy as a closed system, is an arbitrary additional tax for some foreign enterprises, namely, those whose native jurisdictions don't impose a double tax on corporate income earned abroad. Moreover, if a tax treaty partner of the U.S. has bargained for freedom from discrimination against its enterprises doing business in the U.S., the branch tax on its face looks like a breach of the treaty.

The second qualifying statement in the legislative history of the branch tax suspends the branch tax in most cases for enterprises of the U.S. treaty partners. It says:

> Congress generally did not intend to override U.S. income tax treaty obligations that arguably prohibit imposition of the branch profits tax even though as later-enacted legislation the Act's branch tax provisions normally would do so. Congress adopted this position, however, only on the understanding that the Treasury Department will renegotiate outstanding treaties that prohibit imposition of the tax.[6]

And right away the Treasury Department announced lists of treaties it considers in conflict with the branch tax and therefore as not generally overridden.[7]

But this is still not the whole picture. Notwithstanding this acknowledgment of international obligations, the branch tax by its terms still applies enterprise by enterprise, if there is treaty shopping— the statute uses the very term, which is obviously pejorative, clearly for effect. Recall that treaty-shopping means the deliberate use of treaty arrangements to secure tax advantages. But the statute does not inquire into motives. It simply provides that a foreign corporation can claim the benefits of a treaty only if it is a "qualified resident" of the treaty partner. "Qualified resident" corporations are those whose stock is regularly and primarily traded on an established securities exchange, OR those 50% or more of whose stock is beneficially owned by natural persons residing in the treaty partner AND less than 50% of whose income is used to pay liabilities to nonresidents.

What should one think about this shell game of tax imposition, suspension of the tax for treaty partners, and reimposition of the tax on some of their corporations? Does the branch tax legislation, even as qualified by its legislative history, nevertheless abrogate U.S. tax treaties? The key language in the U.S. 1981 Model Treaty antidiscrimination clause is that dealing with "enterprises of a Contracting State":

---

6. Id. at 1038.

7. Treaties that prohibit the tax are those with Aruba, Austria, Belgium, China, Cyprus, Denmark, Egypt, Finland, Germany, Greece, Hungary, Iceland, Ireland, Italy, Jamaica, Japan, Korea, Luxembourg, Malta, Morocco, Netherlands, Netherlands Antilles, Norway, Pakistan, Philippines, Sweden, Switzerland, and the United Kingdom.

Treaties that do not prohibit the tax are those with Australia, Barbados, Canada, France, New Zealand, Poland, Romania, South Africa, the Soviet Union, and Trinidad & Tobago. I.R. Notice 87–56, 1987–2 C.B. 367.

The taxation on a permanent establishment which an enterprise of a Contracting State has in the other Contracting State shall not be less favorably levied in that other State than the taxation levied on enterprises of that other State carrying on the same activities.[8]

It is important to see how investors might take advantage of the privilege thus conferred on "enterprises" of a treaty partner.

Generally, a foreign-owned enterprise that does business in the United States is taxed in accordance with the structure of its ownership. If the alien owner or owners reside here, they are subject to income tax on essentially the same terms as citizens. If they reside elsewhere, they are subject to withholding tax on the profits they withdraw from the domestic business activity, whether it is incorporated or not. (The withholding tax is effectively an income tax and is levied at rates that approximate the highest corporate and individual rates, now roughly 30%.) But the anti-discrimination clause of a tax treaty can displace the withholding tax, because it is effectively an additional tax on the foreign-owned venture. In order to take advantage of the treaty, there must be a "permanent establishment" of the foreign operation in this country, and that requirement is one over which legal wrangling, before the "competent authority" designated by various treaties, has long been a feature of international tax practice. But given a permanent establishment, the treaty can easily become a substantial tax exemption—exemption from the withholding tax on foreign withdrawals of domestic business profits. This benefit may only level the playing field, if the treaty partner's enterprises are as heavily taxed at home as ours are here. Treaty shopping depends essentially on the few exceptions to this general condition. In the not-so-distant past, the exceptions were conspicuous and well used.

To return to the interpretation of the standard U.S. anti-discrimination clause, we should notice that whether a tax on a treaty shopping venture is prohibited by either sentence of Article 24 depends on (a) whether incorporation in a state confers nationality there, and (b) whether incorporation in a state confers the status of "an enterprise of" that State.

The U.S. position has been that a corporation generally has the nationality of the state of incorporation, but there is some variety of opinion within the international community. A widely accepted view associates an incorporated enterprise with the state in which the company's central management is found, the *siège morale*. The authors of the Restatement of U.S. Foreign Relations Law believe the U.S. position is ready to question the nationality of tax haven corporations. Whether that is so or not, the *Nottebohm* decision of the International Court of Justice suggests that in the case of natural persons the link between a person and a state claiming that person as a national must

8. 1981 Model Tax Treaty, Art. XII.

be substantial to merit legal recognition.[9] Since the nationality of legal entities has shallower foundations in custom than that of natural persons, the *Nottebohm* precedent casts doubt on the right of states to extend diplomatic protection to legal entities on grounds of incorporation alone. Presumably, the nondiscrimination clauses of U.S. tax treaties refer to and protect "enterprises of" Contracting parties, rather than corporations as such, precisely because the contracting parties will not lightly be assumed to have intended to create treaty benefits for non-nationals. Indeed, state responsibility for a treaty violation may not extend to injuries to non-nationals.

When may a state claim as its own an "enterprise" linked in some way to it? International law, apart from treaties, has scarcely touched upon the question, which, I suppose, is part of a larger question of which the International Court of Justice in *Barcelona Traction* answered a different part. The holding in that case was that a state does not have *jus standi* to assert the claims of a legally distinct entity in which nationals of the state own less than a 100% interest.[10] The opinion of the Court says in passing that shareholders own mere interests in and not rights to the assets of a corporation, and that states may assert claims on behalf of corporations to which they have granted legal recognition. If recognition by a state for any purpose, and a fortiori the granting of a corporate charter, entitled the entity to privileges under the anti-discrimination clauses of the state's tax treaties, economically weak treaty partners would be under great pressure to invite opportunistic use of their treaties with their economically more attractive counterparts. They would have to take affirmative, and often politically unpopular, steps to avoid becoming tax havens. This implication is not necessary for the holding in *Barcelona Traction* and is perhaps too broad a statement, as the Court's earlier holding in *Nottebohm* warns. But, given the breadth of interpretation to which international law precedents are subject, contrary views are not precluded.

Should the nationality of an incorporated enterprise be determined by ownership at all? Or should the physical location of management be decisive? If ownership counts, does indebtedness figure in the structure of ownership? What body of law will distinguish debt from equity in this connection? Evidently, the treaty shopping provisions of the branch tax represent one view of these matters. Can these provisions be understood as an interpretation of existing treaties? Congress hoped such a view could be defended, I suppose. It seems, however, not to matter so much how we categorize the U.S. position—whether as an abrogation of treaty obligations, interpretation of treaties, or attempted reservation with immediate effect.

9. Liechtenstein v. Guatemala, [1955] I.C.J. Rep. 4 1955 WL 1 (the Nottebohm Case).

10. Belgium v. Spain, [1970] I.C.J. Rep. 3, 1970 WL 1 (Barcelona Traction, Light & Power Co., Ltd.).

The Group of Six—Belgium, France, the German Federal Republic, Great Britain, Luxembourg, and the Netherlands—immediately registered a protest against the U.S. unilateral "action" but otherwise took a remarkably conciliatory approach. The joint memorandum of protest agreed that the problem of treaty-shopping must be addressed; it merely insisted on treaty renegotiation as the preferred means. At least one treaty—the U.S. Belgian treaty—was swiftly renegotiated to include an anti-treaty-shopping provision. Canada and the Netherlands included such a provision in their own new tax treaty. There have been no other protests, and investment planning now proceeds on the assumption that the branch tax can override treaties as threatened.

Why should so many states agree so readily to the principle embodied in this brash departure from treaty obligations? Tax advisers had thought that treaty-shopping would always be a feature of their world. Did the affected treaty partners have reason to join forces to halt the practice that has been the heart of international tax planning?

If the branch tax were simply a means of capturing tax revenue that would otherwise be lost, the treaty partners of the U.S. would certainly not have agreed in principle to renegotiate the affected treaties. Surely, the negotiators of the treaties expected some loss of revenue as a result of the application of the nondiscrimination clauses, and there can be little sympathy for efforts to alter this consequence retroactively.

I suggest that the branch tax is understood by governmental tax advisors on all sides, not as a revenue-raising measure, but as a measure designed to prevent distortion of the international market for investment capital. Much of the world today is effectively a community of countries among which capital may flow freely—at least, without serious governmental inhibition. A natural objective of an economic community is to ensure an efficient allocation of investment resources within the community. Certainly, the perceived cause of much investment and trade distortion has lately been the perceived inefficiency of the international capital market—the Eurodollar phenomenon of the 1970's and the world debt crisis of the 1980's are both examples of this, although they are differently understood in different quarters. What *is* commonly recognized is the danger of investment flows that reflect not the real potential for economic growth of some country's economy but only an overstatement of the return on some otherwise less productive enterprise. Efficient allocation of investment resources would be achieved by equalizing the marginal rate of return on investment in each country of the relevant economic community. As will be discussed further below, these rates of return are finally being seen to depend very significantly on the *structure* as well as the *rate* of capital taxation, which in most cases is corporate taxation.

If the tax treatment of income from capital is on a residence basis, i.e., the tax liability of a resident of any country on a unit of investment income is independent of the country in which the income originates, then capital market equilibrium requires that the pre-tax interest rate be the same in all countries (real interest rate, adjusted for differences in money supply). It won't be the same if the pre-tax rates of return on similar corporate enterprises depend on the country in which the enterprises are carried on. The structure of the applicable corporate tax is what governs this rate of return, for our purposes. Either a classical corporate tax—one comprising two layers of tax at whatever rates—with true economic depreciation, or a cash flow corporate tax with integration will do, if all countries concerned use the same structure in measuring the corporate tax base. (This, by the way, is the announced goal of EC and OECD theorists—everyone seems to agree that similarity of tax structure is in the common international interest.[11])

Treaty-shopping exaggerates the current variety of corporate tax bases in the world economic community. Governments everywhere are seeing strong proof of this, either in the flight of capital from their own best enterprises or in the unwanted influx of de-stabilizing investment in unworthy, already overbid markets—sometimes in both. A tax on treaty-shopping enterprises could be designed not to punish or to raise revenue but simply to remove distortive tax incentives for inefficient investments. Needless to say, other political pressures work alongside whatever idealism there may be concerning the pursuit of more efficient capital markets. People in business, the trade unions, and farmers everywhere seem to favor transnational trade protectionism or retaliation therefor, and taxes are often the chosen means.

If these pressures continue to influence policy-makers, the goal of frustrating treaty-shoppers and of making corporate tax bases more closely comparable from country to country will loom ever larger on the agenda of tax treaty negotiators—even at the expense of nondiscrimination. Before the defects of anti-discrimination clauses were felt, the United States had been engaged in, and had almost completed, a long series of treaty re-negotiations, with the broad purpose of unifying its international tax policy with respect to principal trading and investment partners. While the effort was successful in most respects, it also underscored the awkwardness and delay that will inevitably attend any attempt to rationalize international tax policy by traditional means. It also exposed the existence of vastly different national needs and wants on opposite sides of the negotiating table, especially when the United States was seeking to limit the tax-haven status of a smaller or Third World state.[12] Thus, the legal process is centrally affected by the *lack* of a genuinely international tax policy agenda.

11. See John A. Kay & Mervyn A. King, The British Tax System (5th ed. 1990); Sijbren Cnossen, *Tax Harmonization Issues in the European Community*, 8 Am. J. Tax Policy 259 (1990).

12. Paul D. Reese, *United States Tax Treaty Policy Toward Developing Countries*, 35 U.C.L.A. L. Rev. 369 (1987).

12.3   A RELATIVELY OLD PROBLEM: TAX HAVENS

Treaty overrides are only the tip of the iceberg. Problems due to the awkwardness with which international business transactions fit traditional legal concepts of international sovereignty and jurisdiction crop up in a variety of ways and, given the inventiveness of tax advisors, more can be expected. The reader may need to know at least a minimum about tax havens, a topic briefly mentioned above, and about the perceived problem of abusive transfer pricing between entities belonging to multinational corporate groups.

The term "tax haven" is actually used in two ways in discussions of international tax planning. The more inclusive application of the term extends to all taxing jurisdictions that provide an advantage for individuals or businesses whose income or wealth would be taxed more heavily if they fulfilled the requirements for residence in another jurisdiction. Thus, for example, since 1986 the United States has been a tax haven for some corporate enterprises with European links because U.S. marginal tax rates on corporate income have been reduced to a level below that of several European countries. A U.S. corporation that could, for example, provide services in Great Britain without establishing itself there (in the sense defined by the relevant British tax law) would stand to pay less tax on marginal profits than a British corporation would if it provided the same services in that country. Australia currently has no corporate-level tax on corporate profits, distributions to shareholders being taxed at the same rates and in the same way as other income, and this makes it a tax haven for corporate enterprises that are able to carry on operations in other countries while maintaining Australian residence and avoiding the usual permanent establishment trigger for taxation abroad.

Sometimes "tax haven" is used more restrictively to describe those comparatively few countries that openly foster efforts by their residents to attract tax avoiders. Tax havens in this sense are identifiable by characteristics like a relatively low rate of taxation, high levels of secrecy for banking and other financial transactions, a financial sector disproportionately large for the business operations actually carried on in the country, well-developed communications networks, lack of currency control, political and economic stability, liberal commercial laws, limited participation in tax treaties (because potential treaty partners shun them), and the availability of competent lawyers and accountants to staff tax avoidance operations.[13]

Many countries have adopted laws that deny tax preferences to or impose heavier taxes on enterprises with tax haven residence, defining that concept largely in terms of tax rates.[14] Such anti-tax-haven

13. Vincent P. Belotsky, Jr., *The Prevention of Abusive Tax Havens* 17 Cal. W. Int'l. L. J. 43 (1987).

14. Organization for Economic and Commercial Development, Tax Havens: Measures to Prevent Abuse By Taxpayers: International Tax Avoidance and Evasion 21 (1987).

legislation would thus apply to countries that openly assist tax avoidance schemes as well as to those that inadvertently or in the pursuit of other ends happen to do so. One of the elementary goals of double tax treaties has been to eliminate the unintended use of treaty partners as tax havens. An important element in treaty defenses against unwitting susceptibility of the treaty partners to use as tax havens is the mutual exchange of taxpayer information between the relevant governments, sometimes in exchange for financial aid. The United States has had limited success in just such a foreign-aid-linked campaign to establish information networks with former Caribbean tax haven countries.[15] The tension between the international and domestic political spheres often prevents the easy accomplishment of information exchange. Some countries, like Switzerland, have broad bank or commercial secrecy laws that are not automatically overridden by treaty provisions requiring information exchange. It took years for the United States, which may have been the most aggrieved of Switzerland's allies, to persuade that country to lift its secrecy protections in a limited range of situations. The Swiss business community had first to be convinced by adverse judicial decisions in the United States that secrecy would cost more than it was worth to them as a lure for foreign business.[16] Although many commentators recommend a global tax information exchange treaty as the first and most important step towards defusing tax competition of all sorts, progress in this direction has been small and discouraging for the future.

12.4 A RELATIVELY NEW PROBLEM: TRANSFER PRICING

This brings us to the second of the two related topics mentioned at the beginning of the previous section. In the international tax context it is common to refer to the allocation of costs, revenues, and related items among the entities that make up a multinational enterprise as *transfer pricing*. A parent corporation in Canada, for example, may sell golf carts to a United States subsidiary for resale in this country. If U.S. corporate tax rates are lower than Canadian rates, the parent may be tempted to claim, for Canadian tax purposes, a very low profit on the transfers of goods to the subsidiary, even though the subsidiary declares a correspondingly higher profit on its resale of the transferred goods; the Canadian taxes saved would outweigh the U.S. taxes paid. The Canadian tax authorities might then challenge the transfer pricing as abusive, on the theory that an arm's length price should have been received for the goods sold by parent to subsidiary. It is sometimes said that most countries accept an "arm's length" standard for appropriate international transfer pricing, so that treaties should be interpreted accordingly and the business affairs of MNCs regarded as subject to reclassification if the arm's length standard is violated by treaty part-

15. See Gregory P. Crinion, *Tax Evasion in Tax Haven Countries*, 20 Int'l Law. 1209, 1235 (1986).

16. Crinion, supra note 15, at 1239–42.

ner enterprises.[17]

The trouble with this simple view of how multinational corporate groups ought to allocate their earnings for tax purposes is that MNCs, in particular, are characterized by idiosyncratic exploitation of intangible business assets—patents, knowhow, customer lists, and good will in a host of forms. Unrelated corporations rarely share intangibles in a manner that permits clear comparison with the practice of these related entities.[18] The exploitation of intangibles is often not a matter of separate contractual agreement among related or unrelated parties, and when contracts do commemorate the "transfer" of some or all the value of an intangible, the accounting aspect of the transfer may offer no insight into the ultimate division of profits among the parties.[19]

To illustrate: A Japanese cosmetics firm decides to establish a presence in the U.S. market by having its U.S. subsidiary sell products at extremely low prices to U.S. retailers in the first years of a long-term sales campaign, simultaneously providing an array of marketing assistance to these retailers. The Japanese parent takes a low profit on the transfer of cosmetics to its U.S. subsidiary. The subsidiary receives a very small return on sales. The return is low because U.S. retailers are being allowed to profit from the marketing campaign *despite* the Japanese parent's sacrifice of a considerable profit margin to the subsidiary via its transfer pricing. The achievement of the marketing strategy would perhaps translate immediately into an increase in the value of the subsidiary. The intangibles of market share, product image, department store floor space and trademark would not show up on a balance sheet. They might be recognized in a sale of the subsidiary by the parent to a third party, but again they might not. The example shows that the price of what is transferred between members of an MNC may point in the wrong direction, if what we are concerned with is the creation of value—especially, the creation of a valuable future profits stream. Here, the parent corporation takes less profit than it could on the sale of property to its subsidiary, but it does so as part of a strategy of generating goodwill in the subsidiary that may later increase the value of the parent's manufacturing operations and generate royalties on trademark licenses to other U.S. or foreign

17. Tax authorities here, for example, take that position in support of currently proposed transfer pricing regulations. *See* U.S. Treasury Dept. and Internal Revenue Service, Report on the Application and Administration of Section 482, at 1–3 (April 9, 1992) ("every major industrial nation accepts the arm's-length standard as its frame of reference in transfer pricing cases").

18. This, at least, is the plausible thesis of recent scholarship on the subject. R. Caves, Multinational Enterprise and Economic Analysis (1982); Alan Shapiro, Multi–National Financial Management (1989); Michael Granfield, *An Economic and Strategic Evaluation of the Proposed 482 Regulations,* 92 Tax Notes Today 121–31 (June 11, 1992).

19. Hugh Ault & David Bradford, *Taxing International Income: An Analysis of the U.S. System and Its Economic Premises,* in Taxation and the Global Economy 11, 30–33 (ed. Assaf Razin & Joel Slemrod 1990).

firms.[20]

The lesson of this illustration may be that in order to appraise the economic performance of a multinational we must grasp the business plan of the group and evaluate its success in terms that may be peculiar to the planners' view of what makes business sense. This would forcefully imply that the arms' length standard of correct transfer pricing should be ignored or at best kept as a mere factor in a more complex formula for intra-group profit allocation. Or it may be that the elusiveness of idiosyncratic corporate group business plans should discourage efforts to tax corporate profits equitably. Treasury's recent promulgation of proposed regulations on this matter has elicited sophisticated responses from a variety of theoretical perspectives. As the discussion reaches flood tide, little can be said except that economic sophistication has so far widened and not narrowed the differences of opinion among the participants.[21]

The obscurity of the transfer pricing or, more accurately, the profit allocation problem for MNCs actually affects all other aspects of international tax policy that have been mentioned in this chapter. Antidiscrimination provisions in tax treaties are worthless if they do not take into account the possibility that there may be no ultimate way of analyzing the profitability of corporate groups that do business in several countries at once. If corporations can disguise what really generates profits for them by dividing aspects of their operations among corporations of different nationality or residence for treaty purposes, then nationality or residence is irrelevant, and the attempt to police it by subtle treaty classification is doomed to irrelevance too. Similarly, even cooperation and mutual information exchange among all the countries in which an MNC does business cannot illuminate the rights of those countries to tax the respective parts of the enterprise, if there are no ultimate parts to begin with.

Unfortunately, the only purely diplomatic way out of this theoretical and factual wilderness is arbitrary agreement by taxing jurisdictions to apportion MNC profits so that suitable parts will be taxed by each jurisdiction. And since advance agreement by taxing authorities without the cooperation of the affected corporations might also be futile, because the taxpayers would remain free to change plans and reap profits elsewhere or in a different manner than the governmental negotiators had foreseen, the agreements should, if possible, include the MNCs themselves as parties. The recently announced *advance pricing agreement* (APA) procedures are a step in this direction.[22] But since

20. The illustration is derived from a more elaborate one given in Granfield, supra note 18, at 8.

21. See Dale W. Wickham & Charles J. Kerester, *New Directions Needed For Solution of the International Transfer Pricing Tax Puzzle: Internationally Agreed Rules or Tax Warfare?*, 56 Tax Notes 339 (July 20, 1992); Edward Albert Purnell, *The New Present Value Approach to Intangible Transfer Pricing Under Section 482: An Economic Model Takes the BALRM Floor*, 45 Tax Law. 647 (1992).

22. U.S. Treasury Dept. and I.R.S., Report on the Application and Administra-

they involve only the taxpayer corporations as parties, it was quickly recognized by commentators here and abroad that APAs may provoke retaliation from other taxing jurisdictions if they appear to overreach the "correct" economic result.

12.5 THE COST OF CAPITAL AND TAX COMPETITION

Our brief look at the international law and diplomacy of treaty overrides introduces a few of the elements of international tax policy that now dominate a lively and growing interest among economists in the area. Their focus is the relationship between taxation and trade distortion. To see this in the round, it is useful to recall that *indirect* taxation has often been thought not to distort the economic decisions of firms doing business, although *income* taxation on the other hand does on certain assumptions appear to interfere with those decisions. Whether this is actually so depends on a host of variables, including the sweep of the indirect tax—the more universal its application, the less substitution it can cause [23]—but to the extent that indirect taxes fall most heavily on consumption and direct taxes on "factors of production" such as labor or capital, direct taxes are more likely to affect decisions and hence have the greater opportunity to distort economic behavior.

Having said this, we should note immediately that at international borders some distortions relating to taxes on consumption are conspicuous. Border towns often resemble the "duty-free" lounges of airports, touting the tax advantage of buying in a low-tax jurisdiction for immediate export elsewhere. The endurance of these small areas of distortion by high-tax jurisdictions is often dictated by the political motive of providing foreign aid to the low-tax jurisdictions, but the effect of such tax avoidance may also be *de minimis*. It is easier to change where one produces wealth than to change where one consumes it, and thus the occasional and limited tax holiday that vacationers enjoy causes no headache to taxing authorities. In Europe, where the entire population of a state may live within easy reach of a national border, the problem of sales or VAT tax avoidance looms larger. It has been a significant objective of the European Community to promote closer conformity of VAT tax rates and incidence for member countries in order to forestall serious and destructive tax competition that might undermine the ability of any member of the Community to enforce this near-equivalent of a national sales tax.

Direct taxes pose much greater problems for enforcement in the global context. For example, your occupation may permit you to move to a low-tax jurisdiction in order to shelter your income. Many coun-

tion of Section 482 (April 9, 1992), chapter 3.

23. See the discussion of optimal tax models and their implications for substitution effects in Chapter 14. These considerations are sometimes collectively represented by the so-called "Ramsey rules," which say roughly that commodity taxes should be designed to reduce demand for all commodities in equal proportions. Frank Plumpton Ramsey, *A Contribution to the Theory of Taxation*, 37 Econ. J. 47 (1927).

tries do not assert the right to tax the income of their nationals earned abroad, and so a tax-motivated change of domicile may produce tax savings without costing the taxpayer his or her nationality. The United States takes the broader view that the income of its citizens is subject to U.S. tax, wherever earned, and regardless of nexus with U.S. territory. Still, the avid tax-avoider might sacrifice U.S. citizenship for, say, Liechtenstein citizenship in order to pay less in taxes. Conveniently for tax policy, most people would find this form of tax avoidance impractical.

Investment income is a different matter. An individual who cannot shelter her wages can choose to invest in enterprises in a jurisdiction that does not tax business profits as heavily as the home jurisdiction does. Capital is increasingly mobile. The world economy is becoming ever more integrated, and there are now swift and easy communications networks among major money center markets for corporate securities and other highly liquid investments. The influence of taxes on where money is invested has become of major importance, affecting which goods are manufactured in which countries, and driving isolated markets to extreme and sometimes unstable positions. The internationalization of capital also creates explosive problems of enforcement for tax systems that are geared primarily to the almost closed economic systems of the past.

Since most people still cannot move their homes in order to avoid taxes, the possibility of avoiding taxes on capital investments simmers down to the strategy of investing in corporations that face lower tax rates by effective use of international tax planning. Distributions and the proceeds from the sale of corporate shares are still likely to be taxed at the rates normally applicable to other income in the investor's country.

Some countries deliberately take advantage of gains by tax competition. The Republic of Ireland, for example, adopted a corporate tax rate of 10% for most manufacturing firms, with the express purpose of enticing capital and jobs from other countries. By analogy, the U.S. tax law has long since provided a tax holiday for U.S. corporations that establish business operations in Puerto Rico or another U.S. possession.[24] Domestic corporations have taken relatively cynical advantage of the possession tax credit by transferring the manufacturing aspect of a business to a possession corporation controlled by a mainland parent. Most of the gains from these tax competitive measures are at the expense of the economy of other areas. In some instances at least, established manufacturing enterprises have transferred operations from an original location on the U.S. mainland to Puerto Rico, taking away jobs from specific groups of workers on the mainland. Such tax-

---

24. I.R.C. § 936. The provision allows a credit for that portion of the corporate tax attributable to income from Puerto Rico or another possession of the United States, if 80% of the gross income of the corporation came from sources in a possession for the preceding three years and 75% from the active conduct of a trade or business for the year for which the credit is to be claimed.

motivated geographical moves can have relatively high costs elsewhere in the economy.

Accordingly, the general welfare may be diminished if potentially competitive taxing jurisdictions do not refrain from the practice of undermining one another's tax regimes. The EC has in particular agreed to avoid the use of "state aids" for the purpose of intra-community competition and is seeking, still with little success, to persuade recalcitrant members to bring their corporate tax systems into rough conformity. Simultaneously, and with greater success, the EC has by negotiation among its members achieved a reasonable degree of uniformity in the adoption of value-added taxes as partial surrogates for corporate taxes,[25] and more recently other members of the 24 member countries of the Organization for Economic Cooperation and Development (OECD) have followed suit; only the United States, Switzerland, and Australia have not yet done so.

As chapter 11 pointed out, the principal European countries that did have "classical" corporate tax structures—tax systems that impose a tax on corporate profits *and* on distributions out of those profits—have now moved to various forms of dividend relief, so that corporate income is roughly taxed at rates corresponding to the marginal tax rates of their shareholders. The imposition instead of a value-added tax, which operates as a tax on consumption rather than on production or profits, is considered by many economists a more neutral way to skim a governmental share from the net product of an economy in close interaction with other economies.[26] The prevailing argument from EC tax theorists is that such neutrality follows from the way in which a consumption tax of this design (not all consumption taxes would share the relevant feature) takes geography into account.[27]

What suits the VAT to the purpose in question is primarily the invoice method of collection that is generally used in Europe. (Other methods of VAT collection could achieve the same advantage only by greatly added complexity.) The European VAT is imposed on producers as products are sold (services are taxed in the same way) and collected by reference to invoices filed with the tax authorities. Exports are exempted from the tax by the simple expedient of refunding the tax to purchasers as they cross the border (or thereafter). Importers pay tax on the full value of imports at the VAT rate. The result is that only goods and services consumed in the taxing country are in principle subject to the tax. It is said therefore that the tax is imposed on a *destination basis*. By contrast, eliminating the special provision for imports and exports would have the effect of taxing goods and services where they originate and not necessarily where they are

25. Kay & King, The British Tax System, supra note 9, at 209–17.

26. Hans-Werner Sinn, Capital Income Taxation and International Resource Allocation (1989).

27. See Sijbren Cnossen, *Consumption Taxes and International Competitiveness: The OECD Experience*, 56 Tax Notes 1211 (September 2, 1991); *Tax Harmonization Issues In the European Community*, supra note 9, at 275.

consumed. They would then be said to be taxed on an *origin basis*. What makes the VAT attractive for the purpose of frustrating tax competition is that it is *both* a consumption (not a production) tax *and* destination based. If different countries within an integrated trading community impose taxes at different rates on a destination or residence basis and on the same tax base (e.g., consumption or individual, as opposed to corporate, income), taxes should have no effect on consumer choices.

In contrast with these much vaunted attractions, flat taxes on consumption tend to be regressive and may adversely influence choices between labor and leisure because they "favor" purchases of goods that are in some respects substitutes for work—like camping and sports products. Moreover, a little appreciated fact about the European-style VAT is the comparatively high cost of administering it. In Great Britain, the cost was estimated to be as great as 10% of revenues in the 1970's, when the rate of the tax was relatively low (8%).[28] A part of the cost may have been attributable to the "zero-rating" or exemption of a variety of goods and services. More recent estimates for OECD country administration of VAT taxes are considerably lower—from .35% of revenue in Sweden to 1.09% in Belgium, not taking the rate of tax into account.[29] Nevertheless, the demoralization associated with yet another layer of paperwork for sellers might constitute a greater cost in this country than these nominal European administrative burdens indicate.

It would be difficult to overstate the attention recently devoted essentially to the idea of a shift from profits taxation to consumption taxation in the name of international tax harmonization. Several academic reputations are based on the movement in this direction; learned conferences and several volumes of convergent essays by leading figures have advanced the argument. Much attention has been given to translating what is essentially a set of a priori hypotheses about the effects of taxation on capital and resource flows into econometric models of real world investment phenomena.

If we are correct in thinking that tax competition hinders overall welfare gains, what barometer of international welfare could we use to detect the predicted effects? As one would expect, there is a significant gap between what can be said about the effect of taxes on investment and the effect of taxes (through investment effects) on the income of individuals and ultimately on collective "welfare" (read: gross domestic product). Economic models that represent the effects of taxes on income are highly stylized and have run into insuperable mathematical barriers to great realism. Hence, the use of empirical data in the study of the effect of taxes on welfare is confined to analysis that *assumes* a correlation between economic growth and welfare gains. In other words, the best we can do to discover what effect tax competition or its

28. C.T. Sandford, M. Godwin, P. Hardwick & I. Butterworth, Costs and Benefits of VAT (1982).

29. Cnossen, *Consumption Taxes and International Competitiveness: The OECD Experience,* supra note 25, at 1215.

abatement might have on real people depends on speculative assumptions about the importance for real people of the availability of new capital to existing business firms.

Thus, for example, several researchers have used general equilibrium models to try to ascertain whether a beneficial tax system, viewed from the standpoint of its domestic operation alone, could have such negative effects on incoming foreign investment flows as to make the effects of the tax system bad on the whole, i.e., whether tax effects on foreign investment elasticity could dominate other effects of tax policy on welfare. As we shall see in our discussion of economics models in chapter 14, interesting results can sometimes be derived from the very abstract analysis of mutually dependent functions of the same variables. In order to theorize about the effect of a country's taxes on incoming foreign investment, it is usually necessary simply to assume how the yield on investment, foreign or otherwise, would behave in the absence of taxes—to make some broad assumptions about the "elasticity" of investment flows. It is interesting indeed that some modeling efforts appear to show that the effects of taxes on foreign investment could overwhelm the effects of taxes on domestic welfare, holding foreign investment constant (or assuming no foreign investment).[30] Models thus appear to prove that tax competition can turn an otherwise "good" tax system into a "bad" one.

In order to determine whether that transformation might occur in the real world, much more must be known about actual foreign direct investment (FDI) response to taxes. You might think that in a world as well documented as ours has become, this information would be easy to gather; but it is elusive. A principal reason is that much of the best data about foreign investment flows is collected by governmental agencies like the Department of Commerce without regard to whether foreign ventures in this country use funds brought in from abroad or instead borrow locally. Balance-of-payment figures do not distinguish local borrowing and hence may be deceptive, yet they are virtually all we have. Scholars have disputed the need for, and indeed the very possibility of, making allowance for this aspect of the balance of payment data.[31] The upshot is that we have little reliable information about the actual effect of recent tax law on FDI. A second problem about measuring the effect of taxes on FDI is that empirical research has generally ignored the effect of taxes in the home country of the foreign investor. One investigation concludes that the evidence supports the conclusion either that U.S. taxation of FDI had a negative

30. See Lawrence H. Goulder, John B. Shoven, & John Whalley, *Domestic Tax Policy and the Foreign Sector*, in Behavioral Simulation Methods in Tax Policy Analysis (ed. M. Feldstein 1983); Lawrence Summers, *Tax Policy and International Competitiveness*, National Bureau of Economic Research Working Paper No. 2007 (1986).

31. Joosung Jun, *U.S. Tax Policy and Direct Investment Abroad*, in Taxation in the Global Economy 55 (ed. Assaf Razin & Joel Slemrod 1990) (arguing for the need for general correction to take local borrowing into account); Michael P. Dooley, *Comments on Jun's Paper*, id. at 74–78 (disputing the significance of local borrowing by foreign concerns).

effect on such investment *or* that stagnation of the foreign investor's home country economy had a controlling influence on the amount of FDI in the U.S.; the same study concludes that FDI is not measurably affected by the severity of home country taxation or tax relief for foreign-source income.[32]

Economic models have tended to confirm that tax competition can occur among countries whose economies are highly integrated. The models so far proposed, however, have intriguingly discordant implications for attempts to avoid tax competition.

One study, using a model based on the response of a single national economy to international trade in three goods over two time periods, concluded that the introduction of a VAT would leave trade unaffected only if the tax was rebated on exports. It also concluded that in practice a VAT may not be neutral in its trade effects because in the short run it could simply be a substitute for an income tax and because in the long run it will burden traded output more heavily than non-traded output, thereby tending to shift resources out of the traded good sectors.[33]

Too absolute a shift to VAT or other tax harmonization measures might also adversely affect the welfare of countries that have different environmental problems or other long-term public contingencies to provide for. "Intercountry differences in capital income taxes may ... be necessary to accommodate" the need for different levels of capital accumulation by the public sector to meet public needs.[34] While some level of tax harmonization may well be essential if destructive tax competition is to be avoided and if excessive tax-related bias in favor of investment in some countries is to be avoided, the balance of domestic public concerns must be weighed in deciding when tax biases are excessive.

In summary, the analytical work on which clear conclusions about the effects of interactive tax systems should be based is just beginning. Nevertheless, the urge to harmonize is strongly felt and has the general support of theorists and others who influence tax legislation. The coincidence of business lobby advocacy of capital income tax relief with the goal of preventing tax competition and of promoting efficient international capital markets may prove convincing to decision-makers.

32.   Joel Slemrod, *Tax Effects on Foreign Direct Investment in the United States: Evidence from a Cross–Country Comparison*, in Taxation in the Global Economy, supra note 31, at 79.

33.   Martin Feldstein & Paul Krugman, *International Trade Effects of Value–Added Taxation*, in Taxation in the Global Economy, supra note 31, at 263.

34.   A. Lans Bovenberg, Krister Andersson, Kenji Aramaki & Sheetal K. Chand,

Tax Incentives and International Capital Flows: The Case of the United States and Japan, in Taxation in the Global Economy, supra note 31, at 283, 314; Cnossen, *Tax Harmonization Issues In the European Community*, supra note 27, at 275 (harmonization of the choice of corporate tax base can be viewed as separate from harmonization of the basis of assessment and hence of individual tax rates).

12.6 WHITHER?

International tax policy is arcane enough that its audience is virtually limited to the multinational corporations that sometimes enjoy the advantages of evasive international tax planning and sometimes find themselves stymied by inappropriate treaties or their absence. National populations that sometimes respond to high principle when domestic tax policy is debated, have yet to begin thinking in such terms about admittedly inscrutable international capital flows and their effects on booming and wayward economies.[35] This is especially unfortunate because the effect of ignorance and indifference in this setting can be the de facto endorsement of imprudent and intolerant actions concerning global neighbors. First, second and third worlds definitely collide over trade and tax policy, and this can be to no one's advantage as the earth grows smaller.

---

35. See Jeffrey Birnbaum, *Clinton's Revised Economic Plan Sets Massive Tax Increases for Foreign Firms*, Wall St. J. (June 22, 1992) at A16, col. 1.

Chapter 13

STATE AND LOCAL TAXATION

13.1 THE PUZZLES OF COMBINED NATIONAL AND LOCAL TAXATION

Many countries, of course, have both national and local taxes, with local differences in tax rates or tax base or both. The United States is unusual in its "federal" insistence on the freedom of local taxation from national planning or coordination. Only the danger of driving away residents and locally beneficial enterprises—the "exit option"—apparently discourages geographical idiosyncracies in the taxation of comparably situated individuals or firms. Behind the camouflage of locally disparate tax policy, however, there lurks another political reality. Federal tax policy, given the supremacy of federal political power, can afford to claim the largest share of the pie, but the federal government need not take responsibility for traditionally local benefit programs and can even, when political winds are favorable, transfer its own previous commitments to the states.[1] This gives a special twist to the priority, established by political custom rather than by constitutional or legislative arrangement, of national over local taxes. Thus, federalism in taxation is subject to tensions of several kinds: constitutional liberality and perceived threats to that liberality confront de facto political constraints of several sorts.

At the center of these tensions, however, is uncertainty over the comparative size of federal and state-and-local tax receipts. If the entire national economy is felt now to have become more closely tied to a global economy, state economies have scarcely had separate identities since colonial times. Commerce is supposed to pass freely from the jurisdiction of one state to that of another, and the populace is in fact more mobile than in any other country. Differences in the design of state and local tax systems create the possibility, taken seriously by both theorists and politicians, that people and activities will exercise

---

1. Federal-state "revenue-sharing" in the 1970's camouflaged the shifting of federal responsibility for a variety of programs to the states, along with only a small share of the revenues that had formerly paid for the federal versions of those programs.

the exit option in response to the configuration of tax burdens in a particular place and go elsewhere, at least temporarily. Entire state tax systems have been redesigned in detail to respond to the perceived effect of state corporate tax, or its absence, on the location of corporate headquarters. Several states have a persistent worry that their comparatively broad social service programs are attracting the poor from other states, and they tinker with combined taxing and spending options in the hope of striking a less burdensome balance.

13.2 CRITERIA FOR ACCEPTABLE TAX FEDERALISM

Despite the conflicting principles and pressures just cited, state and local tax policy is a theoretical and practical backwater. The economic literature is tiny; the Commerce Clause is rarely enforced to re-shape state tax law; custom rather than vision seems to guide what state politicians do; tax lawyers, many of whom work extensively on state tax matters, rarely address the public issues of the field. It is at the state level, however, that tax rebellion is most often threatened. The "poll tax" in Great Britain, a local capitation tax that has been levied off and on through a long history,[2] has also, as a recent T-shirt declared, been protested from 1391 through 1991. In the 1970's, the California property tax referendum "Prop 13" changed the shape of state finances nationwide. All this raises the question, by what standards can state and local tax schemes by judged?

Two goals of tax design, familiar from general tax policy studies, have special relevance to state and local taxation. They are tax neutrality and the coordination of tax burdens with tax benefits. Both goals take on special meaning in this context because there are few if any meaningful economic borders between neighborhoods within a unified national economy. Tax neutrality is an affirmative goal for the several local tax authorities because they run the risk of chasing away their taxpayers. Tax neutrality is also an issue, insofar as local tax authorities may hope to attract taxpayers to their own jurisdictions from others, both for the taxes they will pay and for other, principally economic, benefits their presence may bring.

The ideals of benefit taxation have a special place among the natural goals of state and local taxation because the voting public has a plausible chance of forcing local politicians to coordinate local taxation with local benefit programs, and because notably local government benefits give tax districts what little ability they have to resist the flight of taxpaying constituents. If voters and political candidates wish to bargain with each other over who gets which benefits, they can do so more realistically with respect to the kind of benefits that are usually provided at the local level. Local law enforcement, roads, and garbage collection are matters of disproportionately local concern, at least in comparison with many health care or social security benefits.

2. See John A. Kay and Mervyn A. King, The British Tax System 138–41 (5th ed. 1990).

Local taxation in pursuit of benefit taxation ideals, however, makes tax equity among taxpayers in different localities more difficult to attain. If local taxes are successfully designed to apportion tax burden to government benefit, the addition of local to national tax burdens has no effect at all on tax fairness: local taxes are completely offset by the increases in individual welfare they pay for. But benefit taxation is not so easily realized.

In section 2.3(3) we noted that serious study of the objectives of pure and complete benefit taxation generally ignores the problem of determining whose welfare is increased by a government program and by how much. For even ignoring this substantial and perhaps overwhelming practical problem, it has been recognized that there may be no single best solution to the subsequent problem of determining the tradeoff between private and public goods.[3] The tradeoff problem has been studied extensively. The prior theoretical and practical problem of determining the value of public goods to individuals has received less attention, but it too has a special twist in the context of state and local taxation.

If people could move from one locale to another without paying a toll, a market for local government services might arise in which people simply shopped for the local government they preferred. Thus, for example, if all local taxes were poll taxes or income taxes, if housing cost the same everywhere, and if there were no other costs particularly associated with moving one's residence, the resident/consumer might simply "buy" what she wanted by moving to the appropriate jurisdiction. But housing arrangements, and the prevalence of property taxes among other things, can deter someone from moving, even though a preferred combination of tax burden and public goods beckons.

If localities have various tax rates and offer different levels of public services, the individual resident's tax liability (equal to the value of his or her real estate multiplied by the tax rate) is the price of entry into the community, which amounts to the price of consuming the local output of public services. Ideally, if the market for local provision of public services were perfect, the present value of the future stream of benefits from public services would always equal the present value of future tax payments. But local governments are not perfect competitors, in part because they are not all equally good at providing public-good value for revenues received, but also because people are not perfectly mobile. It is not as easy to move if you depend on a job for income than if you depend only on the yield from passive investments. Since labor is less mobile than capital, the reflection of expected government benefits and taxes in housing prices (the *capitalization* of these elements) may make it less likely that local governments will compete to offer what wage earners want than what the independently wealthy want. The market for different local tax-and-expenditure

3. See Richard A. Musgrave, *The Voluntary Exchange Theory of Public Economy*, 52 Q. J. Econ. 213 (1939); Paul A. Samuelson, *The Pure Theory of Public Expenditures*, 36 Rev. Econ. & Stat. 387 (1954).

packages can be imperfect in many other ways.[4] One of the more obvious ways today is through local competition to reach across local borders and tax those who neither vote nor benefit from the full range of local public goods, so-called "tax exporting."

Implicit so far in our discussion of criteria for local taxation is the assumption that it is up to a central despotic government to choose and apply the relevant criteria. This amounts to looking at state taxation in the United States context as if the federal government is presumptively the right authority to control taxing and spending decisions. Much that has been written about state taxation by tax theorists in this country shares this orientation in one way or another. Thus, many writers argue strenuously that even if one is concerned with economic efficiency at the national level, state and local taxation can nevertheless be desirable. Opponents of state autonomy sometimes argue just the reverse, namely, that federalism in taxation is inefficient from a national point of view. But why should the national point of view control? The value of local autonomy may offset national efficiency losses.

When this possibility is raised, it can be seen that the assessment of state and local tax alternatives is complex indeed. The general issue is really not whether federalism is consistent with the efficiency, distributive fairness, and stability of the encompassing economy. It is, instead: With respect to what community or communities should taxation and the provision of government services be judged? Some answers to this question would almost certainly imply very different standards for evaluating tax federalism. For example, since the multilevel structure of federal government requires some duplication of administrative effort at the different levels, federalism is almost certainly somewhat more costly than a single central tax mechanism would be. Unless this additional cost were offset by national efficiency gains under all circumstances, federalism could not be preferable from the national standpoint. If efficiency at the national level is not a controlling value, why is it a value at all? Why should we be talking about national tax policy instead of local tax policy as the presumptive starting point? If we did, the criteria for a satisfactory federalist approach to taxation would give weight to national-level efficiency gains, only if they raised the average welfare of residents of the state or local taxing unit.

A strong solution of this problem of perspective would essentially be a political argument for choosing the national governmental unit as the proper one for the expression of social choices. Not only do political philosophers acknowledge this problem—sometimes called the problem of national self-determination—to be one of fundamental and radical importance to the entire field of political theory, they have also

---

4. See Peter Mieszkowski, *The Property tax: An Excise Tax or a Profits Tax?*, 1 J. Pub. Econ. 73 (1972) (exploring several re- spects in which general equilibrium in this market may be achieved or missed).

failed utterly to come up with even superficially plausible solutions.[5] Long ago, political theorists assumed that political obligation might arise, if it ever did, only when some would-be authority accumulated enough coercive power within the confines of a given territory to be able to monopolize violence and thus, whatever its principles, to have a hope of guaranteeing physical security to the territory's inhabitants. We no longer "hope to distinguish justified claimants ... from unjustified pretenders with [such] crispness and decisiveness," since virtually all claimants have "consciously weaker claims ... and in addition ... have to abandon all hope of monopoly."[6]

Thus, the mechanics of shopping for public goods within a federal, multilevel system of tax authorities are far from straightforward *and* the priority of the concerns of one level of government over those of another is not easily justified. Debates about state and local taxation often concentrate on one of these two aspects of the problem with the covert purpose of establishing something about the other. Useful discussion of the puzzles of state and local taxation requires that both be kept clearly in view.

13.3 TIEBOUT'S MODEL OF LOCAL PUBLIC EXPENDITURES

For thirty years, the relatively simple models proposed by Professor Charles M. Tiebout have dominated writing by economists on the subject of local taxing and spending for public goods.[7] Tiebout's models were all designed to show that if consumer-voters are able to move from one community to another, they will "adopt" the appropriate local governments, and that equilibrium of local government shopping will be efficient for the encompassing political union to which the local governments owe common allegiance.

The models make a number of simplifying assumptions. Revenue-expenditure patterns are fixed for the various local governmental units. Voter-consumers themselves have fixed preferences for revenue and expenditure patterns and know what their preferences are. The consumer-voters are not tied by employment or anything else, apart from their preference patterns, to one community or another. Only local residents enjoy the benefit and suffer the cost of the public services local governments provide. And communities have and know the best population size for their fixed patterns of taxing and expenditure and work to achieve that size.

Before looking into the implications of Tiebout's simplifying assumptions, note that it is from the standpoint of a previously justified national state or encompassing community that his theory appears to

---

5. See, e.g., Avishai Margalit & Joseph Raz, *The Right of National Self–Determination*, 87 J. Phil. 439 (1990).

6. John Dunn, *Political Obligation*, in Political Theory Today 23, 40 (ed. David Held 1991).

7. Charles M. Tiebout, *A Pure Theory of Local Expenditures*, 64 J. Pol. Econ. 416 (1956).

justify permitting local government autonomy in taxing and expenditure patterns. The models assume that matching consumer-voter choices of local government taxing and expenditure patterns is not a sufficient good in itself to withstand criticism of the arrangement on the basis of costs at the level of the encompassing community. This raises the question why local autonomy is thought to be desirable, if it is not a robust enough goal to stand on its own when compared with broader community goals.[8] The answer, if there is one, presumably lies in the ideal of pluralism itself. There is in this country a national constituency for localism short of dissolution into smaller national units. The advantages of local autonomy are taken for granted, as are the advantages of national union. What could motivate one to strive for both advantages at once? Surely not economic efficiency. Even Tiebout's models do not purport to claim greater overall efficiency for multilevel government than for monolithic government. On the contrary, the motivation for Tiebout's theory must lie in the goal of showing that under some circumstances voter-consumers might achieve a perfect match between their desires and what government has to offer, without national coordination. As Tiebout characterized his theory, its point was to show that within a federal system there could be a "market type" solution to the problem of selecting the level of public goods expenditures that increases everyone's welfare.[9]

Further exploration of Tiebout's theory requires the relaxation of some of the assumptions of his models. First, consider the assumption that revenue-expenditure patterns are fixed for the various local governmental units. One of the normal concerns of policy makers at both the national and state levels is the fear that states and localities will alter their tax schemes in response to those of their neighbors, either erecting tariffs against competition or lowering taxes to attract away desirable business. Even Tiebout's most complex model assumed that the city managers or other local authorities would actively seek to influence moves into and out of their jurisdiction in order to arrive at optimal population size for their pre-determined tax-and-expenditure packages. The outcome of competition among communities is not predictable, at least by equilibrium analysis, if communities are allowed to change their offerings.

The assumption that the consumer-voters are fully mobile, detached from the communities in which they live except for the advantages local governments offer in the form of public expenditures, appears to evade a much more complex reality. The type of taxes imposed by a community may affect the mobility of its residents. For instance, a property tax may lead to a less intense use of land there and decrease land values. The result may be to make it more difficult for landowners to exercise the exit option. But if local services are not sufficiently increased to offset the loss in land values, residents have an

---

8. See Daniel N. Shaviro, *An Economic and Political Look at Federalism in Taxation*, 90 Mich. L. Rev. 895, 906 (1992).

9. Tiebout, supra, at 416.

incentive to move. The outcome of the tension between these contrary pressures may depend on how skillful the local city manager is. Moreover, taxes that are partially excise taxes and property taxes may be borne in large part by imperfectly mobile factors of production, such as labor and the owners of highly specialized equipment. It is not clear, however, that mobility is so greatly distorted by these real possibilities as to render Tiebout's models irrelevant. It is possible that relatively high tax rates in some cities may increase the prices of goods and services produced there, but that these price increases will be tempered or swamped by decreases in the value of land and in returns to other factors of production that cannot costlessly relocate. Empirical studies have suggested that something like Tiebout's model may be reflected in actual relocation patterns.[10]

The third major assumption on which Tiebout's models are based is that public benefits are kept within the community providing them and that taxes are paid only by those entitled to enjoy those benefits. Moreover, the benefits must be such that prospective residents have complete knowledge in advance of the benefits they will receive. It is sufficient to note here that these assumptions are designed to eliminate the usual reasons for questioning the goals of benefit taxation—that the benefit of public goods cannot be measured or foreseen with sufficient clarity to make them a fit subject matter for market transactions.

The administrative costs of preventing autonomous taxing authorities from undermining the collective good by striving to outdo each other are also left out of Tiebout's account. The need to suppress conflict among the "states" of the Confederation period was a principal motive for the design and adoption of the Constitution. Although tariffs were the main problem then, and now the problem is a contrary tendency towards "tax competition" or the undercutting of neighboring states' tax systems, the need for federal policing of state and local tax effects, in the interest of a degree of interstate tax neutrality, is still strong. Thus, in this respect as well, Tiebout's models understate the concerns that beset state and local tax policy.

13.4   IS THERE A RATIONAL MIDDLE GROUND FOR ASSESS- ING TAX POLICY WITHIN A FEDERAL SYSTEM?

From the standpoint of central government the relative autonomy of local taxing authorities requires substantial justification. From the local standpoint local autonomy needs no justification, nor are the costs of local autonomy necessarily to be regretted, wherever they may be felt, but especially if they do not wipe out welfare gains from government at the local level. Indeed, national interference in local affairs may be considered a positive evil, to the extent that it does not clearly contribute to local well being. Given the bifocalism of federalism, the

---

10. Wallace E. Oates, *The Effects of Property Taxes and Local Public Spending on Property Values: An Empirical Study of* *Tax Capitalization and the Tiebout Hypotheses*, 77 J. Pol. Econ. 957 (1969).

pursuit of standards for judging the validity and quality of state and local taxation may seemed doomed.

The recent concern over tax competition among states members of the European Community, however, offers a paradigm for assessing split-level tax policy of the sort with which we are concerned. The EC countries so far still cling to their sovereignty, and their citizens by all accounts want local autonomy in some form to survive, no matter what progress toward a "federal" European union may occur. Cultural identity in Europe has obvious economic ramifications; one need think only of the role wine, beer, cheese, fruit and other agricultural products play in the process of defining self-images for the various sub-communities even within the modern European national units. Self-definition as between the European nationalities is even more closely dependent on the viability of preferences for local goods as well as for local accents, art, philosophy and literature. Nevertheless, the value of supra-national coordination of commerce has long claimed wide support. As a consequence, it is not surprising that "the architects of European unity" expect the joint economic policy of the EC, which must necessarily include some coordination of the several member nations' tax policies, to reflect both European and member nations' several interests, with no preference for one or the other perspective. The standards of good European tax policy might therefore be expected to provide a middle-ground approach to the analogous problem of multilevel tax policy in our older, but perhaps less self-conscious, federal order.

The starting point of the European pursuit of tax harmonization is belief in the proposition that the general welfare may be diminished if potentially competitive taxing jurisdictions do not refrain from undermining one another's tax regimes. As we saw in section 12.4 above, the EC countries have promised to avoid the use of "state aids" that result in intra-community competition and hope to persuade themselves collectively to bring their corporate tax systems into rough conformity. So far these promises and efforts have come to little. Simultaneously, however, and with greater success, the members of the EC have negotiated a reasonable degree of uniformity in the adoption of value-added taxes as partial surrogates for corporate taxes,[11] and more recently others of the 24 member countries of the Organization for Economic Cooperation and Development (OECD) have followed suit; only the United States, Switzerland, and Australia have not yet done so.

The principal European countries that did have "classical" corporate tax structures—tax systems that impose a tax on corporate profits *and* on distributions out of those profits—have adopted tax reforms that provide various forms of dividend relief, so that corporate income is roughly taxed at rates corresponding to the marginal tax rates of their shareholders. The imposition instead of a value-added tax (VAT),

11. Kay & King, supra note 2, at 209–17.

which operates as a tax on consumption rather than on production or profits, is considered by many economists a more neutral way to skim a governmental share from the net product of an economy in close interaction with other economies.[12]

What suits the VAT to the purpose in question is primarily the invoice method of collection that is generally used in Europe. (Other methods of VAT collection could achieve the same advantage only by greatly added complexity.) The European VAT is imposed on producers as products are sold (services are taxed in the same way) and collected by reference to invoices filed with the tax authorities. Exports are exempted from the tax by the simple expedient of refunding the tax to purchasers as they cross the border (or thereafter). Importers pay tax on the full value of imports at the VAT rate. The result is that only goods and services consumed in the taxing country are in principle subject to the tax. It is said therefore that the tax is imposed on a *destination basis*. By contrast, eliminating the special provision for imports and exports would have the effect of taxing goods and services where they originate and not necessarily where they are consumed. They would then be said to be taxed on an *origin basis*. The VAT is *both* a consumption (not a production) tax *and* destination based. If different countries within an integrated trading community impose taxes at different rates on a destination or residence basis and on the same tax base (e.g., consumption or individual, as opposed to corporate, income), taxes should have no effect on consumer choices. Hence, the common reliance on VAT of similar design tends to eliminate tax competition.

The shift from profits taxation to consumption taxation has now become emblematic of tax harmonization in the international context. If we are correct in thinking that tax competition hinders overall welfare gains, what barometer of international welfare could we use to detect the predicted effects? As one would expect, there is a significant gap between what can be said about the effect of taxes on investment and the effect of taxes (through investment effects) on the income of individuals and ultimately on collective "welfare" (read: gross domestic product). Economic models that represent the effects of taxes on income are highly stylized and have run into insuperable mathematical barriers to greater realism. Hence, the use of empirical data in the study of the effect of taxes on welfare is confined to analysis that *assumes* a correlation between economic growth and welfare gains. In other words, the best we can do to discover what effect tax competition or its abatement might have on real people depends on speculative assumptions about the importance for real people of the availability of new capital to existing business firms. For the sake of the present discussion of state and local taxation, however, the prevailing view that

12. Hans-Werner Sinn, Capital Income Taxation and International Resource Allocation (1989).

economic prosperity depends on free capital flows is at least a starting point.

On the other hand, much of the general populace as well as many politicians in power in Europe obviously think local concerns should not be overbalanced by a concern for the Common Market in any of its manifestations. As has been pointed out in section 12.4 above, too absolute a shift to VAT or other tax harmonization measures might also adversely affect the welfare of countries that have different environmental problems or other long-term public contingencies to provide for. Different levels of short-term revenue as well as of capital accumulation by the public sector may well be needed to meet different sorts of public needs. While some level of tax harmonization may well be essential if destructive tax competition is to be avoided and if excessive tax-related bias in favor of investment in some countries is to be avoided, the balance of domestic public concerns must be weighed in deciding when tax biases are excessive.

When local and more general welfare measures (or whatever passes for them) differ, which should guide tax policy? Should tax policy be adjusted to maximize either measure under all circumstances, or should some "constitutional" adjustment of the respective claims of the smaller and larger communities be reached in advance and allowed to rule the unforeseen fortunes of both communities? For Europe, the only possible approach has been to begin with an initial constitutional arrangement, one based on the separate constitutions of the member states, and to contemplate what amount to constitutional amendments by treaty from time to time. The Treaty of Rome, which provides the groundwork for this progression of treaty adjustments, effectively gives each member state a veto over each adjustment of the underlying structure. The political and economic turmoil that has accompanied the ratification of the Maastricht treaty underscores the awkwardness as well as the sensitivity of this arrangement to the wishes of minorities within the community. It must be admitted, however, that the European Community has yet to attempt significant revision of local tax policy in the light of common goals.

By comparison, the U.S. federal constitutional framework for the adjustment of smaller and larger community legislation gives clear priority in most instances to larger community interests. Smaller communities retain no veto over structural changes in the interpretation of the federal taxing and spending power. Despite that balance of interests, state and local autonomy exist in the space left unclaimed by the federal legislature and judiciary. It cannot be said, however, that the result is a clear assignment of rights and powers.

Most important is the relatively large ratio of administrative and compliance costs occasioned by state and local taxation. There are approximately 7,000 separate sales tax jurisdictions in the country. The States' separate and unreconciled business tax regimes create a special problem both for the States and for their subject business taxpayers with respect to the allocation of business income that has ties to more than one State's territory. State autonomy in the selection of the types as well as amounts of tax they raise is largely responsible for administrative and compliance costs being out of line with revenues raised.

> Even assuming that everyone generally wants to cooperate, the positive transaction costs of cooperation, along with the occasional countervailing factors motivating legislators, suggest that there will remain at least residual differences between states' tax bases.... Even a small residual degree of variation may impose substantial compliance costs, however, [because these] costs are not purely proportional to the quantum of divergence between states' tax bases; a significant fixed cost results from the bare fact of divergence.[13]

Administrative and compliance costs are currently estimated to be as high as 5% of total state tax revenues, quite apart from the costs of tax planning, litigation, and lobbying for tax law changes.[14]

What the European and American experiences with multilevel tax policy have in common is that both exemplify comparatively large welfare losses due to the constitutional mode of accommodating more than one autonomous policy maker. "We do not yet possess an acceptable political ideal, for reasons which belong to moral and political philosophy. The unsolved problem is the familiar one of reconciling the standpoint of the collectivity with the standpoint of the individual...."[15] If people and not governments were truly sovereign, the discrepancy could be left to local voting, which would serve as a constant referendum on the priority to be given to the interests of the smaller and larger community. The failure of this utopian approach of course led to attempts at federation and large community coordination in the first place. It would seem therefore that the costs of bifocalism must be taken for granted, and that the goal should be to limit those costs.

The most direct expedient is to restrict both the local and the larger community in the types of taxation they may impose, leaving them free only to set the amount of revenue to be collected at their respective levels. The choice of the local tax base would of course have to be such as to eliminate tax exportation—the imposition of local taxes on residents or activities properly claimed by other localities. Uniformity of tax base *among* localities would otherwise remove the danger of discrimination against inter-locality commerce. Tax competition could still take place: the various localities could engage in an inverse bidding war for residents and business activities by setting their tax

---

13. Shaviro, supra note 8, at 920–21.

14. John F. Due & John L. Mikesell, Sales Taxation: State and Local Structure and Administration 323–27 (1983); Shaviro, supra note 8, at 920.

15. Thomas Nagel, Equality and Partiality 3 (1991).

rates lower and lower. But to the extent that the localities depend on tax revenues to provide government services, tax competition should be self-regulating. The locality with the lowest tax rates would be able to provide the fewest services and would, absent natural advantages of climate or other resources, attract fewer residents. If the number of residents were too few to support the provision of public goods in an efficient manner, residents would soon realize that they were paying too much for the little they got and move elsewhere. All this of course follows Tiebout's theory and assumes that voter/customers can move costlessly; things obviously could not be expected to work so well in the real world, but the conditions for Tiebout equilibrium would very nearly obtain.

The constraint we are discussing, however, seems inconsistent as a practical matter with significant local *or national* autonomy in tax design. An example will serve to prove the point. A constitutionally inflexible tax base at the local level would resemble the British "rates" system of local taxation. Its gravest disadvantage is that structural changes in the economy of parts of a country can turn the mandated local tax base into an artificially great disadvantage for the health of the local government and indirectly of the local economy. British rates, for example, were a property tax based on the assessed value of dwellings and business premises. The decline of the industrial sector during the 1970's and 1980's deprived many northern British cities of a significant part of their rates base by bankrupting industrial rates payers. A simultaneous rise in residential and commercial real estate put excess revenues into the pockets of local authorities in the South of England. The only possible response for the national government was to adjust the balance. The lesson is that even relatively stable tax bases like property values, which were in Britain and still are in the United States the quintessential local tax base, can prove unruly enough to destroy all hopes of equilibrium in the "market" for local government and force the hand of the national government.

This of course provides an argument in favor of the tax autonomy accorded the States under the U.S. Constitution. It also leads directly back to the administrative and compliance cost problems that prompted this excursion on the subject of constitutional constraints. Further experimentation with constitutional adjustment of authority between national and local, and for that matter international, levels of government will no doubt ensue. The European Community, for the moment, is the most interesting laboratory for those experiments.

13.5 STATE TAXATION OF MULTI–NATIONAL CORPORATIONS

Multinational corporations pose a problem for national tax systems because their profits cannot practically or theoretically be assigned to or apportioned among the various jurisdictions in which they do business. There simply is no empirical test for dividing a multinational's enterprise into parts associated, as the corporate affiliates are associated, with territorial boundaries. This is so in part because any situs rule for contracts is necessarily arbitrary, and in part because transactions among the component enterprises that make up a multinational corporation do not trade with each other at arm's length. See section 12.3 through 12.4. At any rate, the slipperiness of multinational corporate income has elicited a relatively cynical response from state taxing authorities. Several of them, including some of the larger, more sophisticated states, have levied corporate taxes on multinationals doing business within their territory on a "unitary" basis, i.e., on the basis of worldwide income, without relief for tax burdens borne in other jurisdictions.

Clever taxpayers long ago came up with techniques for circumventing the income taxes levied on legally separate but affiliated firms by distinct geographical jurisdictions, whether national or states belonging to federal nations. If state A has an income tax and state B does not, it is easy for a corporation doing business in both jurisdictions to establish separate but affiliated corporations in the two states and then shift income to B, the state without a tax, by arranging for the two affiliated corporations to sell inventory or services to each other at prices that favor B affiliate, thereby avoiding the income tax of A. To combat abusive "transfer pricing" of this sort, some states have chosen to tax the income of both affiliated corporations if they are engaged in a unitary business. What constitutes a unitary business? There is no commonly accepted definition but the idea is that the several corporate components of the unitary firm both contribute to and benefit from the common ownership of them all. Some cases emphasize the centralization of management of the several firms and the flow of value among them. It might be well for courts dealing with the issue to consider the common creation or exploitation of intangibles such as market share, product image, name recognition, and so forth. In any case, the underlying point of unitary taxation is to respond to the difficulty of isolating the income of the components of a larger whole. As one commentator puts it, "a unitary business exists if (and only if) separate accounting does not adequately isolate the income of an individual corporate entity."[16]

The United States Supreme Court has held that such worldwide unitary taxation does not violate the Constitution—a largely negative holding, given the agnosticism of the Court with regard to the Commerce Clause and the problems of state discrimination against interstate and interference with national commerce.[17] The Reagan Admin-

16. Charles McLure, *Economic Perspectives on State Taxation of Multijurisdictional Corporations* 204 (1986).

17. Container Corporation v. Franchise Tax Board, 463 U.S. 159, 103 S.Ct. 2933, 77 L.Ed.2d 545 (1983).

istration, however, despite its apparently genuine concern over the negative impact of state unitary taxation on the national economy, proposed nothing more than an exchange of federal assistance in state information gathering for state forbearance from unitary taxation.[18]

The worldwide unitary tax strategy presents another aspect of the policy problem that arises from concern for the welfare of more than one community. States that have nominal autonomy in the design of their tax schemes usually have little interest in exercising that authority to the disadvantage of corporations that can remove themselves from the territory of the taxing state. The exit option should limit the availability of worldwide taxation as a means of extortion, and indeed it appears to do that. But the problem of transfer pricing is as real for the states as it is for the federal tax authority.[19] Given multinational corporations' actual or apparent manipulation of the accounts of their separate state units, the states have responded with global sanctions designed to maximize revenue, regardless of the theoretical optimum apportionment of corporate profits among the states and between the United States and other countries. It is important that states may be motivated to adopt worldwide unitary taxation of corporate profits for other than tax competitive reasons. While prudence may restrain tax competition among similarly situated states, it does nothing to restrain the unilateral insistence on what are in effect accounting rules that enterprises of other *countries* may regard as arbitrary.

For this reason, one practical response at the federal level to state worldwide unitary taxation is, as the Reagan Treasury proposed, to offer the states the information available to the national tax authorities. To give the state tax authorities the same enforcement advantages as federal authorities eliminates a part of the problem for the states. This response also appears to respect state autonomy within the federal system. The issue of fairness to nonresidents remains, and it is complicated by the fact that nonresidents will at least consider themselves unfairly treated if the simultaneous pursuit of different tax strategies by several taxing authorities places them at a disadvantage as compared to their competitors (or similarly situated nonresident individuals, as the case may be). But whose responsibility are the cumulative effects of several tax systems? Moreover, one of the advantages of the multinational business enterprise is its ability to shop for better tax treatment than may be available to competitors who have operations within only one tax jurisdiction. See section 12.4 above. Thus, worldwide unitary taxation finds a natural overlap between the problems of state and local taxation and those of internation-

18. U.S. Dept. of Treasury, The Final Report of the Worldwide Unitary Taxation Working Group: Chairman's Report and Supplemental Views (1984).

19. Transfer pricing is one outgrowth of the pervasive difficulty of national tax competition and the underlying difficulty of assessing the income of multinational corporations. See section 12.4.

al taxation, which was inevitable because both sets of problems spring from friction among the interests of several overlapping communities. The difference is that in the international context, the "self-interest" of communities smaller than the national states that are primary members of the community of nations is not at all clear and does not discourage arbitrary and offensive tax measures.

Chapter 14

ECONOMIC MODELS AND PROBLEMS OF TAX DESIGN

14.1 THE PURPOSES OF MODELS

When the staff of the Treasury Department or of the congressional tax committees analyze a tax bill, they sometimes rely on economic models in evaluating its effects. Experts who are not government employees also construct models in order to investigate whether variations in the design of tax systems improve their efficiency or equity. These model studies are evidently intended to be more authoritative than other less comprehensive analyses, and if they indeed take more of the relevant factors into account they deserve respect. Yet even among economists, the authority of tax models is controversial and seems likely to remain permanently in doubt. This chapter attempts to describe what the model builders are up to and to offer some explanation for the limbo to which their results are generally consigned.

The first point that needs to be made is that economic models used in tax policy discussions are of very different kinds. Some are intended to serve as tools for predicting where the dollars will fall if a given tax measure alters current tax burdens. These are of course models of tax incidence but also usually devices for predicting how taxpayers will adjust their behavior in the light of new or modified levies (and how these behavior adjustments will trigger others, and so on). When the Treasury or congressional staff devise and use such models, their purpose is usually to ascertain how much money particular features of the current tax structure raise for the government and how much other features cost in revenues that might be raised if the tax law were simplified so as to eliminate the features in question; the overall purpose includes predicting the revenue yields of the actual tax laws and of alternative versions that might be enacted. This analytical task is obviously closely allied to that of analyzing "tax expenditures," though it does not presuppose the controversial political implications of the tax expenditure doctrine. See Chapter 7, above. The close alliance rests on the fact that revenues forgone because of a particular feature of the tax law are by definition tax expenditures if that feature is not required by a principled delineation of, say, income or of whatever is the tax base under the law.

Other tax models may serve their purposes perfectly well even if they offer no guidance about actual or potential tax revenue yields. They may be constructed solely for the purpose of illustrating how generic features of a tax measure (such as the progressivity of an income tax, or the lump-sum incidence of a commodity tax) affect some standard or goal, and not for the purpose of mimicking in detail how actual tax regimes would work. The latter aspect may be reinforced by the decision to simplify drastically the factual setting against which the effects of the tax are studied. For example, the economy may be pictured as involving only two taxpayers and only two commodities.[1] Obviously, the limitations of such models are the most discussed and important thing about them. How much can we tell about how things would really work if we do not at least try to build all the relevant features of the world into our basic picture? It is an unfortunate shortcoming of the way in which the cognoscenti sometimes discuss such models that little attention is devoted to interpreting them. The vital question of evaluating the implications of these models is thus partly left to the general (and hence usually inexpert) reader.

Among the sort of models just described—those designed to illustrate rather than to aid prediction of real-world results—another division of labor is worth mentioning. Some illustrative models are intended to show under what conditions an economy would be in equilibrium after a tax measure is introduced and the economy has had time to react to the tax; models concerned with the conditions that would characterize equilibrium are called partial or general equilibrium models, depending on whether they attempt to take into account all the information that might in principle influence economic behavior. Others are concerned with the optimization of certain goals of taxation and not primarily with questions of equilibrium conditions; they seek to identify the conditions that would produce optimal results of some desired kind, such as optimal yields from a given kind of tax or optimally small distortions of other features of the economy, and are called optimal tax models. Optimal tax models can be general equilibrium models but need not be.

Perhaps the most important difference between optimal tax models and other models for our purposes is the orientation of optimal tax models towards issues of distributive justice. Other types of economic model often represent participants in an economy in terms of their preferences, especially when the purpose of the model is to show something about the interaction of individual behavior driven by the

---

1. See, e.g., James A. Mirrlees, *The Theory of Optimal Taxation*, in Kenneth Arrow & Michael Intriligator, eds., 3 Handbook of Mathematical Economics 1197 (1986).

preferences in question. But optimal tax theory has from its earliest days conceived of various problems about taxation as problems concerning the maximization of preference satisfaction, at least with regard to some select types of preference. So, for example, the point of a particular model of this sort might be to show that the varying preferences of a large number of individuals for leisure and for other forms of consumption can be maximized if there is a progressive tax on wages.[2] In other words, the optimal tax theorist manipulates the design of his or her model so as to illustrate the widest range of conditions under which some desirable consequence of a tax system for individuals or for the aggregate will consistently occur. By contrast, general equilibrium models, when devised for the purpose of analyzing aspects of tax systems, are usually designed to mimic the actual workings of an economy and the taxes to which it is subject as closely as possible—eliminating much of the generality striven for by optimal tax theorists—with the purpose of showing as specifically as possible how a particular kind of economy will respond to a particular kind of tax structure.

14.2 OPTIMAL TAX MODELS

Optimal tax theory is to be found in a small number of scholarly articles that are surprisingly consistent in their focus. The explanation for this is in part that the area grows directly from one particularly brilliant response to a general puzzle about the design of tax systems. In 1927, Frank Ramsey, a graduate student in philosophy, who was also a mathematician of great sophistication, took up the challenge of an eminent economist to determine what general features a proportionate tax on some or all uses of income would have to possess in order to have the highest yield at the least cost to the consumer.[3] The student's brief essay laid the groundwork for the rest of optimal tax theory, but his unfortunately early death ensured that others would have to find ways of generalizing his assumptions and adapting his solution to more detailed representations of economic life.[4]

The attractive core of Ramsey's paper, however, lay in its already formidable generality. He was able to create a setting in which the problem of tax efficiency could be approached with virtually no extraneous assumptions about the particular characteristics of the society whose tax system was at stake or the peculiarities of the people who made up the society. The basic idea was to choose mathematical functions that could be interpreted as standing for key factors in the

2. This roughly approximates one of the optimal tax model theorems that led to the development of more sophisticated tax models and to results that point in different directions. See Mirrlees, supra note 2, at 1201–09.

3. Frank Plumpton Ramsey, *A Contribution To the Theory of Taxation*, in Foundations: Essays in Philosophy, Logic,

Mathematics and Economics 242 (ed. D.H. Mellor 1978).

4. The literature on optimal taxation began to grow only after 1970. Since that time a number of important papers have appeared. See Agnar Sandmo, *Optimal Taxation: A Survey of the Literature*, 6 J. Pub. Econ. 37 (1976).

behavior of individual economic actors and to assume as little about these functions as possible. It may seem odd, though, to say that little was assumed when some of the basic assumptions are actually revealed. For example, a function of central importance to the model stood for a person's welfare. It was "defined" only to the extent that the function was assumed to depend exclusively on the amounts of various commodities consumed by individuals. It was also assumed that aggregate demand for particular commodities accurately expressed the effect on individual utilities of consuming these commodities, and that the demand and supply curves were straight lines at or near the level of production at which the taxes were to be imposed.[5]

These are big and highly implausible assumptions for the real world, in part for reasons already discussed in Chapter 3. When the Ramsey proof assumes that "utility" for a consumer depends only on amounts of commodities consumed, it streamlines all conceivable aspects of taste and value that make people different from each other and that make individual life plans complex. Although it is true that isolated decisions may plausibly be reduced to the simplicity attributed to the usual stylized utility function, we have as yet no full-blown account of what is peculiar about these rare circumstances. When the proof assumes that supply and demand curves are straight at the level of production to which the tax is to be applied, it posits a lack of variation in marginal utility that may occur in reality, but again a reasonable guess is that it is highly unusual and no empirical study indicates when, if ever, it does occur.

Nevertheless, the addition of relatively slight additional constraints on these functions was sufficient to enable Ramsey to prove his sweeping conclusion about tax design. Before examining that conclusion, let us first notice something about the state of economic theory to which it constituted an addition. It had been assumed that one condition all tax schemes must meet in order to be efficient was that of (what would now be called) Pareto optimality. This is the requirement that the tax measure should improve the aggregate welfare (make everyone better off collectively) without diminishing any individual's welfare (cause someone to be worse off). Efficiency in this sense requires the ideal tax system to be consistent with a Pareto optimal allocation of resources. Resources are allocated in this optimal way if, as compared with the pre-tax situation, the tax alters who owns what but does so in a way that takes nothing away from anyone.

Economists had long since identified one impractical solution to the problem of ideal, Pareto optimal taxation. It was to stick to lump sum taxes. These by their nature must be taken into account once and for all by taxpayers, so that their subsequent decisions about what amounts of leisure to choose and what amounts of labor to sell for what levels of consumption will not be affected "at the margin." (Lump sum taxes have no marginal influence on subsequent well-informed, well-reasoned

---

5. Id. at 243, 249.

decisions about consumption because these taxes realign everyone's starting point for making such decisions only once and then leave the subsequent decisions unaffected.) This "classical solution" to the problem of how to tax without influencing economic decisions was impractical for extremely basic reasons. Governments cannot finance themselves for the indefinite future with only one tax collection effort. The collective wealth of present taxpayers, for one thing, is not great enough to pay for all future government outlays. Even if it were, present taxpayers would not stand for such a draconian exaction. So periodic tax harvests seem inevitable. Reasonable taxpayers will plan with them in mind and adjust their economic decisions accordingly, with the result that lump sum taxes no longer have the admirable neutrality attributed to them in this ideal account.

Against this background, we can see that Ramsey's proof is, strange to say, an effort to bring economic theory into line with real world requirements. It confronts "the second-best problem of making the best of a necessarily distortionary tax system." [6] As such it belongs to the same family as other far less mathematical efforts to analyze the neutrality of various indirect and direct taxes on production and investment decisions. Tax theorists had previously argued in favor of sales taxes on commodities, as opposed to profits or income taxes, as a second-best solution of the kind desired.[7]

What distinguished Ramsey's contribution, again, was the boost it gave to the effort to generalize the conditions under which a tax could be efficient and neutral in the narrow sense of minimizing the aggregate deadweight loss for any given tax revenue or level of public expenditure, a fiscal objective discussed briefly in section 2.2. The terms of Ramsey's generalization served as a platform for further developments by lending themselves to other mathematical theorems about the effects of a tax on individual taxpayer's utility functions. Thus, the Ramsey proof launched efforts to deal in a theoretical way with the interaction between taxes and both group and individual welfare.

14.3 AN OVERVIEW OF RAMSEY'S CONTRIBUTION

The nontechnical reader can get an idea of the strengths and weaknesses of this way of attacking tax policy problems from a simplified overview of Ramsey's problem and his solution. Labor and leisure are alternative uses of one's time, and the model assumes that any labor expended is always a subtraction from leisure. So if leisure is something enjoyable and hence a source of welfare enhancement, it is sensible to treat it as comparable to a commodity that one might purchase. One purchases leisure by forgoing the labor that would earn wages with which other commodities would be bought. We assume more generally that leisure is one of the available commodities; that

6. Sandmo, *Optimal Taxation: An Introduction to the Literature,* supra note 4, at n. 37, 38.

7. Alexandre C. Pigou, The Economics of Welfare (1920).

people derive utility only from the consumption of commodities; and that when a consumer chooses to consume a certain quantity of a commodity, the choice influences other choices only by reducing what the consumer has to spend on other commodities—in other words, the choice of one commodity will not bias the consumer in favor of other commodities, as perhaps swimwear purchases bias one in favor of beach towel purchases (there is, in economic jargon, no cross-elasticity of demand for different commodities). We also assume that amounts of commodities are measurable in the same units, and that includes the commodity leisure, so that we are in effect assuming that amounts of labor have values that can serve as the equivalent of a currency for this little economy.

We also assume that the public sector needs a certain definite level of tax revenue. Total taxes, in units of labor, then must equal the sum of the revenue from taxes on each commodity. If producer prices for all commodities are given, the problem of selecting a tax structure is the same as that of setting consumer prices. The goal of minimizing the drag of the tax on collective welfare—the amount of welfare lost due to tax collection without augmenting the tax revenues—becomes that of choosing a consumer price structure that does not induce consumers to choose what they will consume because of taxes; the optimal tax structure thus avoids "substitution effects."

Ramsey demonstrated that mathematics alone can solve the problem if one additional assumption is made, namely, that in the relevant range the social utility function is "concave," which is to say that as the amount of any commodity that is consumed rises, average social utility increases but at a decreasing rate—total utility goes up more slowly than amounts of consumed commodities. Given the simplified way in which prices and labor correspond, this amounts to an extremely stylized version of the assumption of the decreasing marginal utility of income. The restriction of the assumption to the relevant range means that the marginal utility of consumption must be assumed to diminish only in the neighborhood of the amounts of consumption that may be affected by the imposition of the tax, which is to say, where it matters. The restriction of course does not make the result much more general, since *any* assumption of uniformly diminishing marginal utility is already much more than we are ever likely to be able to ascertain about an actual group of people.

Nevertheless, the Ramsey proof and a range of related theorems derived from Ramsey's way of framing the problem do tell us interesting things. One of the important lessons is that the "idea that indirect taxation at uniform rates is obviously best from an efficiency point of view" is generally false.[8] (It is true only if we assume equal income elasticities for all taxed goods, which is to assume that every consum-

8. Sandmo, *Optimal Taxation: An Introduction to the Literature*, supra note 5, at 42, 44–45.

er's utility from each commodity changes at the same rate as amounts of the commodities change.) More specifically, Ramsey shows that a proportional reduction of prices is not in itself likely to preserve the pre-tax efficiency of an economy in equilibrium. This is because optimal allocation is achieved by preserving the *quantities* of goods consumed in the same proportion both pre- and post-tax, and there is no reason to suppose that adjustment of taxes on different commodities in proportion to their prices will preserve this allocation. (The assumption in question is also equivalent to the assumption that redistribution of income cannot improve the overall distributional effects of the economy.[9]) Otherwise, we learn little of practical importance. So the focus of the theory thus far should be understood to be essentially that of clarifying the assumptions on which crude analytical guesses about tax equity were based. In this regard, we learn a simple but extremely important cautionary lesson: "indirect" taxes, like the familiar state sales taxes and proposed national sales taxes, do *not* have the equity advantage that was once universally claimed for them.

14.4 OTHER LESSONS ABOUT OPTIMAL COMMODITY TAXATION

It is comforting for economists that the results associated with Ramsey's proof confirm other generally accepted propositions about the economics of taxation, such as the "rule" that taxes on commodities with the least elastic (i.e., least declining) demand minimize deviations from pre-tax economic decisions.[10] A corollary is that consumer goods that are linked with the choice to enjoy leisure rather than to work should be taxed at higher rates under a commodity tax than should consumer goods that are substitutes for leisure and complementary to labor.[11] The fact that a place can be found in optimal tax models for home truths is not very informative, however, when the home truths in slightly disguised form provide the skeleton of the model, as is the case with the propositions just mentioned. They are, in other words, close enough to what the models assume about the relationship between taxation and utility-guided choices among commodities to shed relatively little light on public policy.

On grounds of efficiency alone, it would make sense to tax food and the basics of life, for which demand is more or less fixed until one has enough (after which point the thing in question is no longer a necessity), rather than fast cars and other luxuries, for which demand is variable and, in particular, declines the more one already has.[12] How taxes affect the distribution of wealth is, however, a major political and ethical issue. The audience of optimal tax theory is obviously concerned with these distributional effects of taxation as well as with

9. Id. at 48.

10. Sandmo, supra note 5, at 45–46; see Peter Diamond & James A. Mirrlees, *Optimal Taxation and Public Production II*, 6 Am. Econ. Rev. 261 (1971).

11. H.V. Corlett and G.H. Hague, *Complementarity and the Excess Burden of Taxation*, 21 Rev. Econ. Stud. 21 (1953–54).

12. A.B. Atkinson & J.E. Stiglitz, *The Structure of Indirect Taxation and Economic Efficiency*, 1 J. Pub. Econ. 97 (1972).

efficiency. If the good of society as a whole were measured as a simple sum of the satisfactions of its members, and if people had identical utility functions (if the enjoyment of commodities and leisure affected everyone's welfare in the same way and to the same extent), optimal commodity taxation would set different tax rates on different commodities, with the highest rates on commodities favored by the rich.[13]

Other contributions to the field have focused on special features of how the provision of public goods interacts with the consumption of taxed commodities; how subsidies improve the competitive allocation of resources when not all the benefit or harm associated with individual consumption flows to the consumer (when there are externalities of consumption); and how to set prices of public utilities.[14] Since the revival of interest in optimal taxation in the early 1970's, the whole of public economics has been more or less taken over by reference to models for optimizing efficiency and distributional effects, more or less all of them extensions of Ramsey's original conception.

14.5 THE MIRRLEES INCOME TAX MODEL

Although others had previously built upon Ramsey's work,[15] James Mirrlees constructed an optimal income tax model that now virtually defines the field. Its primary purpose is to determine the optimal income tax rate structure for a society in which all income is derived from labor. The nature of the tax—a tax on income—is thus taken for granted; lump sum and commodity sales taxes alone are not considered as alternatives (in one extension of the model Mirrlees does consider combining commodity taxes with an income tax[16]). Although the model depends on a host of simplifying assumptions and for these and other reasons does not, as some admirers have supposed, "ground ... progressive taxation ... in a theory of distributive justice,"[17] it does illustrate relationships between social welfare and tax burdens that have heuristic value for tax policy issues in the real world.

The model, like Ramsey's before it, makes drastically simplifying assumptions about welfare. In particular, it incorporates an individual

13. Peter Diamond, *A Many–Person Ramsey Tax Rule*, 4 J. Pub. Econ. 335 (1975); James A. Mirrlees, *Optimal Commodity Taxation in a Two–Class Economy*, 4 J. Pub. Econ. 27 (1975).

14. S. Kolm, Cours d'Economie Publique (1971) (public utility pricing as an extension of optimal tax theory); A.B. Atkinson & N.H. Stern, *Pigou, Taxation and Public Goods*, 41 Rev. Econ. Stud. 119 (1974) (public goods in competition with taxed private commodities); Agnar Sandmo, *Optimal Taxation in the Presence of Externalities*, 77 Swed. J. Econ. 86 (1975).

15. Most of this work was closer to Ramsey's in that it concentrated on optimal commodity taxation. S. Kolm, *L'Etat et le Systeme des Prix* (1969); Boiteux, *Sur la gestion des monopoles publics asteints a l'equilibre budgetaire*, 24 Econometrica 22 (1956); Green, *The Social Optimum in the Presence of Monopoly and Taxation*, 29 Rev. Econ. Stud. 66 (1961). Other theoretical studies, however, also dealt with balancing losses due to efficiency against more equitable distribution of income, as does Mirrlees model. Ray C. Fair, *The Optimal Distribution of Income*, 85 Q.J. Econ. 551 (1971).

16. James A. Mirrlees, *Optimal Tax Theory: A Synthesis*, 6 J. Pub. Econ. 327 (1976).

17. Joseph Bankman & Thomas E. Griffith, *Social Welfare and the Rate Structure: A New Look at Progressive Taxation*, 75 Cal. L. Rev. 1905, 1966 (1987).

utility function that increases with the sum of consumption and leisure, and further assumes that consumption equals income (i.e., that all income is spent on consumption). Mirrlees' model also assumes that all individuals have the same utility function, and that its values are measured in terms of the same units (they are in effect units of labor). Moreover, the curve of the utility function is assumed to be concave: although utility increases with the sum of consumption and utility, it increases more slowly than that sum does. We should pause here to note that these assumptions led, in the generalized implications of Ramsey's proof, to the counter-intuitive conclusion that in order to optimize social welfare, viewed as a simple utilitarian sum of individual utilities, the highest rates of commodity tax should apply to necessities and the lowest to luxuries. Obviously, the truth of these assumptions or their adequacy as the premises for policy analysis deserve close attention.

One of the attractions of Mirrlees' model is that it permits different assumptions about the choice of a social welfare function to be compared with respect to their tax policy implications. Classical utilitarians had assumed, for example, that social welfare is a simple sum of individual utilities. Current defenders of a utilitarian approach in ethics regularly abandon this seemingly neutral approach for one that discounts differences among individuals by "weighting" the values of their utility functions differently before summing them to determine collective or social welfare values. If individual utility functions were capable of taking on different values for different sums of leisure and consumption, which is not possible on the assumptions built into the model, weighting might be used to correct for distortions considered not in the interest of the individual, injurious to others, or otherwise morally or politically unacceptable. No such need arises here because individuals have identical utility functions. But they may choose to work different numbers of hours and hence have different levels of consumption. The weighted social welfare function examined under the model is therefore only of the sort that differentiates between amounts of consumption and leisure, giving less weight to greater total amounts and more weight to lower total amounts. (It should be noted that this is an odd thing to consider doing, because utility is presumably of value in itself; we are not discounting to reflect the declining value of greater amounts of utility, but more of this later.)

Mirrlees considered yet a third choice of social welfare function, one suggested by Rawls's second principle of justice, that any reduction in the welfare of an individual member of society is justifiable only if it improves the welfare of the person whose welfare happens to rank last. Although Rawls did not intend this "difference" principle to be translated into traditional utilitarian terms, for reasons we considered in Chapter 4, the only expression it can be given on this model is that of assuming that the social welfare function varies with the *product* of the utilities of individual members of society, and does so to improve the welfare of the person whose welfare is lowest.

The model provides a means of calculating the schedule of tax rates that maximizes social welfare under these three views (or closely related variants) of how the social welfare function should be chosen. We will not examine the mathematical apparatus of the model here, other than to note that inherent limitations on its extension to more realistic settings may tell us something about the very possibility of basing tax policy on welfare judgments conceived in classical or modified utilitarian terms. (The mathematics offers no conceptual illumination of the policy problem at issue.) For the moment, it is enough to note that if we know the amounts of pre-tax income of all the individuals who make up a society, the model permits us to calculate which tax will maximize social welfare, given that the tax will induce the individuals to change their working hours by reducing the utility they derive from their labor. Thus, the model highlights the peculiar type of distortion income taxes cause in giving people a reason to substitute untaxed leisure for taxed consumption. This point will become important in our later discussion.

The model can be illustrated with a two-person economy in which individual A earns the minimum wage $4.55 per hour and individual B earns $100 per hour. Suppose that neither can work more than 16 hours a day because for each hour worked he or she must spend a half-hour in welfare-neutral activities like preparing for work, sleeping, etc. We will assume with Mirrlees that the shared utility function is the sum of an arbitrarily chosen function of consumption (which is assumed equal to income) and the same function of leisure, or [18]

$$C = \ln(nh) + \ln(24 - 1.5h).$$

If there is no tax on income, both will work an eight-hour day.[19]

With no income or other tax on the workers' earnings, the utilities of each and the total utility of their society are as follows:

No Tax Economy

Individual	Wage rate	Total wages	Utility
A	$4.55	$51.20	7.869123
B	$100.00	$800.00	9.169518
		Total	17.038641

If a 25% flat tax is imposed, the utilities of each and total utility are as follows:

---

18. The arbitrarily chosen function ln is the so-called natural logarithm, a concave function in terms of which any other concave function of a single argument can easily be expressed as the sum of the products of real numbers and the natural logarithm of algebraic functions of that argument.

19. The highest values of the utility functions of the two workers differ but these highest values occur for the same number of hours worked each day. If $U = \ln(nh) + \ln(24 - 1.5h)$, where n is the wage rate of the worker and h is the number of hours worked, then the utility function is maximized when $dU/dh = 24n - 3hn = 0$, and the value of H that makes this true is 8, regardless of the value of n.

25% Flat Tax Economy

Individual	Wage rate	Total wages	Utility
A	$4.55	$47.32	7.253471
B	$100.00	$735.00	8.912534
		Total	16.166005

As has been mentioned, what is especially interesting about the Mirrlees model is that it enables one to select the tax rate structure that will maximize social welfare—under any of several definitions, including the traditional utilitarian, weighted utilitarian and Rawlsian social welfare functions mentioned above. The mathematics is beyond the scope of this text. The results, however, reveal surprising implications of the assumptions and constraints of the model.

It is important that the Mirrlees model depicts a society with indefinitely many taxpayers who are paid at different wage rates. It can accommodate the analysis, moreover, of variable marginal tax rates, not only flat rates or even rates that vary in constant or linear fashion in relation to total income. The results of this comparison have rightly attracted the attention of tax policy experts outside the narrow field of optimal tax theory.

A peculiar feature of the Mirrlees model should be noted first. In order to portray the effects of various income tax rate structures on various conceptions of social welfare, the model focuses on the combination of possible progressive tax rates with something like a refundable personal exemption or standard deduction (called "demogrants"). The decision to examine an income tax with just these features is of course an arbitrary one. Nothing about the model or its objectives requires that the focus be narrowed to exclude, say, the combination of an income tax with something like the U.S. alternative minimum tax (a tax that effectively denies a portion of certain deductions to those with incomes above a certain level). Nevertheless, the combination of tax features that Mirrlees chose to consider provides a reasonable illustration of what can be accomplished by progressive taxation. In particular, the "demogrant" idea generalizes a common feature of most income tax systems. They permit all taxpayers, or those with low levels of tax, substantial exemptions (in the United States, this is called the "personal exemption") that are designed to insure that everyone may receive some level of income without any tax obligation, the level being set with a view to what is required for subsistence. The exemption scheme is historically linked with the argument that no tax should be levied on the consumption of the necessities of life.[20] But these exemptions are limited to people who have income. In a tax model that leaves out of account any governmental welfare scheme for those without any income, demogrants must play a role in order to duplicate the effect of welfare transfer payments.

The model under discussion has several moving parts. It permits us to ask how the tax rate structure should be set treating as variables (1) the revenue yield government requires, (2) the conception of social welfare that is to be maximized (the only alternatives are the three described above), and (3) the distribution of earning ability among members of society (in particular, the model gives results for a society in which everyone has the same earning potential and a society in which earning potential (which could also be interpreted as willingness to work) is differently distributed).[21] Results of calculations concerning the model are otherwise good for all variations that the model permits. It is in this respect that the model offers a serious approach to conclusions that should be good for all circumstances. But more of the limitations of the model in a moment.

As Mirrlees commented in his first paper on the subject, he expected that high marginal tax rates for the highest income earners would be optimal. It turned out, however, that whether social welfare is defined simply as the sum of individual utilities or as the product of individual utilities (Rawls's "difference principle" being a special case of the latter, if we equate welfare with utility), setting the highest marginal rates for the lowest income earners is the way to maximize social welfare. The demogrant system lessens the burden of these high marginal rates. The rich still pay a higher average tax than do the poor, and they continue to have the highest incomes, although the optimal tax structure would redistribute wealth to a small extent. The model is moreover capable of generating precise figures for the optimal demogrant and specific tax rate structures, of which Mirrlees offers a generous sampling of specific results.[22]

What then can we conclude? It is tempting to suppose that the model demonstrates the superiority of progressive income taxation to other tax schemes, or at least to other taxes on income. This is not quite the case.[23] First, there is nothing about the model that supports a preference for the combination of demogrants and income taxes at different marginal rates. Mirrlees considers other combinations of taxes elsewhere in order to reach conclusions about the optimal tax structure, given that another combination is to be used.[24] But given that there is to be an income tax with demogrants, the model seems

21. Mirrlees presents results for a society in which skill distribution is at four levels corresponding to the 10th, 50th, 90th, and 99th percentiles within the society. James A. Mirrlees, *An Exploration in the Theory of Optimum Income Taxation*, 38 Rev. Econ. Stud. 175, 206 (1971); see also *Optimal Tax Theory: A Synthesis*, 6 J. Pub. Econ. 105 at 328, 337–38 (1976).

22. Mirrlees, *Exploration*, supra note 21, at 202–04 (Tables I through XII).

23. *Contra* Bankman & Griffith, supra note 17, at 1907, 1958; but see id. at 1958–64 (authors attempt to explain away Mirrlees' marginal rate and other counter-intuitive conclusions while preserving the argument for progressive rate structures; no general argument emerges).

24. See Mirrlees, *Optimal Tax Theory: A Synthesis*, supra note 21.

quite positive about the implications of a consensus of social welfare views: there should be a progressive income tax and it should tax the lowest levels of income at the highest marginal rates.

Objections to these conclusions naturally focus on the model's assumptions. Most conspicuously, assumptions about individual utility functions cast doubt on the significance of the whole enterprise. We have seen that separability, continuity, identity of preference with interest, and the mutual independence of different individuals' utility functions are characteristics of traditional utility analysis that vitiate the equivalence of utility so defined with human welfare.

Furthermore, two peculiar characteristics of traditionally defined utility functions on which the Mirrlees model is based have such odd consequences in this context that we should question the relevance of the model altogether. First, the model assumes that taxpayers are free to choose just how much to work and make that choice "rationally", i.e., so as to maximize personal utility. All the model's implications for marginal tax rates depend heavily on this highly unrealistic assumption. In fact, it is a platitude of empirical research on actual economic behavior that most taxpayers are unable to express a reaction to changing tax burdens by rearranging their work schedules. The substitution effects of taxes on the choice between labor and leisure are not at all what a simplistic model would lead one to expect, and the Mirrlees model is unfortunately among the most simplistic in this regard. (To put this objection differently, our intuitions about what tax rate structures should be would probably accord with the implications of the model if labor and leisure were completely substitutable; we would then surely see the human predicament very differently.)[25] Varying the ease with which a taxpayer can replace labor with leisure is equivalent to varying the cost of that replacement. If a taxpayer is stuck with certain work hours under a wide range of circumstances, then the cost of replacing labor with leisure is prohibitively high under those circumstances. The size of the optimal demogrant and marginal tax rates change under the Mirrlees model if the elasticity of substitution between labor and leisure is assumed to be lower than 1.0 as in Mirrlees' original computations.[26] But, in order to mimic the world we know, the model would have to accommodate highly differentiated elasticities of substitution between labor and leisure. Social classes are defined as much by these as by different rates of compensation for their labor. Thus, the assumption of a common elasticity in this regard is crucially unrealistic and affects the consequences of the model significantly.

Second, the model ignores what benefits are returned to taxpayers apart from demogrants. In the wealthier industrial democracies, taxes pay largely for "entitlement" programs whose benefits flow to predicta-

---

25. Cf. Bankman & Griffith, id. at 1962–65 (criticizing the Mirrlees model's assumption of a constant elasticity of substitution of 1.0 between labor and leisure).

26. Bankman & Griffith, id. at 1965.

ble portions of the populace. Political scientists are inclined to point out that this may account in part for the stability of tax incidence and the majority's acquiescence in a certain tax burden. The Mirrlees model treats government outlays as if they provided public goods in which everyone benefited equally. This is not the usual case, and our intuitions certainly reflect what we know about the disproportionate sharing in health, retirement, education, and other governmental benefits to which the bulk of governmental levies are dedicated.

Further work on the Mirrlees model has corrected its implications in the light of the probable effect of envy and sympathy on individual welfare in societies like ours. One's position in the income hierarchy obviously influences most people to some extent. Envy of those who are apparently better off and sympathy for those who are apparently less well off can thus lower the utility a person would otherwise derive from a certain income. On the other hand, contempt for those less well off and awe of the wealthy are also present in the human comedy. On the assumption again that individual utility functions are identical, but with provision for the welfare of others to influence the welfare of any individual by a uniform measure of envy for those better off and sympathy for those faring worse, a revised version of the Mirrlees model indicates, as one would expect, that a more progressive tax rate structure maximizes social welfare on both utilitarian and Rawlsian definitions. Lower levels of income still call for higher marginal rates.

Finally, important limitations of the model leave us essentially without a clue about how an income tax influences certain real-world determinants of welfare. Recall that wages were taken as given and assumed not to be affected by the imposition of the tax. In economists' jargon, wage levels are exogenous variables (quantities whose values have their source outside the model). The model also excludes the phenomenon of accumulated and unearned wealth and assumes that prices are independent of the distribution of income (prices are taken to be equal to individuals' independent utility valuations of commodities in labor units). But taxes may of course influence all of these. When a tax is imposed or an existing tax is revised, price, wage and savings levels may be affected as individuals maximize utility for themselves against the changed backdrop of alternatives. Their responses may indeed influence each other. To put it more technically, general equilibrium effects may affect the results of the model that we have so far discussed. (We turn to general equilibrium models in the next section.)

Attempts to extend the model to general equilibrium analysis of wages have yielded positive, though in some ways conflicting, conclusions. Assuming that different types of labor are substitutes rather than complements (i.e., that the same job can be done by differently skilled workers), and making other plausible assumptions about the labor supply, some have argued that Mirrlees's results are confirmed.[27]

---

27. Allingham, *Inequality and Progressive Taxation*, 11 J. Pub. Econ. 273 (1979); Feldstein, *On the Optimal Progressivity of the Income Tax*, 2 J. Pub. Econ. 357 (1973).

Assuming negative labor supply elasiticity and complementary rather that substitutable types of labor, the model can be made to indicate that progressivity increases the gap between the the highest and lowest income levels.[28]

Accumulation of wealth and the possible influence of income distribution on individual utilities have yet to be introduced into the model. What efforts have been made to consider less direct effects of taxation (through the general equilibrium studies mentioned in the last paragraph, for example) already point to a wall of computational complexity that will probably limit further developments in these directions. Some of those committed to the effort have already given up the hope of dealing with these additional variables for any but a linear tax structure.

What is to be learned from optimal tax theory, in the light of these limitations? The relatively drastic stylization of people and their economic interaction that is fundamental to the Mirrlees model and its variants is typical of many economic analyses. Understood as first approximations to predictive theories, they fall so short of practical application that their constructive suggestions simply cannot be assessed. I think that is the wrong way to regard economic models of this general category. "The purpose of all applied welfare economics is to draw out the implications of alternative economic assumptions."[29] The mid-air goal of revealing conceptual connections has of course been well served by the Mirrlees model. But it of course points the way for a long and demanding journey.

A central lesson to be derived from the study of optimal tax models, however, is that the journey's prospects are themselves drastically limited. Inexorable mathematical difficulties stand in the way of further elaboration of the models to reflect many of the essential elements of the problem of distribution and the impact of taxes. Optimal tax theory is incontrovertibly a theory of second-best. If there were no real world constraints, lump sum taxes would be best. Income and commodity taxes are worse. But we are not in a position to scrap what we have, restore the world to a just state, and then impose an optimal tax system. The societies with which tax policy is concerned already have tax systems. Distributional concerns apply not only to the positions of individuals after a tax is imposed but to the shift from earlier positions.[30] But every addition to the model, including many that would incorporate very ordinary features of simple realistic societies, burdens the mathematical capacity of the model builder. It is generally concluded, for example, that nonlinear marginal income

28. Allen, *Optimal Linear Income Taxation with General Equilibrium Effects on Wages*, 17 J. Pub. Econ. 135 (1982); Carruth, *On the Role of the Production and Consumption Assumptions for Optimal Taxation*, 17 J. Pub. Econ. 145 (1982).

29. Martin Feldstein, *On the Theory of Tax Reform*, 6 J. Pub. Econ. 77 (1976).

30. Id. at 77–78.

tax rate structures are too complex to be modeled, once any distribution of earning capacity is taken into account.

What significance attaches to the mathematical dead end, if that is indeed what optimal tax theory faces? Formal models in other theoretical areas have sometimes run up against a similar problem, and it has gradually doomed the research projects of which these models were a part. The jury never comes in on the merits because the court is dissolved. It is probably too early to say whether this fate awaits optimal tax theory. A cloud of uncertainty, however, hangs over the area.

14.6 GENERAL EQUILIBRIUM MODELS AND TAXES IN GENERAL

Economic models have been used to investigate consequences of tax systems quite apart from distributional effects. One goal of this sort of analysis is to measure the efficiency of particular kinds of tax levy, as a ratio of revenue raised to distortionary cost borne by the economy (see Chapter 2). Some of these models, arguably the most persuasive, attempt to portray economic quantities in mutual interdependence, with sufficient inclusiveness to forestall the common objection in other areas of economic thought that indirect effects of the primary economic behavior may offset and utterly change the outcome associated with the primary behavior. These are general equilibrium models.

Equilibrium analysis in economics is the attempt to describe an economic system at a single moment in time (static analysis) or as it changes over a period of time (dynamic analysis) by means of a large number of quantitative relations or equations involving economic variables (prices, quantities of consumable and productive goods or services) which, by hypothesis and as represented in the model, simultaneously determine one another. It is usually thought to be a strength of general equilibrium models that they assume very little about the specific values of variables but instead represent how economic relations are affected by minimal restrictions on the behavior of the functions that define the model. Typical restrictions are those about the slope, monotonicity, and curvature of these functions, such as the so-called "law" of diminishing returns or of the diminishing marginal utility of income.[31]

General equilibrium analysis is so called in contrast with partial equilibrium analysis. The latter assumes that economic phenomena observed in small sectors of the economy, for example, in a particular industry such as tire manufacturing, exert no appreciable influence on the rest of the economy; or, more simply, that some variables included in the model are to be taken as given and not subject to the influence of changes in other variables. Thus, in the optimal tax models described

31. Mark Blaug, Outlines of the History of Economics (1960); Paul A. Samuelson, Foundations of Economic Analysis 7–17 (2d ed. 1983); Joseph Schumpeter, History of Economic Analysis 963–98 (1954).

in the previous section, wages were taken for granted and considered immune to change as a result of changes in tax rates, even though a more general analysis of the influence of taxes would allow for such influence. In other partial equilibrium models, changes in wages might be assumed to have no influence beyond the industry immediately affected, i.e., it would be assumed that national income and market demand schedules were not affected by changes in wage schedules.[32]

The standard example of partial equilibrium analysis is historically one of the oldest: the representation of an industry by its supply and demand curves. A typical industry is assumed to be one that faces a downward sloping demand curve, perhaps one that declines faster than it increases (a convex curve). The typical industry also cannot lower the cost of producing additional units of the product beyond a certain level; there is a minimal cost per marginal unit of product. The industry supply curve represents this by showing that the cost per additional unit does not decrease for levels of production above a certain minimum number of units. In these circumstances, the downward sloping demand curve must eventually intersect the upward or at least nondeclining supply curve. The intersection is located by reference to a certain level of production. If the industry were to increase production beyond the level marked by the intersection, it would do so at a financial loss, because the cost of producing additional units would be above the price at which additional units can be sold; the position of the demand curve below the supply curve beyond the point of intersection tells us this.

The supply and demand analysis, usually summarized with a diagram of the supply and demand curves and little further information, is partial equilibrium analysis because it purports to show that, apart from indirect effects, the output of the industry should rise to the level indicated by the intersection of the supply and demand curves, when all rational moves along the two curves have been accomplished by the relevant producers and consumers, i.e., when the behavior of producers and consumers is in equilibrium.

This example illustrates the importance for equilibrium analysis of a few simple assumptions about the curvature of the functions chosen to represent relevant economic variables. The analysis does not show that only supply and demand determine the equilibrium level of output. This is assumed. Nor does the analysis show that there must be an equilibrium level for industry production. This is broadly assumed as well, in the form of the assumption that the supply and demand curves have a certain shape. What motivates these assumptions is the economist's general knowledge of economic behavior—armchair observation, if not speculation. If the assumptions are plausible, the unforeseen characteristics of the interacting variables (the intersection of the supply and demand curves) may be illuminating, or that at least is the hope of the discipline.

---

32. J. Schumpeter, id. at 990–94.

General equilibrium analysis pushes this method of analysis as far as it can go. It too postulates that certain relations among variables, represented by a range of largely undefined mathematical functions, simultaneously determine the values of the variables in question. A model may hypothesize entrepreneurs who buy raw materials from other entrepreneurs, hire land from landowners, hire workers with certain skills and utility functions, purchase capital goods from capitalists, and sell products for profit to consumers or other entrepreneurs. The model will represent the markets in which these transactions occur, such as those of capital, of the products themselves and of the productive services that contribute to their production, by specifying the functions of supply and demand that determine their equilibrium.

The equilibria of the several markets are determined by their mutual interaction. More precisely, general equilibrium occurs *if* the assumptions on which the model is based sufficiently confine the behavior of the largely unspecified mathematical functions. Thus general equilibrium analysis becomes a search for restrictive assumptions that will determine *some* overall equilibrium, and it had better be one that corresponds to a description of the relevant markets that is a plausible reflection of the world as we know it.

The call for general equilibrium analysis of how taxes affect actual economic behavior has often come from those who survey the problems of excess burden and related distortionary effects of taxation.[33] Recently, general equilibrium models have been offered to ascertain the private costs of a marginal government dollar in tax revenues, how the general efficiency of the economy would be affected by replacement of a battery of disparate taxes with a single general sales tax, and how it would be affected by the integration of personal and corporate income taxes.[34] As has been mentioned, general equilibrium analysis of optimal income tax progressivity is represented by several competing analyses.[35]

Most attempts to apply general equilibrium analysis to tax policy issues are apparently designed to persuade politicians and the public of the value of certain reforms. The limited realism of the models is fatal for that purpose.[36] One feature that seems less objectionable in more theoretical work is the analysis of overall welfare effects. The general equilibrium analysts typically assume that welfare gains and losses may be treated as if winners, under some change in the tax structure,

33. See, e.g., Carl S. Shoup, Public Finance 28–31 (1969).

34. John B. Shoven & John Whalley, Applying General Equilibrium 153093 (1992); Don Fullerton, John Kind, John B. Shoven & John Whalley, *Corporate Tax Interpretation in the United States: A General Equilibrium Approach*, 71 Am. Econ. Rev. (1981); Alfred Piggot & John Whalley, *Economic Effects of U.K. Tax-subsidy Policies;: A General Equilibrium Analysis,* in their New Developments in Applied General Equilibrium Analysis (1985); John B. Shoven, *Applied General Equilibrium Tax Modeling,* 30 IMF Staff Papers No. 2 (1983).

35. See notes 30–31 supra.

36. Alan A. Tait, *Not So General Equilibrium and Not So Optimal Taxation,* 44 Pub. Fin. 169 (1989).

compensated losers. This really amounts to a reliance on the utilitarian social welfare function, according to which aggregate utility is considered to be improved even though some individuals are injured more than anyone is benefited, a criterion of improvement that has little appeal in ethical or public policy debate.

In addition to this central problem with the very concept of welfare, general equilibrium analysis also suffers in the practical context from what had seemed a strength for the development of theory. As we have seen, equilibrium analysis is strongly typified by the use of as little information as possible about the specific values of the functional equations that define relevant economic behavior. But information linking an economic model to the facts of a particular country's economy is essential if the model's implications are to convince policy makers.

At this point, it is important to note that when a model is adapted to the task of predicting the future of an actual economic system, the Turkish domestic economy, for example, it takes on a methodological dimension not shared by classic economic models. In order to grasp the shift, it is useful to reflect for a moment on what is involved in the specification of models.

A model is said to be "specified" to some extent when its defining mathematical functions are made sufficiently specific to yield actual values under a wide range of circumstances, at least when the specific values of some variables are determined. Thus, for example, the Mirrlees model was specified to an extent even in its original form by the assumption that individual utility functions varied with the sum of the natural logarithms of leisure and consumption. The model could be differently specified by assuming different rates for the substitution of leisure and consumption by different individuals, for example, the rates of substitution could be estimated to be between 0.5 and 0.75 for most people, on the basis of empirical study of employment decisions around the time of a change in tax rates. Changing the specification of the model in this way would not increase its specification, though it would make the mathematics more complex. It *would* specify the model to a greater extent to fix the number of consumer/taxpayers to be represented by the model. In Mirrlees' original model, the number was left open by means of the assumption that there were indefinitely many (i.e., "countably infinite") individuals represented. Greater specificity here does not aggravate the difficulty of mathematical solutions to questions about how the model functions but may even make matters simpler.

A model must be specified to some extent if it is to offer predictions about particular economic phenomena, for example, about the effects of corporate taxes on Swedish industry. But specification presupposes that sometimes highly theoretical variables have been accurately measured or otherwise determined for sometimes unwieldy real-world people and institutions. Although the typical equilibrium model takes for granted that the notion of equilibrium is meaningful in the abstract, there is no simple test for deciding whether a given national economy is indeed in equilibrium at a given moment at or near the present time. Looking back, and given a wealth of information about past economic behavior, deciding whether the economy *was* in equilibrium ten years ago may be possible, but even that is not so easy a matter to establish. Some applied general equilibrium analysts, for example, have assumed that in 1973 the U.S. economy was in equilibrium, although not in the prior or subsequent years. Yet the reason for the choice is largely that this was the last year in which sufficient information was available for the question of equilibrium even to be assessed. It has been pointed out that the first great oil price hike took place late in 1973, and that its distortionary effect would certainly have been felt in the last quarter of that year. This of course tells against the equilibrium of the economy at the time. The information was obviously available to the equilibrium theorists, and yet they *had* to choose this most recent fully documented year of economic behavior if the model was to offer interesting predictions for subsequent years.[37]

The methodological weakness of this instance of specification is obvious. It is also obviously likely to afflict other applied uses of general equilibrium theory. The problem is twofold: economic data are at best scant for such rarefied theoretical issues as the occurrence of equilibrium, and concepts like equilibrium are inherently hard to apply to fully specific situations. The difficulty is an inevitable consequence of the fact that we have only one or at most a few laboratories for economic testing on the grand scale; and experiments in these labs are hard to schedule and exceedingly slow to complete. Life refuses to speed up to facilitate econometric studies. The conceptual difficulty may be a reflection of a broad (and deep) difficulty about all kinds of social theory and their theoretical terms. It has long been recognized that making social scientific hypotheses testable is harder than it was to make hypotheses in the basic physical sciences testable. Whether that greater difficulty for the social sciences is a fundamental or a transient feature has yet to be decided.

At any rate, the use of models to analyze broad features of economic phenomena and the use of economic models to predict what will happen (or to explain the past) are very different. Economists themselves usually commemorate the difference by referring to models in the former sort of employ as models without qualification and to the latter as *econometric* models.

The econometric version of general equilibrium models faces an initial hurdle, in the need to establish an equilibrium point of reference in the history of some real economy. It is commonly thought, even among experts, that real economies are in permanent disequilibrium and that this is crucial to their tendency to change as well as to the direction in which they do so. The seemingly inevitable doubts sur-

---

37. Id. at 171.

rounding the basics of equilibrium modeling of actual economic change thus "leaves the 'ordinary' policymaker wondering about the time, effort, and (frequently public) money spent on economic research." [38]

Having emphasized the limits of general equilibrium models, it is vital to take note of their valuable contribution to tax policy. The study of the effect of taxes on capital markets, by means of applied general equilibrium modeling, has prospered since the early 1980's.

Several powerful models have been deployed to illustrate the consequences of sweeping tax base changes, with detailed information about the United States economy as a starting point. Not only do these models aspire to realism by using that input, they also model widely discussed structural features of the U.S. economy in a reasonably detailed manner. Thus, the models in question typically use Department of Commerce data to obtain the payments for labor and capital of a number of industries. They take into account differences among consumers grouped according to income range. All major existing taxes are taken into account, including the federal personal and corporate income taxes, excise taxes, and indirect business taxes. One of the striking improvements of these over earlier general equilibrium models is their attempt to represent the effects of taxes that discriminate among capital income flows to individuals from different industries. Depreciation allowances for investment in tangible personal property are higher than for investment in certain intangibles and lower than for investment in other intangibles. See section 8.1, above. This, among other peculiarities of the U.S. tax system, causes capital income from industries that invest in different proportions in these forms of property to be taxed at different rates. Finally, the models also refine the representation of government sector expenditures and transfers. Detailed information about lump-sum transfers for social security, welfare, government retirement, food stamps, and similar programs are included. So are government demands for raw materials, labor and manufactures.

In brief, the heightened realism of these recent models far outstrips that of earlier, weaker general equilibrium models that were never really intended to illustrate realistic economic change for a country as complex as this. Before considering the more interesting of the implications of these models, it is important to note that some of the more drastic simplifications of previously discussed models survive in them. Importantly, they assume that consumers save for future consumption based on the assumption that prices will not rise, whereas during a large part of the period the models cover, based on the actual data used as input, consumers could be anything but confident that this would be so, given uncertainties due to inflation. The models also assume that consumers of all income groups can vary their choices of labor and leisure to the same, rather high extent.

38. Id. at 173.

Despite this and other inevitable respects in which they stylize the economic system, these models greatly improve our ability to evaluate the consequences of some popular tax policy proposals, including capital gain tax reductions and the shift from a hybrid income-and-consumption tax, like the current federal income tax, to a pure consumption tax. A reasoned approximation of the long-term revenue and welfare effects of broad alternative ways of designing the national tax base is a suitable and, happily, an apparently attainable goal of this latest generation of applied general equilibrium models. One family of models yields the result that corporate tax integration with indexation of capital gains would yield the same gains for the economy as would the substitution of a pure consumption tax for the existing hybrid tax, and that both alternative tax schemes would have yielded substantial gains over the last twenty year period (on the order of $400 billion).[39] These gains are of course relatively small in comparison with the federal budget deficit, which has been increasing annually by amounts of the same magnitude.

The comparison is of interest, because a different perspective on the choice of a tax base might be inferred from the obsessive attention that has been devoted to capital income taxation and consumption tax alternatives to the income tax. Determining the order of magnitude of the consequences of tax alternatives seems a defensible use of stylized assumptions about consumer and producer behavior. It is to be hoped that further development of models like those described here will have a similarly illuminating effect on discussions like those described in Chapters 9 and 11, and perhaps other tax policy areas.

14.7 MACROECONOMIC AND OTHER ECONOMETRIC MODELS IN REVENUE ESTIMATION

The task of estimating the revenue effects of tax legislation is essential to the purpose of coordinating government spending with tax effort and national debt. As we have seen, borrowing and taxing can be equally effective means of supporting public expenditure, if conditions are right. Avoidance of inflation and imbalance of payments nonetheless give taxation the advantage in most circumstances. While it is no longer realistic to suppose that government spending must be curtailed if current revenue is not there to support it, governments usually need to have as accurate a forecast as possible of the extent to which taxes will cover expenditures, so that the costs of any necessary borrowing can be included in fiscal planning. When the calculation of individual tax liability is indexed for inflation or made to depend on other economic conditions, revenue estimation becomes more difficult but also more urgent, because the chance of budget deficits becomes more volatile.

39. John B. Shoven & John Whalley, Applying General Equilibrium 153–93, esp. 166 (1992) (presenting the results of models based on 1973 Department of Commerce data); see Charles L. Ballard, Don Fullerton, John B. Shoven & John Walley, A General Equilibrium Model For Tax Policy Evaluation (1985) (forerunner of the models used in the previously cited work).

Accuracy of prediction is the only goal of revenue estimation, and the future to be predicted is usually near at hand. Since conceptually interesting models of economic relations cannot do the job, all models are ad hoc. Moreover, such broad features of the economy as gross national product, average price levels, and rates of inflation and unemployment—economic variables that reflect macroeconomic change rather than individual behavior—are those in terms of which it is easiest (and for want of alternatives, inevitable) to frame the problem of making government outlays and receipts comparable. Economic theory has struggled with the role of macroeconomic quantities like these but has failed to come up with general models relating them to microeconomic variables like price and individual consumer preference. As a consequence, revenue estimation uses models that are not only far more specifically tied than theoretical models to present knowledge of the state of the economy but that are not even translatable into the same fundamental terms.

For example, an increase in gasoline tax may be expected to reduce gasoline sales but also automobile and tourist industry sales. On the other hand, reduced oil imports should strengthen the dollar and perhaps result in lower domestic interest rates, thus strengthening the economy. The magnitude of these related effects can also roughly be expected to depend on the national employment level, the current national budget deficit, and the accumulated national debt, each to a different degree. Estimating the net effect of a 1% increase in the gas tax should therefore involve the modeling of the complex interaction of these macroeconomic variables. Microeconomic changes ultimately control the result; individual budget decisions will finally register the changes that must be netted to produce a revenue estimate. But revenue models rarely represent the behavior of individuals as such (although they may use individual tax return data to compute tax effects on selected categories of taxpayer). The theoretical framework for that level of detail is not available.

It is largely for this reason that budget estimates are highly controversial and seem likely to express political preferences. Since the best models for this purpose blur the concrete level at which the economy can be most neutrally observed, all predictions are correctly seen as grounded in assumptions about likely changes or lack of change in broad economic characteristics (GNP, employment levels, etc.). The model builders could only defend assumptions about change in these macroeconomic variables with anecdotal and impressionistic argument, and so the established practice among federal government revenue estimators in this country is to "hold constant" a startling range of macroeconomic variables: GNP, interest rates, employee compensaton, investment, the overall price level, and the total level of state and local taxes.[40] Sometimes, this assumption, which is largely motivated by the

---

40. Emil Sunley & Randall D. Weiss, *The Revenue Estimating Process*, 55 Tax Notes 1299, 1301 (June 10, 1991).

need for the appearance of political neutrality, boldly distorts a revenue estimate. For example, the assumption that GNP will be constant distorts estimates of excise tax revenues because excise taxes have partially offsetting effects on income and payroll tax collections.[41]

Almost as important a source of inaccuracy in revenue estimates is the problem of allowing for defects in the administrative and legal implementation of a prospective tax measure. The Treasury and the tax-writing congressional committees often entertain "tax bills" in one form, make decisions based on the anticipated effect of these provisions, and then leave it to legislative or administrative staff to make final technical changes. The gulf between bills as they appear during legislative debate and final tax acts has become more pronounced as the tax laws grow more complex. A good reason for the "before and after" transformation of some bills is the difficulty of integrating amendments to the tax law with mutually dependent existing legislation. The game of tax avoidance aggravates the legislative process further by making it impractical for even well informed legislators and Treasury officials to foresee in detail what will be necessary to the final formulation of possible tax law change, while the possibility is under scrutiny.

By custom congressional revenue estimators ignore the difference in revenue effect between defective legislation and the legislation that was intended.[42] Treasury revenue estimators on the other hand take enacted law at the letter and hence regard "technical corrections" legislation as having a sometimes significant revenue effect. In recent years technical amendments have been frequent and vast in their sweep. As a result, revenue estimates of the executive and legislative branches are now systematically out of step, sometimes to a considerable extent.

Another aspect of revenue estimate modeling that deserves mention here is its largely confidential nature. Given the current climate of tax lobbying in this country, officials in charge of the revenue estimation process have for some time told their staffs not to reveal basic assumptions and structural features of their revenue models, fearing that private revenue estimators will criticize aspects of the models that they consider unfavorable to their economic interests, without correcting mistakes that are favorable to them. As a result, private firms regularly employ former government revenue estimators in order to have access to their residual knowledge of how the process

41. Tolley & Steuerle, *The Effect of Excises on the Taxation and Measurement of Income*, in Office of Tax Analysis, U.S. Treasury, 1978 Compendium of Tax Research 67 (1978).

42. Id. at 1302.

works. Since only larger firms and well organized trade groups can afford to take advantage of this privileged source of information, the very measure taken by government officials to preserve their neutrality has elicited a new threat to it.[43]

43. Sunley & Weiss, supra note 40, at 1305–06.

Appendix

TAXES AND THE TIME VALUE OF MONEY

If a taxpayer can defer the payment of taxes, it is almost always in his or her best interest to do so. This is obviously true where a taxpayer can put off payment of a tax until next year when she knows that her rate of tax will be lower next year than it is this year. It is equally true if she knows that she will have a loss next year against which she can net the gain upon which she is facing tax this year. Generally, the ability to defer tax may mean that a taxpayer can control how much tax will eventually have to be paid.

But in a world where interest is a fact of life, deferment of taxation will benefit the taxpayer in another way. This is because the deferral of a tax payment for any substantial amount of time will result in a reduction of the amount of tax. The ability to invest money at interest means that the value of a tax dollar payable tomorrow can be obtained by investing an amount of money smaller than a dollar, today. This phenomenon is now widely known as the "time value of money" and it can obviously contribute to the evaluation of tax policy.

An example will illustrate the point. If taxpayer Bob is in a 50% tax bracket and has $2,000 taxable income, he will pay $1,000 tax this year. If he can defer payment of that $1,000 for one year and instead invest all his taxable income at 10%, he will make $200, $100 of which would have been otherwise unavailable had he not deferred his tax. Even if the earned $200 is then also taxed at 50%, the original %2,000 will have generated $100 after tax as opposed to $50 without the deferment. If this difference does not seem significant yet, consider a more weighty example. Bob could invest in his own business, where he might hope for a ˙return on his funds. He might also have $100,000 to invest instead of $1,000. Even for a year of deferment, Bob can save $4,000, and this number grows quite rapidly the longer he can avoid the payment of tax. Obviously, the importance of the deferment will depend on the interest rate and also to some extent on whether Bob can defer tax payment on his interest earned, as well as his original income.

A quick rule of thumb can approximate the effect of interest on the growth of money. It is called the "Rule of 72" and it works like this: If Bob invest money at x%, with interest compounded annually, his money will double in 72/x years. One hundred dollars invested at 9% will double to $200 in eight years, and at 6% it will double in twelve years, and so on. This rule is fairly accurate for periods of time longer than three years, and it becomes more accurate the more frequently the interest is compounded.

We might now look at Bob's tax situation from a different angle, that of present discounted value. This measures the amount that would have to be put away today to pay a certain amount of tax tomorrow. If Bob knows that he will have to pay $100 in tax next year, and he can invest at 10% today, he will be able to invest about $90 now to pay the $100 in tax next year. If the $100 tax can be delayed for ten years, and funds can be invested at 20% with interest compounded annually, he need only invest $16.20 today to pay the $100 ten years hence. According to these figures, Bob can avoid paying 83.8% of the tax altogether by deferring the payment. That represents a huge tax savings, all due to interest and deferment.

Deferring a present tax on some item will result in the same amount of tax saving as will exempting from tax the yield from the investment of the same taxable item. In other words, exemption of the interest and deferment of taxation on the principle yield the same amount of tax saving. Another example will illustrate the point. Betty has $100 this year, but she can defer recognition of that amount for a year. The interest rate available to Betty is 10%. If Betty defers recognition and so avoids the subsequent tax and then invests at 10%, she will earn $10 on her invested amount. She will receive $110 ($100 original investment income and $10 interest on that income) at the end of the year and at a 50% tax rate, she will still have $55 after tax. If, on the other hand, she recognizes the $100 in the first year, pays a tax of 50% or $50, and invests the remaining $50 at 10%, she will realize a total of $55 at the end of the year if her investment return is untaxed. Notice that under the consumption tax ideal, neither the original investment nor the resultant interest return would be taxable, since both would be considered saving. Under the present income tax system, however, both the amount invested and the interest would be taxed.

The important points to keep in mind for tax policy analysis are these: first, the further into the future the taxpayer can push the payment of tax, the lower will be the present value of that tax. This is true whether the tax regime is based on income or consumption. Second, while deferring tax payment results in savings to the taxpayer, it results in revenue lost to the government, in a portion equal to the taxpayer's benefit. Finally, while deferment depends on the available rates of interest for its value, it always depends on other factors, such as the rate of inflation and the availability of accelerated depreciation.

Index

✝